THE
GREAT
GLEN

Do

Fhreadaidh Dhòmhnaill Bhàin

Fred Macaulay
(1925-2003)

THE
GREAT
GLEN

From Columba to Telford

CATRIONA FFORDE

Neil Wilson Publishing • Glasgow

First published by:

Neil Wilson Publishing

www.nwp.co.uk

© Catriona Fforde, 2011

A catalogue record for this book is available from the British Library

The author has asserted her moral right under the Copyright,
Designs and Patents Act, 1988, to be identified as Author of this Work

Maps by Rob & Rhoda Burns, Drawing Attention

Print edition ISBN: 978-1-906476-66-3

Ebook ISBN: 978-1-906476-67-0

Printed and bound in the UK by Bell & Bain, Glasgow

CONTENTS

Acknowledgements

I would like to thank Sybil Macaulay for the great help she gave me in reading and criticising the whole manuscript of this book; without her encouragement it might never have seen the light.

I also want to thank Ray Burnett for first arousing my interest in Columba, Christian Aikman for telling me about the Sharpening Stone, Ronnie Campbell for showing me where it was and my publisher Neil Wilson for all his help and his soothing advice about maps. Finally I must not forget my two dear black Labradors, Clova and Phemie, who walked about in the Great Glen with me and spent so much time squeezed under my desk while I worked.

Author's Note

The reader may feel a little confused by the many Gaelic names of people and places they will encounter in these pages, some of which appear in pure Gaelic. some in an English equivalent and some halfway between the two. I have tried to give these names the forms in which they are most often found in the literature and hope that the result is not too aggravating.

I
The Great Glen

This great opening is called by the generall name of Glenmore [Gleann Mòr]. The extremitys of these mountains gradually declyning from their several summitts, open into glens or outlets, where yow have various views of woods, rivers, plains, and laiks, and the torrents, or falls of water, which every here and there tumble down the presipices, and, in many places, seem to breck through the cliffs and cracks of the rocks, strick the eye more agreeably than the most curious artificiall cascades.

In a word, the number, extent, and variety of the several prospects; the verdure of the trees, shrubs, and greens; the odd wildness of the hills, rocks, and precipeces; with the noise of the rivoletts and torrents, brecking and foaming among the stones, in such a diversity of collowrs and figures; the shineing smoothness of the seas and laiks, the rapidity and rumling of the rivers falling from shelve to shelve, and forceing their streams through a multitude of obstructions, have something so charmingly wild and romantick as even exceeds discription.

John Drummond of Balhaldy

IF THE TSAR of all the Russias had drawn a line on the map with a ruler from Inverness to Fort William to show where a new railway was to run, as we are told Tsars were wont to do, it could hardly have been straighter than Gleann Mòr (the Great Glen). It is a glen formed not by the action of water seeking its way forward along the easiest path, but by the movement of the earth's crust ruthlessly splitting rocks asunder along a fault line. It was formed nearly 400 million years ago by a colossal upheaval during which the most northerly part of the land mass was sheared and pulled away roughly 65 miles towards the south-west. The wide and relatively flat bottom of the glen was then carved out by glaciers during the Ice Age, but rock movement is not yet complete and many earthquakes are still recorded, most of them, fortunately, only very small ones.

After the Ice Age the glaciers melted – their progress is charted by the parallel 'roads' of Glen Roy – leaving what eventually became a series of lochs with the rivers that drain and feed them, the whole creating an almost continuous watery boundary between this furthest section of what is now Scotland – the last slice we might term it – and the rest of Great Britain. It is rather as though a giant had placed his right hand on the major land mass and torn the top portion away with his left hand and had then, instead of discarding it, put it back, but out of alignment. It is still grinding its way south-westwards.

As the Ice Age receded the earth warmed up and plant life began to appear. The monocultures of spruce with their tightly packed trees and dark, barren forest floors, which cover many of the hills today, were mercifully absent until the last century, but the magnificent Scots pines, which can reach 50 to 70 feet in height, early began to clothe the slopes of the glen, followed by the Druids' sacred tree, the oak, and by other species such as birch, willow and alder. Smaller bushes – bog myrtle and juniper – pushed up and fragile flowers began to spread over the floor of the glen. Then came the animals – reindeer, lynx and brown bear, probably all gone by the tenth century. Wild boar and beaver persisted for longer. Deer too were there but perhaps in smaller numbers than today because of the presence of wolves which did not die out until the 18th century, the last having been killed, it is said, in 1743.

The modern motorist might well be forgiven for thinking the glen far from straight as he weaves his way round interminable twists and bends to avoid outcrops of rock or invasive loch or river, but there are places where he is bound to acknowledge its straightness; at the foot of Loch Ness, for instance, where that great water stretches away to the north, further than the eye can see; or at the slope by Aberchalder where the four miles of Loch Oich and the dry land which separates it from Loch Lochy and, on a clear day, Loch Lochy itself are laid out before him, while from somewhere south of Corriegour beside Loch Lochy there is another straight vista down to the hills opposite Fort William and to the Ardgour hills fringing the Firth of Lorne.

The water levels in the lochs and rivers have altered down the centuries and we can only guess what they were at any particular time. These levels have been influenced recently by the dams built to supply electricity, but before then they were subject only to natural processes, to rainfall and rock movements and the unceasing force of the wind.

The glen is bounded on either side by great hills, in the south including Ben

Nevis, the greatest of them all. In winter there are wide snowfields on the slopes of these hills and even in midsummer patches of snow remain on the northern faces. A fall of snow shows up every undulation, every rock, every hollow which the softer days of spring and summer hide in clouds of heather and deer grass.

In fierce winds the lochs turn grey and fringe their tossed waves with spumes of white. On still, damp days they pull down thick mists and hide beneath them, drawing the shining birches and the dark heather into their fitful whiteness to wait, unseen or partly seen, until the sun breaks through. Sometimes the lochs are still and, like giant looking-glasses, hold the trees and the hills in a spell beneath their waters.

Ptolemy (Claudius Ptolemaeus), the astronomer and geographer who lived from 90-168AD recognised the Caledones, who lived along the Great Glen, as the dominant tribe in the north of Scotland, whereas the Romans gave the name of Caledonia to the whole area which, from their point of view, was inhabited by totally barbarous tribes. These 'barbarous tribes' came to be known as Picts – Latin 'picti' (painted people) – perhaps from their delight in painting their bodies, which they may well have done to frighten their enemies and not merely as a decoration, though whether they were as highly decorated as some illustrations suggest we may never know.

One might think that the Great Glen must have been welcome as a highway for travellers from the broken rock-strewn coastline of the south-west to the cold waters of the North Sea, from the fertile plains of Moray to Moluag's blessed isle of Lismore, yet a look at the many maps plotting the presence of, for instance, Pictish monuments and archeological sites, thanes, nunneries and monasteries, would suggest that not very much was going on there in the early Christian period although plenty of Bronze Age remains have been uncovered. There was little good agricultural land and most of the glen was, of course, a long way from the sea, which was the favoured medium for the transport of people and goods until the last two hundred years or so. As journeys through this glen must have involved fighting one's way over hills and rocks and negotiating lochs, rivers, waterfalls and bogs there may have been little settlement along this apparently favourable route in earlier centuries.

A journey up the Great Glen from the south is generally regarded as beginning at corpach by Fort William where the waters of Loch Eil and Loch Linnhe meet, but I cannot help thinking of the glen as beginning eight miles further south at the Corran Narrows where Upper Loch Linnhe is very nearly enclosed and shut off from the salt tides which rule its lower half. The water rushes strongly through this small gap and the ferry boats crossing to and from Ardgour have to make a detour up the loch and then turn back again into the current, which is too strong for them to make their way straight across. It is here that the traveller from the north first finds himself in or beside the open sea and here that the southerner, if he is travelling by water or on the west bank, has his first clear view of the highest hills. The east bank has the busy road, but on the west bank is a charming, narrow, single-track road leading through the little settlements of Inverscaddle, Goirtean a' Chladaich, Stronchreggan, Trislaig, Camus nan Gall and so, round the corner into Loch Eil, to Achaphubuil. All the way up the loch this little western road gives wonderful views of Ben Nevis and, it must be confessed, less wonderful ones of Fort William which, for all its advantages of water and mountains, has sadly missed its chance of being an attractive town.

The next ten to 15 miles (16-24km) up the glen from Fort William are dominated by the great mass of Ben Nevis and its companion, Aonach Mor. Ben Nevis, the highest hill in the British Isles, is all the more impressive because it rises from sea level, whereas the next highest hill, Ben MacDhui in the Cairngorms, starts from a base of 1400ft (427m) above sea level. There is snow on Nevis's north-east face even in the middle of summer. Its peaks and corries are again best appreciated from the west side of the glen or from the relatively flat land of the strath where the river Lochy runs between fields of green grass or of heather and juniper and where we find Tom a'Charich, Brackletter and Highbridge (General Wade's construction, now broken down and unusable).

Halfway up the slope above Spean Bridge is the church of Kilmonivaig (the largest parish in the Highlands) and at the top of the slope is the Commando Memorial, erected to remember those Commandos who trained in this area during the Second World War. In its elevated position, for the land falls away sharply to the west here, the dark figures on the monument stand out clearly against the paler sky. A few years ago someone, for what reason I cannot remember, wanted to plant trees round it, which would have greatly lessened its impact, but every Commando and ex-Commando in the world wrote in to protest and the site was left as it was. The road divides here, the main branch continuing up the east bank and the other going west over the canal at the foot of Loch Lochy where it meets the road to Achnacarry – Cameron of Lochiel's stronghold. Here is Bunarkaig where the river Arkaig joins Loch Lochy; the little bridge there looks over the shining water of the bay and the wide sweep of the loch towards the great hills.

On the east bank of the glen the main road passes on the right the huge gash of Glen Gloy going up to join the Corrieyairack Pass and forming part of an ancient highway between west and east. The road moves close to the loch here and sweeps up to Laggan Locks along stretches where great trees rise above occasional white houses and make of the road a green tunnel letting the sunlight or the mist in through their leaves and branches.

Laggan Locks is at the north end of Loch Lochy and the canal takes over here, but only for two miles, when Loch Oich begins. It is only four miles (6.5km) long and on average 350 yards (320m) wide and at its deepest point 133ft (40m) deep, whereas Loch Lochy is ten miles (16km) long and 1050 yards (965m) wide on average, with a mean depth of 229ft (70m). Half way up Loch Oich on the west bank are the ruins of old Invergarry Castle, the seat of the MacDonalds of Glengarry. The River Garry flows in here from the west and the loch continues to Bridge of Oich and Aberchalder, where the canal begins again, running close to the River Oich (it is hard to disentangle them on the map) and between banks of heather to Fort Augustus on the south shore of Loch Ness.

This loch easily eclipses the other two in size, being about 24 miles (38km) long and one mile (1.6km) wide, and its maximum depth is somewhere between 750 and 1000ft (238-305m). It is quite devoid of islands, apart from Cherry Island at the south end near Fort Augustus Abbey. This is not a real island but a crannog, an artificial island, built perhaps as a place of refuge in times of danger; it may be 2500 years old. There were cherry trees on it at one time, perhaps visited by the soldiers at the fort and it is also thought that there was once a mediaeval castle there, but now there is room only for a single pine tree and a few bushes, for the water level of the loch is much higher than it used to be. Somewhere in the surrounding water is a causeway that linked Cherry Island to the west bank. One of the monks at the Abbey, Dom Odo Blundell (fl.1910), went down in an old-style diving suit – one of those vast metal suits roughly following the lines of head and body and with a large glass window at face level – to see how the crannog was constructed and found it to be made of layers of different-sized stones kept in place with logs of wood which will have hardened to an iron-like consistency during their long sojourn in the water.

From Fort Augustus there are two roads to Inverness. The main road follows the west bank of Loch Ness and goes through the small settlement of Invermoriston and the somewhat larger one of Drumnadrochit. Invermoriston is flanked by two massive hills, Sron na Muic (the promontory of the pig) to the south and Craig nan Eun (crag of the birds) to the north, which stand like substantial sentinels at the mouth of Glenmoriston. To the south of Drumnadrochit is the great rounded hill of Meallfuarmhonaidh which dominates the whole of the west bank. The village itself is heralded by the ruins of ancient Castle Urquhart on Strome Point where there has been some kind of fort or castle since the Iron Age. Quite apart from the interest to be found in the castle itself, its position is an excellent one for observing the loch and spotting or not spotting the Monster – first seen, as far as we know, by St Columba in the 6th century. Columba acually saw it in the River Ness and not in the loch, but its habitat seems to have slipped south since then and there is a museum in the village dealing with every known fact, or fiction, about it.

The last settlement before Inverness is Lochend, where a line of houses stands across the top of the loch like a bastion holding back that great sheet of water. Here on the east bank, are the towers and pinnacles of Aldourie Castle, looking, amongst its trees, like something out of a fairy tale.

The east bank of Loch Ness looks rather unexciting from across the water, but this is far from being the case, for there are so many different kinds of landscape to be found there. First, from the Fort Augustus end, there is the road along the south shore of the loch near the former Abbey buildings. Not much more than half of the loch can be seen from here; the rest of it seems to have slipped over the curve of the earth and disappeared. The road strikes away from the water and to the north-east behind a curtain of low hills and through hilly but soft, green agricultural land.

Then comes Loch Tarff with its pretty wooded islands and the long climb up to a viewpoint from which an amazing landscape of lochs is visible – Loch Knockie, Loch Kemp, Loch Mhòr, Loch Ruthven, Loch Duntelchaig, Loch Ashie, and a host of smaller ones. They lie as it were in a lost landscape, hidden from the Great Glen itself yet part of it, sheltered by a line of low hills which have their feet in Ness waters.

Beyond the viewpoint and at a much lower level is Whitebridge, with its Wade bridge and the hotel that was once a kingshouse,[1] and then Gorthleck amidst scattered houses overlooking Loch Mhòr. There are charming narrow roads between Errogie, Foyers and Inverfarigaig leading up and down steep hillsides, beside groves of trees and great mossy boulders, always with some little burn below them seeking a path, this way and that, down to the great loch itself.

Round Croachy and Brin there is farm land, dull and flat in itself but enlivened by huge and grotesque rocks like the one at Brin where the curlew still make their bubbling calls. To the west lie all the lochs visible from the viewpoint. Loch Ruthven is the special haunt of birds, watched over by the RSPB. At Loch Ashie ghostly armies have been seen in the sky and the clash of their swords and beating of their drums are heard, but no-one knows in what cause they are fighting. Dores, on the shore of Loch Ness, is nearby and from here there is an impressive view down the loch of Mealfuarmhonaidh on the further side of Urquhart Bay. It is only a few miles now to Inverness.

The River Ness flows out of its loch past the Pictish fort at Torvean (behind the golf course club house), past the islands and the castle at the main bridge and out into the Moray Firth and its leaping dolphins. The islands are full of paths and trees with flowers and bushes in between and places where one can observe the flow of the river and see the towers of St Andrews Cathedral or the roofs of Eden Court Theatre, part of which was once the Palace of the Bishop. It is a great place for walking a dog and for meeting other dogs and the paths wind about and cross little bridges to other islands or to the east bank; there is a big ornamental metal bridge across the river here which bounces up and down as one walks, rather to the surprise of the dog. It is one of three similar bridges, attractive and useful to the pedestrian, who can cross the river without using the main bridge. The river slides on beneath them and beneath two road bridges taking traffic into Inverness. The hills flatten out, the sky widens, the wind blows more strongly, Ben Wyvis spreads herself across the horizon, looking like a film set. We have reached the northern end of the Great Glen.

The following chapters introduce human life into this lovely prospect of plants and flowers, of mountain, loch and river. The people who lived there before the Christian era – the Caledones – had responded to the call of Calgacus and sent their men to join him at Mons Graupius, where he confronted the Roman legions but did not win a victory. Yet the Romans did not settle in the north of Scotland; they established camps in this place and in that and then moved on, leaving those they had called Picts still in possession of their land. Later the Picts intermingled with Irish Gaels heralded by St Columba. It was the Irish tongue that prevailed although how different it was from the (probably Celtic) tongue spoken by the Picts it is impossible to say.

When Calum Cille (St Columba) went up the Great Glen in the sixth century he went to visit the King of the Picts and represented a small colony of Irish settled along the western seaboard of Scotland, roughly where Argyll now is. This colony was to grow to include the western isles and to creep up the Great Glen to the north-east, eventually absorbing the Pictish peoples and creating the Kingdom of the Scots, as the Irish settlers came to be called. We do not actually know whether the Picts melted into the Scots or the Scots into the Picts or indeed exactly when or how this came about. As a famous spoof history book tells us:

> The Scots (originally Irish, but by now Scotch) were at this time inhabiting Ireland, having driven the Irish (Picts) out of Scotland; while the Picts (originally Scots) were now Irish (living in brackets) and vice versa. It is essential to keep these distinctions clearly in mind (and verce visa).[2]

The people and events described in the following pages, starting with Columba, are scattered very intermittently along the years from 550 to 1850AD, a period beginning at a time when some of the mists of antiquity were being dispelled and ending at a time which almost touches the lives of our grandparents or certainly great-grandparents.

After Columba and the struggles between Macbeth and the Canmore kings for the ancient kingship comes the great era of the clans. The main Great Glen clans were the Frasers, the Camerons, the MacDonalds of Glengarry and of Keppoch and the Grants.

The Fraser lands lay to the west of Inverness (they included a small enclave of Chisholms) and along the east bank of Loch Ness. The Camerons held much of Lochaber, the stronghold of their chief being at first on the bank of the River Lochy at Tor Castle and later at Achnacarry, at the junction between Loch Arkaig and Loch Lochy. The Glengarry MacDonalds' fortress, Invergarry Castle, was beside Loch Oich with lands supporting it stretching westwards down Glen Garry and beyond, while the Keppoch MacDonalds' lands lay around Glen Spean, an offshoot to the east from the Great Glen. The Great Glen Grants, who were part of a larger clan based in Strathspey, were to be found in Glenmoriston and Glen Urquhart which both run westwards from Loch Ness.

These clans sometimes fell out but on the whole stuck together, following the same political line and supporting the Stewarts from Charles I to Prince Charles Edward, although earlier Stewart kings had shown little understanding of them and had never ceased trying to subdue their wild spirits and chain them within a Lowland code. Their support for the Stewart kings is illustrated in the chapter on

Montrose and in those dealing with the Jacobite Risings. After this we come to the 19th century and the entry of modern engineering in the shape of the Caledonian Canal and finally to a consideration of some of the poets and musicians of the glen.

The Great Glen today is a busier place than it was, but the road which winds its way from south to north only has much in the way of traffic on it in the summer. If you find the traffic upsetting you need only step aside a little and up the brae amongst the trees or the heather or through the wide stretches of whin and broom which turn the fields gold in the spring. The noise of the traffic will die away, be absorbed somehow into the vast blue cavern of the sky, or into the convocation of clouds which gathers between these two lines of hills. The burns will murmur or roar, according to the season, the wind will stir the trees and the birds call, whatever the march of history. The Great Glen will be as it was.

II
Calum Cille (Columba)

Thi tha chomhnadh nan ard.
Tiuirich duinn do bheannachd aigh,
Iomchair leinn air bharr an t-sal,
Iomchair sinn gu cala tamh,
Beannaich ar sgioba agus bat,
Beannaich gach acair agus ramh,
Gach stadh is tarruinn agus rac,
Ar siuil-mhora ri crainn ard
Cum a Righ nan dul'n an air
Run 's gu 'n till sinn dachaidh sIan;
Suidhidh mi fein air an stiuir,
Is e Mac De a bheir domh iuil,
Mar a' thug e Chalum ciuin,
'N am dha stadh a chur ri siuil.

O Thou who pervadest the heights,
Imprint on us thy gracious blessing,
Carry us over the surface of the sea,
Carry us safely to a haven of peace.
Bless our boatman and our boat,
Bless our anchors and our oars,
Each stay and halyard and traveller,
Our mainsails to our tall masts
Keep, O King of the elements, in their place
That we may return home in peace;
I myself will sit down at the helm,
It is God's own Son who will give me guidance,
As he gave to Columba the mild
What time he set stay to sails.

Carmina Gadelica

CALUM CILLE FIRST went up the Great Glen in 565AD to visit Brude mac Maelchon, King of the Picts, at his fort near Inverness. Calum Cille – Calum (or Colum) of the Church – is better known to the English-speaking world by his Latin name, Columba, a name signifying a dove, but he was certainly not a dove.

Much of what little we know of him is hazy or contradictory or distorted by time and the tongues of eager storytellers. This is true to some extent for any biography but in Calum Cille's case we have to look back 15 centuries, to an age 900 years before Johann Gutenberg perfected the art of printing and to a culture which prized the oral tradition and relied on its druids, bards and historians to keep the memories of people and events alive.

The first account of his life was written down by Cummene the Fair, 7th Abbot of Iona, 50 years after Calum Cille's death, but this was included, almost verbatim, in the *Vita Columbae* written by Adamnan, 9th Abbot of Iona, another fifty years later. Besides this written evidence Adamnan had access to a vast treasure of stories handed down orally by his monks. One might therefore imagine that he would have been peculiarly well situated to give a full account of the saint's life. As far as practical details are concerned, however, we can glean very little from Adamnan, in fact the 7th Duke of Argyll, writing in 1884, tells us that he was so exasperated with the book that he was tempted, to throw it across the room.[1] One can understand his frustration. This is not a biography as we would normally understand the term but a hagiography. It is divided into three books, the first dealing with Calum Cille's prophecies, the second with his miracles and the third with his visions of angels. Practical matters are scarcely mentioned. It is only in Book III that we have a fuller and more human glimpse of Calum Cille's life on Iona in the moving description of his last days and death there, nor are the miracles, which sometimes provide pointers to where the saint was and what he was doing, presented in any sort of order as regards time or place. As Dr William Reeves puts it in the Preface to his translation of Adamnan:

> ... he probably turned his attention rather to the marvels than
> the sober realities of the Saint's life, and consulted more for
> the excitement of admiration in a Simple and credulous age,
> than for the supply of historical materials to meet the stern
> demands of remote posterity.[2]

Subsequent accounts of the saint are to be found in the Venerable Bede's *Historia*

Ecclesiastica Gentis Anglorum written at the end of the 8th and beginning of the 9th centuries, in the *Annals of Tigernach*, Abbot of Clonmacnoise, dating from the 11th century, in the Old Irish Life, appearing in the *Leabhar Breac* and dating from the third quarter of the 12th century and, perhaps most important, in Manus O'Donnell's *Beatha Colaim Chille*, finished in 1532 – a wonderful collection of stories, myths and legends about Calum Cille, some based on Adamnan but most coming from we know not where, yet still perhaps containing a core of truth. There have been many other contributions since then but mostly of relatively recent date. The Viking raids on Iona and other monasteries in Britain and Ireland which began in the late 8th century may well have caused the destruction of written evidence concerning Calum Cille, although it is doubtful whether this will have contained any more solid or any more reliable information than that provided by Adamnan.

We can be reasonably certain however that Calum Cille was born at Gartan, Co Donegal, Ireland, in the year 521 and on the 7th December – a Thursday – which makes Thursday a very good day for doing anything.

> *Daorn Chalum-chille chaoimh*
> *La chur chaorach air seilbh*
> *La chur ba air a laogh*
> *La chur aodach an deilbh*
>
> *La chur churach air sal,*
> *La chur gais chon a meirgh,*
> *La chon breith, la chon bais.*
> *La chon ardu a sheilg.*[3]

> Thursday of Columba benign,
> Day to send sheep on prosperity.
> Day to send cow on calf,
> Day to put the web in the warp.
>
> Day to put curragh on the brine,
> Day to place the staff to the flag.
> Day to bear. day to die,
> Day to hunt the heights.

... as Carmichael's *Carmina Gadelica* records it. He came of a powerful princely family in the north of Ireland, the Ui Neill, his particular branch being the Cinél Conaill (the kindred of Conall). He was directly descended from Niall of the Nine Hostages, High King of Ireland from 379 to 405 and, as Manus O'Donnell proudly declares, ' ... we could trace the pedigree of Colum Cille back to Adam were it not that it would take too long.[4] He thus had considerable political power in Ireland, being of the kindred from amongst whom the High Kings were elected, but he had put this potential honour behind him by becoming a cleric. After his years as a student and postulant he devoted the rest of his life to the church. His royal background and impressive mien helped to make him a very powerful cleric and he founded many monasteries while in Ireland, his favourites being Durrow (the oak plain) in Co Offaly, and Derry (the oak grove) on the north coast. The *Martyrology of Oengus* describes him as:

> A well-formed man with powerful frame, his skin was white, his face was broad and fair and radiant, lit up with large grey, luminous eyes, his large and well-shaped head was crowned, except where he wore his frontal tonsure, with close and curling hair. His voice was clear and resonant, so that he could be heard at the distance of fifteen hundred paces, yet sweet with more than the sweetness of the bards.[5a]

Adamnan says of him:

> ... he was angelic in appearance, graceful in speech. holy in work, with talents of the highest order. and consummate prudence; he lived a soldier of Christ during thirty-four years in an island. He never could spend the space of even one hour without study, or prayer, or writing, or some other holy occupation. So incessantly was he engaged night and day in the unwearied exercise of fasting and watching, that the burden of each of these austerities would seem beyond the power of all human endurance. And still in all these he was beloved by all, for a holy joy ever beaming on his face revealed the joy and gladness with which the Holy Spirit filled his inmost soul.[5b]

As the first of these descriptions reveals he, like all the Celtic monks. had a tonsure which differed from that of the monks of Rome; it went from ear to ear just above the forehead. This was a characteristic which, along with the method of calculating the date of Easter, was discussed at the Synod of Whitby in 664. After this Synod the Columban Church was gradually persuaded to abandon its distinctive characteristics and fall in with the usages of Rome.

Calum Cille's view of God and the Christian faith was very different from ours today. Before conversion the Irish followed a pantheistic religion, that is, they found a god in everything and imagined one for every aspect and feature of the natural world. Calum Cille was still in thrall to the past and to the beliefs of paganism and nature worship. He may well still have believed in the Celtic gods and their magic as exemplified by the words and actions of the Druids, whilst at the same time regarding the God of the Christians as more powerful than all the old gods put together. and more attractive. As John A. Duke says in his study of the Columban Church:

> The truth of the matter seems to have been that St Columba himself had not advanced very far out of the darkness which surrounded him; and that his own mind was shadowed by many of the superstitions of his age.[6]

Should we not acknowledge that the Christian view of heaven is still something like the old Celtic view of the world of their gods? God is not there alone; with him are God the Son and God the Holy Ghost and there are also the angels and archangels, the seraphim and cherubim 'and all the company of heaven'. And to these we must also add the Blesssed Virgin Mary and the Saints, to all of whom many Christians pray. Does this not suggest that residues of pre-Christian beliefs still cling to us, 16 centuries after Calum Cille? That aspects of the natural world are still perceived as with the old Celtic pantheon? The voice in the wind, the leaf stirring in the forest, the water smoothing the rock, the moon pulling at the tides with its hard, silvery light – to Calum Cille all these were still as ancient gods, gods who yet had their parts to play in the cycle of the seasons but were subservient to the Christian God. This closeness to the natural world which was and is a vital quality of the work of all Gaelic, Irish and Welsh poets, is to be found in writings such as the *Breastplate*[7] of St Patrick, who flourished in the century before Calum Cille:

I bind unto myself this day
The virtues of the star-lit heaven,
The glorious sun's life-giving ray
The whiteness of the moon at even.
The flashing of the lightning free,
The whirling wind's tempestuous shocks,
The stable earth, the deep salt sea
Around the old diurnal rocks ... [8]

and in writings attributed to Calum Cille himself:

Delightful would it be to me to be in Uchd Ailuin*
That I might often see
The face of the ocean;
That I might see its heaving waves
Over the wide ocean,
When they chant music to their Father
Upon the world's course;
That I might see its level sparkling strand,
It would be no cause of sorrow;
That I might hear the thunder of the drowning waves
Upon the rocks;
That I might hear the roar by the side of the church
Of the surrounding sea;
That I might see its noble flocks
Over the watery ocean;
That I might see the sea-monsters,
The greatest of all wonders;
That I might see its ebb and flood
In their career ... [9]

* an Irish headland

There is no written evidence to prove that Calum Cille wrote these or any other
of the many lines of poetry attributed to him, any more than we can prove that
the *Breastplate* had anything much to do with Patrick, but the tradition attached

to their production is very strong. We do know that Calum Cille revered the bards, had spent some time in his youth studying with the bard Gemman and spoke favourably of the poets at the Convention of Drumceatt in 585, when there was talk of banishing them from Ireland.

Throughout Adamnan's account of the journey up the Great Glen it is evident that Calum Cille did not underestimate the magic power of Brude's druids. He himself however regarded his own magic as more powerful, proceeding as it did from the Christian God, and as beneficial for the same reason, whereas that of the druids he viewed as malevolent. Brude's chief druid was Broichan but Calum's was Christ himself, as he revealed, according to the *Annals of the Four Masters*, before the Battle of Cùl Dreimhne: 'My Druid – he will not refuse me – is the Son of God, and may he side with me'.[10]

Bargaining between Calum Cille and God suggests that the Celtic saints were men with very decided views who were not to be argued with, in fact they could be very belligerent and determined and not prepared to swallow any insult or overlook any difference of opinion. Even Christ Himself could not stand up against them, if we are to trust O'Donnell's narrative. He tells us of a description by Calum Cille of an imagined encounter between Christ and St Patrick who, on the Judgement Day, is bringing all the men and women of Ireland to Christ. (Ailbhe speaks for Patrick). But Christ is doubtful about all these people and says:

> 'There are many sinners and evil men with him.'
> 'He imagines' Ailbhe will say: 'That they are martyrs and penitents.'
> 'Tell him to leave behind those of his company who are evil', Christ will say.
> 'I don't think he will do that,' Ailbhe will say 'for he is an angry and wrathful man ... '.
> Ailbhe then goes back to Patrick and says: ' ... He instructed you to leave behind those of your followers who are evil.'
> 'That's not a welcoming beginning' Patrick will say, 'and that's not how it will be.'

Christ, having remembered that He promised to judge the men of Ireland at the Day of Judgement, finally says:

'Well if that's the case, let Patrick come to us with all his followers until we ... see what we will do with him and his people.'[11]

This amusing story, and many other similar ones, must, one feels, be based on
some very strong traditions about the characters of the Irish saints. They seldom,
if ever, had any of the humble, suffering, sickly-sweet characteristics to be seen so
often in the portraiture of later centuries. And in Calum Cille, besides his kindness and gentleness, particularly evident in Adamnan's description of his last
days,[12] we must never forget the powerful cleric, the darling of Ireland, founder
of monasteries, the Prince who might have been King, the tall, imperious figure
with the commanding voice. Nor should we forget his occasional vindictiveness.
When, for instance, he was copying Finnian's psalter (as described below), he
sent a crane to peck out the eye of a youth who was spying on him through the
keyhole on Finnian's instructions.[13] Fortunately Finnian was able to put the eye
back. Nor should his curses be overlooked, for instance on the rich but very
stingy man, Uigene, who had been lacking in hospitality to his guests.[14]

At that time it was quite common for clerics to take part in or even initiate
battles, even where their objectives were of a worldly nature. For them the welfare
of their clan was as important as that of the church. Calum Cille was involved in
at least three battles – Cùl Dreimhne, the most important of the three, which will
be discussed later, Cùl Rathain in 579, which arose from a quarrel he had with
his friend Comgall about a church near Coleraine (the two men are said to have
come to blows over this) and Cùl Fedha near Clonard in 587. William Reeves in
the introduction to his translation of Adamnan's *Vita* tells us:

> If we may judge from the biographical records which have
> descended to us, primitive ecclesiastics, and especially the
> superior class, commonly known as saints, were very impa-
> tient of contradiction, and very resentful of injury.
> Excommunication, fasting against, and cursing, were in fre-
> quent employment ... St Columba, who seems to have inher-
> ited the high bearing of his race, was not disposed to receive
> injuries, or even affronts, in silence.[15]

Yet Adamnan speaks of him as 'a simple and innocent' man[16] presumably on the basis of what was known of him from his years on Iona and certainly differing from the 'turbulent priest' of earlier years.

The overwhelmingly benevolent part of his character is well represented by his efforts to free women slaves from their obligation to fight in battles and his desire to provide a code of conduct for the treatment of women and civilians in general in time of war. This was later enshrined in the Law of Innocents (*Lex Innocentium*) drawn up by Adamnan himself and enacted in 697 at the Synod of Birr, Co Offaly. It is also known as the *Cain Adamnan* or Law of Adamnan. It protected non-combatants (women, children, clerics, etc) from violence. It was signed by 51 kings of Ireland and northern Britain, including the Pictish king, and by 40 leading churchmen of the Gaelic world. Calum Cille, and Patrick before him, were both written out of the text as it was a product of the monastery of Raphoe of which Adamnan was the patron.

Yet Calum Cille, this great cleric, with his burning love for the green Irish countryside, above all for Derry and its groves and the tumultuous sea carving out its coasts, suddenly abandoned all his power and in 563 when he was 42 left his native land, never to return except for short visits.

Several reasons have been suggested for this journey. The traditional story is that it was the result of a quarrel with Diarmaid mac Cerbaill, the High King. Diarmaid had at his court as a hostage Curnan, the son of the King of Connaught. It was normal for High Kings to take hostages from their dependent sub-kings to ensure their continued support and good behaviour. The name given to Calum Cille's ancestor, Niall 'of the Nine Hostages', indicates the extent of his power. During a game of shinty, or hurley as it was once called in Ireland, and in a manner resembling what occurs on our modern football pitches, Curnan had an argument with another player and hit him on the head with his shinty stick, killing him. He fled to Calum Cille and begged for his protection, which was given to him. However, Diarmaid, the High King – and one of the best of them, though very unlucky in the events of his reign – required the laws to be observed without exception. He had Curnan arrested and executed, thus violating the sanctuary granted by Calum Cille, not to mention causing a diplomatic incident between himself and the King of Connaught. This alone was enough to upset Calum Cille, but there was a further cause for anger.

Diarmaid had given judgement against Calum in a dispute over the ownership of the *Cathach* (the Battler), which was a copy made by Calum Cille of part of a book of psalms brought from Rome by Finnian of Moville, the Abbot of a monastery near the northern shore of Strangford Lough in the present county of Down (Moville from Ma Bhile = the plain of the tree). Calum Cille had been a pupil of Finnian's. The psalter was so beautiful a book and appealed so much to him that when Finnian refused to allow him to copy it he crept into the church where it was kept and copied it secretly over a number of nights. The Abbot, when he became aware of this, claimed the copy as his own. Calum Cille disputed this and the dispute was referred to the High King, Diarmaid, who supported the Abbot saying ' ... le gach boin a boinin is le gach lebur a lebran ... ' (to each cow its calf and to each book its son-book [copy];[17] an early judgement in the history of copyright infringement. Calum Cille was so incensed at this judgement and by the killing of Curnan that he went off to the north of Ireland and raised his people, the Cinél Conaill, who, with the Cinél Eoghain, an associated branch of the Ui Neill, and the army of the King of Connaught, Curnan's father, fought against the High King at the battle of Cùl Dreimhne, near Ben Bulben in Co Sligo.

The High King had an *airbre* – a druidical fence (invisible of course) – placed round his army to protect it and Finnian of Moville stood in a cross-vigil (arms outstretched) behind it. Calum Cille adopted the same posture behind his allies while St Michael, brandishing his sword, stood in the front rank. Calum Cille prayed to God to give him the victory, but God was unwilling to intervene in such a worldly affair. However he eventually let Calum Cille have his own way.[18] The High King's army was defeated, suffering hundreds of casualties for which Calum Cille was held responsible. A penance was imposed on him: he must leave Ireland and never again see it or set foot in it. It is for this reason, the traditional story tells us, that he sailed away from Derry until he came to a place from which he could no longer see Ireland. This turned out to be the island of Iona where he settled and founded an Abbey from which he and his monks went out to bring the Christian message to the rest of Scotland. This explanation quite overlooks the fact that he did visit Ireland several times after settling in Iona, but the difficulty is overcome by describing him as travelling with a black cloth over his eyes and clods of earth from Iona tied to his feet.

Although this traditional story can be discounted, that is, as a reason for Calum Cille's exile from Ireland, the execution of Curnan did take place and the psalter copied by Calum Cille still exists. At some time in the 11th century it was placed in a shrine described in 1532 by Manus O'Donnell as being

... covered with silver under gold. It is not lawful to open it,
and if it is taken three times righthand-wise around the host
of the Cinel Conaill when they are going into battle they will
come back safe and triumphant. And it is on the chest of an
abbot or cleric, who, so far as possible, is without mortal sin,
that the Cathach should be carried around that host.[19]

By the 16th century the Cinél Conaill was represented by the O'Donnell family
of which Manus, as Lord of Tir Conaill, was then the chief and thus the guardian
of the Cathach. It is said to have been carried round an army for the last time at
the battle of the Boyne in 1690 but sadly did not give victory to the O'Donnells
and thus to James VII and II, who was very decisively beaten by William of
Orange. However, if the O'Donnells did still have any Cinél Conaill blood in
their veins it must have become very adulterated by that time; we also do not
know the moral state of the cleric who carried it at this battle, so it would be
unwise to discount the continuing power of this relic. The shrine in which the
Cathach was placed is now to be seen in Dublin amongst the antiquities in the
National Museum of Ireland.[20] On its golden front is a seated figure of Christ
with a bishop at his right hand and a crucifixion scene at his left. Unfortunately
the psalter itself was damaged because the shrine was not big enough for it and
there are now only 58 legible pages left.

Another possible reason for Calum Cille's departure from Ireland which can
easily be fitted into the traditional story or can exist on its own, is that he left
Ireland to set out across the sea in search of the green or white martyrdom. The
Cambrai Homily, a Gaelic text of the late 7th century, sets out three kinds of martyrdom: *baanmartre* white martyrdom or withdrawal, for instance, into a
monastery, *glasmartre* - green martyrdom or asceticism far from home and *dercmartre* - red martyrdom or death for one's beliefs. The teachers of the Celtic
Church thought, refreshingly, that this last form of martyrdom should not be
sought, whereas other Christian churches seem to have gloried in the miseries
and martyrdoms of their adherents. This brought a certain lightness and cheer-
fulness into the Celtic Church and helped to blur the dividing line between the
old and the new faith - but this is a personal view. In any case, for its clerics, who
were adept at telling the Christian story in terms not incompatible with pagan
beliefs, red martyrdom scarcely came in question until the Viking raids began in
the 790s.

After that time dercmartre almost always meant death at their hands. Thomas Cahill pointed out in his charming book *How the Irish Saved Civilisation* that green martyrdom had been a failure in Ireland because the Irish have an 'unquenchable tendency to sociability' and because Ireland itself is so fertile[21] offering none of those arid conditions which the desert fathers found so necessary to their ascetic lives. Even in such remote places as the Garvellachs – the Isles of the Sea – lying between Jura and the Firth of Lorne, or on Skellig Michael, an isolated rock off the west coast of Ireland, they 'were surrounded by fish and were able to create small patches of cultivated ground by the constant application of seaweed. The little beehive huts, each the cell of a single monk, multiplied as more brothers joined them and from their eremitical beginnings developed into small communities. There is nothing here about living alone in holes in the ground or on half a pomegranate a day, as we find with the desert fathers.

Adamnan certainly presents the saint's journey to Alba as a quest for martyrdom and says nothing about its being a penance imposed on him. He writes that 'in the forty-second year [of his age] St Columba, resolving to seek a foreign country for the love of Christ [*pro Christo peregrinari volens*] sailed from Scotia (Ireland) to Britain.[22] Not at all a startling thing to do, for the Irish monks were always on the move, tramping the roads of France and Italy to gather or spread knowledge or rowing up and down the Irish Sea and northwards to the furthest islands seeking, as they put it, 'a desert in the pathless sea', that is, some remote corner where they could be alone with God. They were fearless seafarers and accomplished all their voyages in frail boats with no help from chart or ship's compass. During Calum Cille's lifetime St Brendan the Navigator sailed off to the north, reaching Iceland and Greenland and perhaps even Newfoundland. We have an account of his journey (some: regard it as purely fictional), giving so much detailed information about the construction of his boat that it could be used to build a replica in the 20th century.

But there was another important reason for Calum's journey. Before the time of his birth some of the people living in the Glens of Antrim, in a district called Dàl Riada (Riada's share – after Cairbre Riada, an early king of this district), had left Ireland, led by Fergus Mòr mac Eirc (from whom incidentally Calum Cille's mother was descended) and had settled on the west coast of Scotland in the area now known as Argyll (from Earraghàidheal, the coastland of the Gael). This new homeland they also called Dàl Riada/Dalriada. Like all the inhabitants of Ireland at that time they were usually referred to as 'Scotti', a word thought to be derived from an old Irish word meaning 'raider', which is how they will have been seen by the inhabitants of Britain. Although the date of Fergus Mòr's expedition is given as 498 it is possible that migration from Ireland to Argyll began as early as the third century. In Argyll their immediate neighbours were the Picts who then inhabited much of what we now call Scotland, although their main centres of power lay further east. The Picts are also believed to have been a Celtic race, though whether they spoke a Celtic language, possibly of the P-Celtic or Brythonic variety, as opposed to the Q-Celtic spoken by Calum Cille, is unclear. The few traces of their civilisation that have been discovered so far include forts, a monastery and beautiful stones incised with symbols, to which we do not as yet have the key.

In 557 the Picts had defeated the Dalriadans in battle and killed their King Gabran.[23] Cut off from the rest of their people and clinging to a comparatively small area of coastline in a country otherwise inhabited by an alien and largely pagan people who had recently shown their power in war against them, the people of Scottish Dalriada were bound to feel in need of support and Calum Cille was the very person to give it to them. Even if he had not been of royal birth or a powerful figure in the church his rich, strong voice, his height, his charismatic force, his holiness combined with strength in practical matters, his diplomacy without weakness, all combined to provide an ideal prop to a nervous and ailing state. His journey may have had some idea of *glasmartre* behind it or may have coincided with a need to obey an imposed penance, but it was first and foremost a political and diplomatic mission. In short, it was probably not direct to Iona that he was going when he left Derry but to the court of Conall, the successor of the slain Gabran, whose main power centre was the hill fort of Dunadd.

Dunadd lies roughly three miles (4.8km) to the north of Lochgilphead in the north-east corner of the Mòine Mhòr (the Great Moss). It is an Iron Age fort only about 180ft (54.8m) high, yet it dominates the vast and totally flat area of the Moss which stretches away westwards to Loch Crinan and the sea. The fort itself would be easy to defend and commands a wide, clear view all round. The River Add runs past it, its source far away to the north-east amongst the rocks and lochans on the south side of Loch Awe. As it gets near Dunadd and the Mòine Mhòr it describes countless twists and turns, after the manner of quiet rivers making their way lethargically across level land, and, passing the fort, eventually joins Loch Crinan beside the Crinan Canal. The fort may once have been entirely surrounded by water overflowing from the river and forming a stagnant or semi-stagnant lake which later developed into the Moss. The Moss began to form 4000 to 5000 years ago and may therefore have looked much the same as it does today in Calum Cille's time. Although the Add was probably navigable as far as Dunadd it may not have taken larger sea-going ships.

The fort was therefore not only easy to defend, it also gave easy access to the sea and it was the sea that then offered the most convenient highways to all parts of the new Dalriada, to the lands of the Picts, to Ireland and to the wider world, known and unknown.

In 565, two years after his departure from Derry, Calum Cille set off on a visit to the Pictish King, Brude (or Bridei), whose fort was at the north end of the Great Glen. What he had been doing during this two-year interval we do not know. Much of the time may have been spent in discussion, in mastering the politics of this new land, in considering its geography; perhaps he paid a first visit to Iona, perhaps he even began his journey to the north from Iona and not from Dunadd, for it is possible that Conall was in a position to offer Iona to him as a suitable site for a monastery. We do not know how far Conall's power had spread or whether the inhabitants of Iona were at that time Gaels (Scotti) or Picts, although there is some evidence of Christian settlement on Iona a century before Calum Cille. It is said that when he first arrived there he was met by a party of bishops, although no religious foundation is known to have existed there at that time, nor were bishops then much of a feature of the Irish Celtic Church, which was organised largely on monastic lines. The 'bishops' are more likely to have been Pictish druids, although Oran, who died in 548 and to whom a 12th-century chapel on Iona is dedicated, seems to have had some connection with Iona and was possibly already there more than 15 years before Calum Cille left Ireland.

In visiting the Pictish king there must have been a hope of fostering friendly relations between the Dalriadans and the Picts and perhaps of improving conditions for the eventual spread of Christianity in the Pictish lands. One very important aim was to obtain Brude's consent to Calum Cille's residence on Iona or, if Conall had felt able to give him the island already, then to obtain Brude's confirmation of that gift, as would be usual between an over-king and a tributary king – if Conall would consider himself one of the latter.

But whichever of these explanations is true or whether they are all partly true and whether, at the beginning of this great mission, Calum Cille and his companions stepped into a curragh moored by the Iona shore, or whether it was moored in the River Add at the foot of Conall's fort, they will in either case have sailed into the Firth of Lorne and up Loch Linnhe to the southern entrance to the Great Glen.

Curraghs were boats with a wickerwork frame covered with animal skins, very light and easy to handle and invaluable where portage was needed, that is, carrying the boat over dry land to the next stretch of water. They are still to be seen on the west coast of Ireland, although canvas is used today instead of animal skins. They varied immensely in size, from the tiny round coracles that held one person to the large ocean-going ships with sails as well as oars.[24]

A hoard of Celtic artefacts uncovered in Broighter, Co Derry, included a model boat of beaten gold from the 1st century B.C. The boat has seven pairs of oars, a steering oar and a mast. The model is 7½ inches (19cm) long and the original vessel from which it was copied is thought to have been 50 feet (15.2m) long. It would have needed a minimum of 16 men to crew it, 14 to row, one to steer and one to manage the sail. This style of boat has been suggested as the one used by the Irish Dalriadans for their expeditions to Argyll and perhaps for other raids on the British mainland.[25] Calum Cille's curragh is likely to have been of this type and may have been 60 feet (18.3m) long.

Calum Cille is said to have taken 12 companions with him on his journey up the Great Glen. Twelve is the usual number given for the entourage of a saint, remembering the 12 apostles of Christ. An appendix to the 'B' manuscript of Adamnan's *Vita Columbae* gives a list of them:

> Baithene, Calum Cille's successor
> Cobthach, his brother
> Ernan, Calum Cille's uncle, brother of his mother Eithne
> Diormit, Calum Cille's attendant
> Rus and Fechno, two sons of Rodan
> Scandal, son of Bressal, son of Ende, son of Niall
> Luguid mocu-Theimne
> Echoid
> Tochannu mocu-fir-Chetea
> Cairnan, son of Brandub, son of Meilge
> Grillan[26]

Manus O'Donnell also gives a list from which Luguid mocu-Theimne is missing, but Mochonna, said to be the son of an Irish King, is included. He is not mentioned in Adamnan's text. Both lists include Diarmaid (Diormit), Calum Cille's faithful servant for many years. Neither list includes Lugne Mocumin (unless, which is very likely, he is Luguid mocu-Theimne), who is mentioned several times by Adamnan and who was the man attacked by the 'aquatic monster'. He subsequently became Prior of Eilean Naoimh (Nave Island off Islay).[27]

The Latin life of St Comgall of Bangor, Co Down, says that he and St Cainneach (Kenneth) of Aghaboe, Co Laois, accompanied their friend Calum Cille mainly because they could speak Pictish and he could not. In the life of Comgall the miracles performed in the Great Glen are therefore fairly apportioned between the three saints. Adamnan does not however mention Cainneach or Comgall, presumably because he wished what he was writing to redound entirely to the glory of Calum Cille.

Comgall was about five years older than Calum Cille. He came from south Armagh/north Down and was an Irish Pict, that is, he belonged to the *Cruithni* and specifically to the Ulster *Cruithni* dynasty, Dál nAraidi. They inhabited various parts of Ireland but apparently their language did not differ from that of the rest of Ireland.[28] Comgall may therefore have learnt his Pictish during the time he spent on Tiree, where he founded a monastery but had to abandon it because of attacks from the people and their druids. But we do not know if this was before his journey up the Great Glen or after it. He founded his monastery at Bangor, Co Down, in about 557 and seven years later, in about 564, he began his only visit to Scotland, that is, in the year before Calum Cille's visit to Brude.

Cainneach was four years younger than Calum Cille and was the son of a bard from Derry. He had studied under Finnian of Clonard (not to be confused with Finnian of Moville with whom Calum had had the disagreement about the book of psalms) and in a number of other monasteries, including Glasnevin near Dublin and Llancarfan in south Wales. He had taught the Picts in Mull, but whether before or after accompanying Calum Cille to Brude is unclear. He was rather absent-minded and once, after staying on Iona, left his staff behind there. Calum Cille however used the power of prayer to have it conveyed to him at the Mull of Oa in the south of Islay (this is Adamnan's story).[29] According to Manus O'Donnell Cainneach was very short, which worried him a lot. Calum Cille made the ground rise under him on one occasion so that he was as tall as everyone else. The resultant hillock could still be seen in Manus's time but he does not say where it was.[30] St David of Wales (Dewi Sant), who was roughly contemporary with Calum Cille (he died in 589), was also short and once caused the ground to rise to bring him up to a desired level. The church of Llanddewi Brefi is said to have been built on this ground. He had a loud, penetrating voice, like Calum Cille's but perhaps not so sweet.

Given our doubts about the extent of the knowledge of Pictish of Cainneach and Comgall it is very likely that they would have been of little use to Calum Cille as interpreters. In this case, did he take other interpreters with him, perhaps men of less elevated position? Or might it suggest that Pictish was a form of P-Celtic, akin to the ancestor of Welsh, and not so very difficult for an Irishman to understand? The two saints were in any case friends of Calum Cille and no other reason for their accompanying him is really necessary.

III
Brude mac Maelchon

Teanga Chalum-chille 'na mo cheann,
Agail Chalum-chille 'na mo chainn;
Foisneachd Mhic bhuadhaich nan gras
Dhol thugam-sa an lathair sluaigh.

The tongue of Columba in my head,
The eloquence of Columba in my speech;
The composure of the Victorious Son of grace
Be mine in presence of the multitude.

Carmina Gadelica

SO CALLUM CILLE set out with his companions in his curragh – or curraghs, for we cannot really be sure how many people he had with him – rowing or blowing up the Firth of Lorne in the year 565 and in the springtime of the year, for the *Annals of Innisfallen* say that 'At Pentecost [Whit Sunday] he spent his first night in Britain.[1]

They passed the long, narrow island of Lismore, lying in the extended jaws of the Great Glen, where Moluag, a contemporary of Calum Cille, had founded a monastery in the previous year.

Lam luoc glan geldai, Grian Lissmoir di Alba (Moluag the clear and brilliant, the sun of Lismore of Alba) was, like St Comgall of Bangor, of the Irish *Cruithni*. In Irish the Picts and the Irish *Cruithni* are given the same name, but in Latin the former are referred to as *Picti*; what real connection they had with one another, if any, is far from clear. Moluag seems to have been given the job of opening up the Great Glen with a view to converting the Picts to Christianity and it is possible that Comgall of Bangor, whom he knew well, went up the Great Glen with Calum Cille in order to obtain permission for Moluag's work from King Brude. Adamnan does not of course say anything about this for, as we have seen, he does not admi t that Comgall and Cainneach were with Calum Cille.

Lismore is a very fertile island; its rich green fields might be in the west of England and its hedgerows, dripping with the flowers of the wild fuchsia, might be in the west of Ireland, yet all around it, beyond the shining water, are the great hills of Appin and of Morvern with their heathery braes and tumbling waterfalls, their mossy rocks and scree-filled ravines. Tradition has it that Calum Cille wanted Lismore and that when, in their respective curraghs, he and Moluag were racing towards it and Calum Cille seemed to be winning, Moluag cut off his little finger and threw it ashore, thus establishing his claim. He later went up the Great Glen and beyond into the east of Scotland on his mission to convert the Picts and there are many churches or church sites there which he founded or which were founded in his memory.

One might have expected that Calum Cille would have called in at Lismore when passing it (if only to curse the resident saint, for there are several traditional stories suggesting that he did not forgive Moluag for beating him in the curragh race), but Adamnan does not suggest a visit and this is perhaps only another example of his 'forgetfulness' of other saints who might draw our attention away from his main object of praise.

Ahead now on the starboard bow came the narrow entrance to Loch Leven, ringed by the Mamore hills and the jagged tops of Glencoe. All around the boat lay the bright sea, its winds and tides and waves familiar to the travellers from their voyages amongst the islands of the west, for they used seaways whenever they could to avoid travelling through the stony, roadless land. Soon another entrance lay ahead of them, this time at the Corran Narrows leading into Upper Loch Linnhe. The rowers rested on their oars, gazing at the great land mass ahead of them and the strong tide roaring through the narrows. Calum Cille must have been amazed at the majesty of these great hills, so different from the softer hills of Ireland where he had lived all his life, apart from the last year or two in Argyll; the hills he knew best were Erragall and Sliabh Sneachta near his birthplace in Donegal, the Sperrins near the abbey he founded in Derry and the hills he could see to the south-west down the length of Strangford Lough from the Abbey of Moville. Of this last group, in the Kingdom of Mourne, the greatest is Sliabh Donard at about 2860 feet (872m). Now the huge rocks and corries of Ben Nevis, the piled clouds resting on its summit, the sharp spring air, the fresh scent of the pines and the fragile leaves in their bright new green on the trees which clothed all the slopes around them, all these brought them delight and dread in equal proportions, for they must make their way up this great unknown glen to the very top, to the stronghold of Brude mac Maelchon, the King of the Picts. They must travel 70 miles (112km) on land or through confined waterways, amongst a people who spoke a different language and might well fear and resent their presence and at the mercy of wild animals – bears, wolves and lynx.

Strangely, in spite of all the dangers one might reasonably imagine possible, Adamnan does not say a word about dangerous animals or unfriendly natives. The people Calum Cille meets on his way up and down the glen are all pleased to see him; even Brude's druids, though nervous and resentful, look forward to battles of wits and to pitting their knowledge of magic against his. Wild animals hardly feature at all. There is, of course, the 'aquatic monster' which will be discussed later. Serpents also were encountered[2] and he dealt with them by making their venom harmless. He must have found them alarming as there were and are none in Ireland, St Patrick having dealt very decisively with them; he called them to the shore where he made them take their tails in their mouths, thus turning themselves into hoops which he trundled down into the sea, telling them not to come back again; and so far they haven't. Calum Cille's relations with the animal kingdom included his meetings with cranes. He must have had a pet crane beside him as he copied Finnian of Moville's psalter, since he said to it: 'It's alright with me, if it's alright with God, for you to pluck out the eye of that youth',[3] (sent by Finnian to spy on him). On another occasion he foretold the arrival in Iona of a crane from Ireland who would be exhausted by the journey and unable ·to struggle out of the water when it landed. He sent a monk to help it and feed it, but it would take food only from Calum Cille himself. It stayed for several days eating out of his hand and then with great shrieks and laments, because it knew it would not see him again, set off for home. This was a cause of great sorrow to the saint too, not only because he was losing its company but because he could not himself take flight and return to his beloved Ireland.[4]

It seems unlikely that Calum Cille would have started on his visit to Brude without first preparing the ground, without an invitation in however vague a form from this powerful king, 'rex potentissimus' as the Venerable Bede calls him. The absence of any aggression from the native population of the Great Glen has already been touched on and although those he met must have been awed by this impressive personage and his train of interesting attendants, this might not have been enough to prevent attacks arising from ignorance or fear unless some edict had gone out from Brude ordering that the visitors should be treated hospitably.

Such an edict seems to have worked later on in the case of Cormac, the restless seafaring monk, for whom Calum Cille asked this very consideration from Brude in regard to the people of Orkney. Stories about Calum Cille may already have been bruited about in the Pictish lands and the king would be intrigued by what he had heard and no doubt pleased to have an opportunity of meeting a person of such importance from amongst a people with whom he had not always had friendly relations.

It is difficult to describe this journey up the Great Glen, given the very sketchy information we have on Calum Cille himself and on the physical characteristics of Scotland at that date. By now rivers must have changed direction, water levels altered, lochs dried up and others been formed; the size of the population has increased markedly, small though it may still be, and many man-made structures have been introduced, all due to climatic or geological change or to the intervention of technology or politics. The indications Adamnan gives as to the places visited are vague, nor does he make it clear whether the incidents connected with these places occurred during the outward journey to Brude or on the way back, or indeed during some later journey up the glen, as Calum visited Brude at least twice. For the sake of simplicity I am placing all the incidents in the first outward journey.

Adamnan refers to the Lake of Apor (*stagnum aporicum*) which seems to have occupied a position somewhat to the west of what today is the mouth of the River Lochy;[5] *stagnum* means a lake or marsh produced by water overflowing from a river. Since that time the lake has dried up leaving us with Corpach Moss. This vanished loch may have given its name to the district of Lochaber, which has the present-day Fort William as its centre.

Corpach is thought to mean the 'field of bodies' and it is believed to be a name given at a later time to the place where the bodies of those awaiting burial on Iona or on Eilean Fhianan in Loch Shiel, also known as the Green Isle, rested until a boat came to take them on their last journey. However, Dwelly's Gaelic dictionary gives an alternative meaning for *corpach* – 'Ground under which there is decayed wood',[6] which could certainly describe Corpach Moss. The modern village of Corpach is to the west of the Moss and slightly round the corner into Loch Eil, which may suggest that the sandy area surrounding Caol and Inverlochy has been there for many centuries. This, combined with the presence of the Moss or rather the loch it replaced, would have been a considerable barrier to travellers who would have had to go round to the west and up the west bank of the River Lochy to get up the Great Glen.[7] Calum Cille is thought to have visited Corpach and later on established what is known as a mission house there, and this too makes the west bank of the river the more likely route for him to take.

Somewhere near Lake Apor they met Nessan the Crooked, who was very poor but gladly offered them hospitality for the night. In the morning Calum Cille blessed his five heifers and promised that they would increase to a hundred and five.[8] He gave a similar blessing to Columban, who may or may not have been living in the Great Glen; he gave generous hospitality to Calum Cille and became a great friend. In his case any animals produced over the number of 105 were always lost by accident or disease. This is not regarded by Adamnan as part of the miracle but as demonstrating Calum Cille's ability to foresee events.[9] In the same district they encountered another very poor man who appears not even to have had any cattle or other livestock to support life.

Calum Cille took a stake and blessed it and gave it to the man, telling him: 'Preserve this stake with great care and it, I believe, will never hurt men or cattle, but only wild beasts and fishes; and as long as thou preservest this stake thou shalt never be without abundance of venison in thy house'. The stake carried out its work with great enthusiasm, impaling so many wild animals and fishes that the man's family could all be fed leaving plenty of surplus meat to be sold. It was, however, so efficient that the man's wife became frightened it might kill their children, having no trust in Calum Cille's promise that it would never kill men or cattle. In spite of her husband's efforts to find a safe place to keep it he was eventually obliged to cut it into pieces and burn them in the fire, thus reducing his family again to abject poverty.[10]

These miracles and other good works in the area must no doubt have absorbed quite a lot of time. They stayed at least one night with Nessan and perhaps several more, but once they resumed their journey and left the immediate vicinity of Lake Apor their aim was to get to the River Lochy and to go up by boat as far as possible. There may well have been stretches of the river far too shallow or too turbulent to allow passage to any sort of craft and there may also have been large rocks or changes in level or sudden twists which would have defeated the most enterprising boatman. So they proceeded up the Lochy river, sometimes on the water, sometimes on or near the bank, carrying their boat. I have seen boatmen on the west coast of Ireland striding down the strand towards the sea carrying their curraghs on their heads – two or three men to a curragh. But Calum Cille's curragh, if it was of a larger size and with a mast in the middle of it, would be difficult to carry in this way.

Being on or beside the river positioned them at the very lowest part of the glen and Ben Nevis and Aonach Mòr would have looked their most majestic towering up above them on their right. These great hills cut off the land to the east entirely and in winter fill the whole glen with their cold, snowy influences, chilling and enchanting the traveller at the same time. But Calum Cille and his companions did not see them in winter although much of the snow on their tops would have been left untouched by the cool suns of spring.

The west bank of the river now presents a very confused picture on a map because of the insertion to the west of it of the Caledonian Canal, which was so placed that thin slices of land and virtual islands were left between the two waterways. Tor Castle would have been a likely place for taking the curragh out of the water for here the river has to make a great detour round the rock on which the castle was later built. There are great changes in depth here and huge boulders lying in turbulent water. Further on in quieter water they passed the two spurs of land where later the farmhouses of Strone and Moy were built. Sometimes in one and sometimes in the other Bonnie Dundee sat late into the night, eleven centuries later, writing his interminable letters in support of the cause of his King, while further on, at the place we now call Gairlochy, his Highland army camped amongst the heather, coming or going as circumstances dictated but always, for 6-8 weeks, leaving the nucleus of a camp there.

Gairlochy stands at the southern end of Loch Lochy and here they could float their boat on its broad waters and sail or row past the site of the later Cameron stronghold at Achnacarry. Near the northern end of Loch Lochy is Kilfinnan where there was a church dedicated to Saint Finnan, also active in the sixth century. He is said to have landed at Kilchoan in the Ardnamurchan peninsula and to have settled on the Green Isle (Eilean Fhianain) in Loch Shiel. He also taught in the Great Glen and ended his ministry at Invergarry.[11] Watson recalls that, according to the Presbytery of Inverness, there was in 1643 ' … in the Paroch of Dunlichity [near the north-east shore of Loch Ness] an Idolatrous Image called St. Finane, keepit in a private house obscurely'. It was burned at the Market Cross in Inverness.[12]

Loch Lochy ends at what is now called Laggan Locks where the Caledonian Canal resumes its duty of providing an unbroken highway to Inverness. Here a famous battle took place between Frasers and MacDonalds in the 16th century in which the slaughter was so terrible that the water of the loch was red for many days and only a handful of warriors remained alive on either side.

It is only about two miles from Laggan Locks to Loch Oich where they could put their boat back in the water. A little way up on the west bank is the Well of the Heads where, in the 17th century, a Gaelic poet washed the heads of the murderers of a chief of Keppoch before presenting them to MacDonell of Glengarry as a reproach because he had done nothing to help in their capture. The loch is joined half way up its length by the river Garry coming in from the west. Near this junction are the ruins of Invergarry Castle, the seat of the Glengarry MacDonald chiefs, whose lands stretched away to the western sea past Loch Garry and Loch Quoich and so to Kinlochhourn, hidden at the narrow, eastern end of its loch among rocks and heather and patches of bright green pasture. After Invergarry they came to Aberchalder where the loch ends and there are only 3 miles of the River Oich to follow before reaching Loch Ness.

The church which later stood near the south end of Loch Ness, close beside the burial ground (still in use), was dedicated to Cummene the Fair, 6th Abbot of Iona who, as we have already seen, wrote a life of Calum Cille 50 years after Calum's death. The old name for the village – Cill Chuimein (the church of Cummen) – was altered in the mid-18th century to Fort Augustus, the fort that had by then been built here being part of a plan of road and fort building to control the Highlands after the 1715 Jacobite Rising. It was named after William Augustus, Duke of Cumberland, of evil memory (he was then a small child). Very little of it now remains. On its site is a 19th-century Benedictine abbey from which the monks have recently, for financial reasons, been obliged to withdraw, leaving a sad gap in the community.

At Cill Chuimein the curragh could have returned to the water for its long journey up to Lochend, from where they might have been able to make use of the River Ness all the way to Brude's fort. After the first ten miles on Loch Ness they drew in to the western shore by the little settlement of Invermoriston where they must have made more than just a brief stay.

There were contests here with the local druids in all of which Calum Cille came off best, but the only one that Adamnan describes is the blessing of St.Columba's Well (Fuaran Chaluim Chille) which can still be seen not far from the river and a little beyond the north end of the bridge. Adamnan's account of what happened here runs as follows:

> Again, while the blessed man was stopping for some days in
> the province of the Picts, he heard that there was a fountain

famous amongst this heathen people, which foolish men, having their senses blinded by the devil, worshipped as a god. For those who drank of this fountain or purposely washed their hands or feet in it, were allowed by God to be struck by demoniacal art, and went home either leprous or purblind, or at least suffering from weakness or other kinds of infirmity. By all these things the Pagans were seduced, and paid divine honour to the fountain. Having ascertained this, the saint one day went up to the fountain fearlessly; and, on seeing this, the Druids whom he had often sent away from him vanquished and confounded, were greatly rejoiced, thinking that he would suffer like others from the touch of that baleful water. But he, having first raised his holy hand and invoked the name of Christ, washed his hands and feet; and then with his companions, drank of the water which he had blessed. And from that day the demons departed from the fountain; and not only was it not allowed to injure anyone, but even many diseases amongst the people were cured by this same fountain, after it had been blessed and washed in by the saint.[13]

William Mackay reports that the well ...

' ... has continued to be in a sense worshipped until our own time [end of the 19th century] and searchers after health may not even yet have entirely ceased to sprinkle themselves with its water and leave their little offerings by its side.'[14]

The church that once stood not far from the well was one of the many places consecrated by Calum Cille during his visits to the country of the Picts.[15] There is no sign of it now but the burial ground (Cladh Chaluim Chille) is still there, a couple of hundreds of yards away from the well, with the ancient standing stones at its entrance and towering above it to the south-west the vast green hump of Sron na Muic (the promontory of the pig), forming one of the jaws of narrow, tree-filled Glenmoriston.

Another ten miles (16km) or so up the loch brought them to the headland on the west bank on which Urquhart Castle is now perched. There must have been a fort of some kind on this site since at least the Iron Age and some regard it as the site of Brude mac Maelchon's stronghold, but I am more inclined to believe that his centre of power must have been nearer Inverness. In its earlier years (12th to 15th century) the castle was involved in the struggles between the Kings of Scots and the Lords of the Isles and men from the islands were constantly raiding down Glen Urquhart to attack it.

While they were somewhere in the vicinity of this fort Calum Cille, 'inspired by the Holy Ghost', heard that there was an old man, Emchat, lying ill and about to die not far away. He hurried his companions along in the hope of getting to the old man in time to baptise him before he died. This took them some way up Glen Urquhart to a house where the old man

> ... on hearing the word of God preached by the saint, believed
> and was baptised, and immediately after, full of joy, and safe
> from evil, and accompanied by the angels, who came to meet
> him, passed to the Lord. His son Virolec also believed and
> was baptised with all his house.[16]

When they eventually returned to their curragh they had only about ten miles (16km) to travel to reach the northern shore of Loch Ness at Lochend. Once they had arrived there Calum Cille and his companions could continue either on or beside the River Ness in the direction of Brude's fort. There are five possible sites for it. One, as already mentioned, is Urquhart Castle which has been found to have all the requirements, archaeologically speaking, for a fort of that period but is not ideally placed to be the centre of power of a king who controlled almost the whole of the eastern and western Highlands. Somewhere nearer the coast might be more appropriate. Then there is Craig Phadrig to the west of Inverness and overlooking the Beauly Firth. This site used to be a prime favourite but it suffers from some of the disadvantages of the Urquhart Castle site and has revealed insufficient archaeological evidence to suggest that it might have been the fort of a king.[17]

Next there is the present site of Inverness Castle, but this has never had much support, nor has the Crown area at the highest point of Inverness. The favourite at the moment seems to be the low hill of Torvean behind Inverness Golf Club. It is close to the river, which would have given it extra protection and also provides easy access to a highway down the Great Glen, and up to the Moray Firth and the whole eastern coastline of northern Scotland. Interest in this site increased when in 1807, during the building of the Caledonian Canal, a heavy silver chain, likely to have been the chain of office of a Pictish king, was found in this area; it had double links, was 18in (46cm) long and weighed 6½ lbs (2.95kg).[18] This does not necessarily mean that it belonged to Brude or even, as it was found near Torvean,. that his fort must have stood here, but it is an extra point to consider along with the excellent position of Torvean for defence and control purposes.

Whichever of these sites Calum Cille was heading for however, he could hope to reach it by sailing on or walking beside the River Ness, depending on the water levels and the condition of the river bed. When they did arrive at Brude's fort they found that they could not enter it as the king would not open the gates to them.

The general picture given by Adamnan and by other writers down to the present day is of a heathen king surrounded by his druids and afraid to let this impressive visitor, of whom he may well have heard many stories, into his court. A 19th-century painting of the event shows a nervous king and his frightened druids cowering with baleful looks in the doorway. If we examine Brude's background, however, the picture changes.

Most moden historians are prepared to agree that Brude may well have been the son of Maelgwn Gwynedd, the King of North Wales. Maelchon can be interpreted as the Goidelic form of the Brythonic Maelgwn. His Latin name was Maglocunus (Princely Hound). Maelgwn's family hailed from the kingdom of the Gododdin (Votadini) which lay near the head of the Firth of Forth and was the subject of the poem Y Gododdin by the early seventh-century poet Aneirin. They were Britons who had moved south into Wales, possibly with the aim of expelling Irish raiders who had settled in that region.

Maelgwn unwisely began his career by killing a kinsman and then entered a monastery to repent of this crime. Later however he abandoned the religious life and returned to the power struggle, in which he was very successful, but he continued to support the church and the advancement of Christianity very strongly. Gildas, a Romano-British monk and contemporary of Calum Cille, storms at all the kings of western Britain in his De Excidio et Conquestu Britanniae (The Ruin and Conquest of Britain), but it is Maelgwn ' ... the dragon of the island ... ' who comes off the worst:

... last in my list, but the first in evil, mightier than many, and mightier still in malice. profuse in gifts and in sin, strong in arms, but stronger still in what kills the soul ... greater than almost all the generals of the British in the size of your kingdom, as of your physical stature ... [19]

Gildas may have been particularly critical of Maelgwn because he deplored the fact that he had abandoned his calling and returned to the fleshpots which he had once foresworn. With the departure of the Romans from Britain in order to defend Rome itself, British society had entered a violent period with each warlord struggling to crush his neighbour and gain more power for himself; so Gildas may also have hoped that Maelgwn would at least make up for his failure as a monk by reducing the chaos left behind by the departing troops and civil administrators. His opinion of Maelgwn is certainly very different from that of others who call him ' ... a great and generous prince and a patron of music and poetry' [20] and ' ... a splendid and impressive figure, like an heroic age prince'.[21] Perhaps his son was like him.

Brude may have been chosen by the Picts as their king, rather than gaining the position by conquest; according to Welsh tradition he had a Pictish grandmother and could have inherited the kingship through her, as Pictish titles were sometimes, but not always as was once thought, passed on down the female line, in the theory perhaps that you know who your mother is but you cannot be sure about your father.

The most important point is, however, (although I have never seen this suggested by any other writer), that as the son of a Christian king, especially one who had once been sufficiently advanced in Christian beliefs to become a monk, Brude was almost certain to have been a Christian himself, but perhaps with sufficient understanding of Pictish culture and ideas to be able to fall in with the practices of a Pictish people, whilst at the same time retaining his Christian faith, even if only very tenuously. (I find it strange that I have never seen this suggested in any literature on the subject.) There is also the possibility, already touched on, that the line dividing Christian belief and pre-Christian practices in the Celtic world was a very vague one and that, just as Calum Cille himself was still influenced by, still walked as it were in the aura of the old Celtic gods, so Brude found it possible to accept the beliefs and the 'magic' of his Druids, and to play them along, should the circumstances call for it. Interestingly Manus O'Donnell says that Brude ' ... didn't have the faith fully' [22] when he first met Calum Cille, which must surely indicate that he thought of him as a Christian. Brude's willingness to allow two Christian missionaries, Moluag and Calum Cille, to establiish religious centres in his territory certainly does not suggest that he was a die-hard or even enthusiastic pagan.

Most people today are inclined to think of Druids either as wicked wizards or as benevolent gentlemen in billowing white cloaks at Welsh Eisteddfodau. They were in fact the learned ones, the repository of all knowledge and tradition, the interpreters of all signs and portents; they were feared by those with little or no understanding of these matters as one might fear anybody capable of performing magic tricks.

Adamnan relates:

> ... when the saint made his first journey to King Brude, it happened that the king, elated by the pride of royalty, acted haughtily, and would not open his gates on the first arrival of the blessed man.[23]

It would not be politic to show too much eagerness to meet a Prince of the Christian church, so the gates were shut, which gave Calum Cille the opportunity to exhibit his strength. Did this occur to Brude? Or did he himself need to have his own opinion of Calum Cille confirmed by some show of strength on Calum's part? When Calum Cille found the doors locked he approached them

> ... and having first formed the sign of the cross of our lord, he then knocked at and laid his hand upon the gate, which instantly flew open of its own accord, the bolts having been driven back with great force. The saint and his companions then passed through the gate thus speedily opened. And when the king learned what had occurred, he and his councillors were filled with alarm, and immediately setting out from the palace, he advanced to meet with due respect the blessed man, whom he addressed in the most conciliating and respectful language ... And ever after from that day, so long as he lived, the king held this holy and reverend man in very great honour, as was due.[24]

It was while Calum Cille and his monks were staying with or near Brude that the 'aquatic monster' was seen for the first recorded time, but in the River Ness not in the loch. Calum Cille wanted to cross the river and told one of his party, a young man called Lugne Mocumin, to swim across and bring back a boat that was on the other side. Adamnan continues:

> But the monster ... was lying at the bottom of the stream and when it felt the water disturbed above by the man swimming, suddenly rushed out and, giving an awful roar, darted after him, with its mouth wide open ... Then the blessed man ... raised his holy hand, while all the rest, brethren as well as strangers, were stupefied with terror ... Invoking the name of God [he] formed the saving sign of the cross in the air and commanded the ferocious monster, saying, 'Thou shallt go no further, nor touch the man'; ... Then at the voice of the saint, the monster was terrified, and fled ... Then the brethren ... were struck with admiration, and gave glory to God in the blessed man. And even the barbarous heathens who were present, were forced by the greatness of the miracle, which they themselves had seen, to magnify the God of the Christians.[25]

In Manus O' Donnell's description of this encounter Calum Cille ordered the monster not to do the monk, or anyone else, harm ever again ... 'And at the words of Colum Cille, the monster went off quietly and gently under the water ... '[26] And so he still remains, living quietly and gently in the waters of the loch, all those who search for him being more of a danger to him than he to them.

But this was only one of the many miracles Calum Cille performed during his visit to Brude. In one case the son of a peasant who had believed in God and been baptised fell ill and died:

> When the Druids saw him in a dying state they began with great bitterness to upbraid his parents, and to extol their own gods as more powerful than the God of the Christians, and thus to despise God as though He were weaker than their gods ...

The saint, however, visited the family and asked to see the body of the boy, whom he then raised from the dead just as Christ raised Lazarus.[27]

On another occasion, – this is Manus's story which he may have found in the Old Irish Life – Calum Cille and his companions were crossing the River Ness when he told them that they must hurry to get to the house of a young man before he died. The angels were waiting to carry his soul to heaven, but he had not been baptised. Calum Cille seemed to know exactly where the man lay and was able to reach him and baptise him in time for the angels to carry his soul away.[28]

Muirchu moccu Macthen in his life of Patrick tells a delightful story about the saint's visit to the High King of Ireland at Tara; he is already *persona non grata* there. He sits down at the king's table and accepts a goblet of wine. The king's druid leans over and puts a drop of something into the wine and they all sit back to see what will happen. Patrick blesses the wine, which freezes in the glass and he turns the glass upside-down whereupon one drop – the drop added by the druid – falls out and the wine becomes as it was and Patrick drinks it without harm.[29] In contrast to this the miracles Calum Cille performs are of a fairly predictable nature, blessing and increasing numbers of cattle, giving curative properties to poisoned water, raising a boy from the dead, turning water into wine (this was done in Ireland), and we find little to match this story of Patrick, although perhaps there were more exciting miracles amongst those left unreported since Adamnan ends his second book by saying that 'many well-authenticated miracles have been omitted in order not to fatigue the reader'.[30]

The nearest we get to the story of the 'one drop' is that of Broichan and the white pebble. Broichan was Brude's chief druid and he had an Irish slave girl whom Calum Cille wished him to release, but he would not. Calum Cille went to the River Ness and took from it a white pebble and predicted that Broichan would fall ill and that the king would send two messengers to him (Calum Cille) asking him to return and help the druid. He also predicted that Broichan would agree to free the girl. The king's messengers duly arrived and Calum Cille sent two of his monks back to the king with the pebble and this message:

> If Broichan shall first promise to set the maiden free, then at
> once immerse this little stone in water, and let him drink
> from it and he shall be instantly cured; but if he break his vow
> and refuse to liberate her, he shall die that instant.[31]

These instructions were followed and it was found that when put into water the stone did not sink to the bottom but floated. Once Broichan had released the slave girl and been restored to health by drinking the pebble water the king kept the little stone and it was used to cure diseases in many people, but whenever the person treated had come to the end of his term of life the pebble could never be found. This was so when Brude himself lay dying; the pebble was sought but not discovered.[32]

We do not know the subjects discussed between Brude and Calum Cille. They were perhaps all too mundane for the 9th Abbot of Iona to pay much attention to them. The position of Conall of Dalriada in relation to this powerful king is likely to have been at the top of the list. As dear to Calum Cille's heart was the question of Iona – whether he might build a monastery there. These problems must have been settled satisfactorily, for Brude and Conall never went to war with each other again and the monastery on Iona became one of the most famous in the world, in spite of the Viking raids which killed many of the monks and destroyed the buildings but could not destroy the spiritual legacy of Calum Cille to his church.

When at last it was time for the visitors to go back down the Great Glen the druid Broichan could not resist one more trial of strength with Calum Cille and told him that he would not be able to leave because he (Broichan) would raise such a wind on Loch Ness that the curragh would be blown back to where it started. Calum Cille took no notice. He went down to where the curragh was moored. It had become very dark and the wind was very violent and contrary but Calum Cille told his people to hoist the sail and once this was done the vessel, instead of being blown back to the shore, sailed out into the loch against the wind.

So the saint went off in his curragh, leaving Brude's great fortress behind him, bearing out into the loch against the force of Broichan's magic storm, the sky a dark slatey blue, the huge round summit of Meallfuarmhonaidh rising up behind the tossing water. How the druids on the bank must have despaired at his brave defiance of the elements and how they must have marvelled when the wind changed in his favour, the waters became calm and the sky bright. Did they question their own faith? And did Brude secretly rejoice at this last show of strength on the part of Calum Cille and his God?

They must have gone back first to Conall in Dalriada and then eventually have made their way to the sea again and across the Firth of Lorne to Iona off the south west corner of the Isle of Mull. But Calum Cille visited Brude at least once more, possibly several times, and it is said by some that when Brude died in 584 his body was brought down the Great Glen to Corpach and put on a ship for Iona where he was buried by Calum Cille. If this is so then he must have been a Christian, either from the very beginning or recently converted and he lies there in Reilig Odhrain near the Abbey church amongst the early Kings of Scots, including Macbeth, and amongst the Kings of Lochlann (Norway) and the Lords of the Isles.

Of Calum Cille's own final place of rest we are by no means certain. He was buried first in his abbey but his bones were removed for safety after the Viking raids began and probably taken to Ireland. The exquisitely made shrine known as the Monymusk Reliquary was believed to contain some relic of the saint and was carried round the Scots army before the battle of Bannockburn in 1314. It now rests, minus its contents, in the National Museum of Scotland in Edinburgh.

Another story explains that Calum Cille had always wanted to be buried in his own country and had told his monks to place his coffin on the Iona strand and leave it for the sea to carry away. It was washed up on the Irish coast some time afterwards and found to contain not only his body but a number of writings and artefacts proving who he was. The coffin was taken to Downpatrick and buried there beside Patrick and Brigid, under the flagstones of the monastery church. The monastery was plundered and destroyed many times, mostly by the Norse, and was rebuilt so often that no-one now knows where the bones of the three saints might be or whether they were ever buried there at all. They certainly do not rest under the great granite stone outside the cathedral which is popularly regarded as their burial place; it dates back only to 1900. But perhaps they are somewhere there all the same, for the prophecy of Berchan, speaking of Calum Cille, says:

> His grace in Hii* without stain,
> And his soul in Derry;
> And his body under the flagstone
> Under which are Brigid and Patrick.[33]

* Iona

But the whereabouts of his bones are of less moment when we have his spirit everywhere around us – in Derry and Donegal and the holy places of Ireland and in the Great Glen and the western islands of Scotland. But most of all in Iona which became a magnet to the whole Christian world. An old Gaelic prophecy about it reminds us of his significance:

Seachd bliadhna roimh 'n bhràth
Thig muir air Eirinn rè aon tràth
'S thar Ile ghuirm ghlais
Ach snàmhaidh I Choluim Chlèirich.

Seven years before the end of the world a deluge
Shall drown the nations; the sea at one tide
Shall cover Ireland and green-headed Islay.
But Columba's Island shall swim above the flood.

IV
Macbeth

The strong one was fair, yellow-haired and tall.
Very pleasant was the handsome youth to me.
Brimful of food was Scotland, east and west,
During the reign of the ruddy, brave king.

The Prophecy of Berchan

BY THE ELEVENTH century Scotland was greatly altered from the land Calum Cille had known. The Pictish kings and their Druids had disappeared, leaving only their enigmatic stones behind them. It used to be generally thought that the Scots had killed every single Pict and expanded into all their territories, but of course it was nothing like this. The Scots of Dalriada[1] had certainly increased greatly in numbers and had moved eastwards so that Dunadd was no longer their main centre of power, but the Picts, far from being slaughtered to the last man, had melted into the population of Scots (or the Scots into the population of Picts) and the two become indistinguishable. The Gaelic language however, although more recently introduced, had prevailed and this may have been because the Picts had never committed their language – whether some form of P-Celtic or something quite different – to paper, whereas the Scots had done so to some extent although their culture too was a mainly oral one. Calum Cille's Gaelic-speaking priests and monks may also have had some influence here.

In the Great Glen, as elsewhere in what we now call Scotland, the Druids' sacred groves had become Christian shrines or places of prayer. The Iron Age and Pictish forts in and around Inverness had been deserted or later defences built on their sites and where there had once been war, or at the best tension between the Picts and the Scots, the combined peoples were now threatened from the north and west by the fierce Vikings. The first Viking raids on Scotland came in the

790s, two hundred years after the death of Calum Cille. They attacked his blessed island of Iona, destroying buildings, seizing precious artefacts and killing many of the monks. By the year 807 the situation was so bad that most of the monks sought refuge in Ireland at Kells (Ceanannus Mor), Co Meath, well away from the coastline, taking with them their precious manuscripts including what came to be known as *The Book of Kells*. As the *Annals of Innisfallen* record: 'Cellach, Abbot of Ia-Columcille, came to Ireland after the slaying of his people by the *lochlannaibh* [Norse]; and the monastery of Columcille was constructed by him at Kells of Meath'.[2]

When Calum Cille first visited the Great Glen in 565 there were already a few Christians there but by the eleventh century the whole population had been converted. After the Synod of Whitby in 663, which dealt mainly with differences between the Columban church and the church in Rome, there had been a reluctant and gradual change amongst the Celtic clergy, eventually bringing their observances – in particular calculation of the date of Easter and the way of cutting the tonsure – into line with Rome.

Calum Cille had negotiated a peace between the Picts under Brude mac Maelchon, and the people of Dalriada, a peace which lasted at least until the death of Brude in 584. Subsequent Pictish kings were engaged in a struggle with the Angles in Northumbria but in 685 Bridei mac Bili defeated them at the battle of Nechtansmere. This kept the Angles quiet for a time enabling a later Pictish King, Oengus mac Fergus, to turn his attention to Dalriada over which he had gained control by 741. Dalriada however, under its King Aed Finn, won back its independence by 778.

Unfortunately there is a gap in the records at this point, but we do know that in 839 the Dalriadic Scots fought alongside the Picts in a battle against the Norse and that in this battle the Pictish king, his brother and the king of Dalriada were all killed. A struggle for the kingship followed from which Cinaed mac Alpin (Kenneth I) emerged as leader. His background is obscure although he is believed to have belonged to the Cenél Gabhrain branch of the Dalriadic people. In 843 he was able to unite the Scots and the *Cruithni tuath* (Pictish people) and establish a ceremonial capital at Sgáin (Scone). Cinaed was enthroned there on the Moot Hill, now close to the 13th/19th-century Palace of Scone. He was known as *rex Pictorum* (King of the Picts), as were his successors until about 900 when, during the reign of Constantine II, the title changed to *righ Albain*, subsequently to become King of Scots. The words 'of Scots' reflect the old Celtic concept of the king as guardian of his people rather than owner of the land; this the people shared in common under his guidance.

One hundred and forty years after Constantine II's reign began a much more famous king was enthroned on the Moot Hill with the ancient Stone of Destiny beneath him. This was Mac Beatha mac Fhindlaech or, to give him the name by which he is best known, Macbeth. He was to rule for 17 years.

In his time the kingdom of the Scots covered the whole of the Scottish mainland down to the Forth/Clyde line plus some of the islands, but minus Sutherland, Caithness, Skye, Orkney and the Western Isles which were all under Norse control. This kingdom was divided into provinces, the largest of which were Moray and Atholl. The province of Moray covered a vastly wider area than the county of the same name today. It stretched from the east coast right across to the west and from Ross southwards to the River Dee and included the Great Glen. These lands were all to the west and north of the Mounth (Grampians) and were the former territory of the northern Picts. The province of Atholl in which Scone is situated lay to the south and east of the Mounth and had belonged to the southern Picts.

The power centres of Moray were at Elgin, Forres, Nairn and Inverness, Inverness probably being the most important, at least during Macbeth's lifetime.

In Gaelic Macbeth is *mac bheatha* (son of life). Originally this would have been a devotional name like, for instance, Gillebride (servant of Brigid), but had perhaps lost its full religious significance by the 11th century. We have no reliable information about Macbeth's date of birth but it was probably about 1005. His father was Findlaech mac Ruadhri, descended from the Cenél Loairn branch of the Dalriadic kings; members of the Cenél Gabhrain had moved across eastwards into what became the province of Atholl, eventually the main sphere of influence of the Kings of Scots, but the Cenél Loairn had gone up the Great Glen into Moray and it was from this branch that the mormaers of that province, including Macbeth, were descended. The title of mormaer seems to have been first used at the beginning of the 10th century; it signified sub-king or regulus. Mormaers were part of the royal kin group and held their provinces by right from the king.

Macbeth's mother was probably a daughter of Malcolm II, King of Scots, though some think she was his sister; in either case she was a very close relative. Macbeth was therefore of royal blood on both sides. His father, Findlaech was killed in 1020 by his nephews Malcolm and Gillecomghain, the sons of his brother Maelbride; Malcolm then became mormaer until his death in 1029, to be followed by his brother Gillecomghain.[3] This pattern of succession fits in well with the alternating succession between collaterals which seems to have been practised in Celtic society from ancient times. Under this system a man was more likely to be succeeded by his brother or nephew than by his son. But it should also be borne in mind that, although a king or mormaer could name his *tànaiste* (heir), his choice would not necessarily be recognised after his death and the assumption of power of his *tànaiste* depended finally on election.

Macbeth may have spent part of his youth, particularly after the death of his father, at the court of Malcolm II, his grandfather, and, if so, is likely to have been there at the same time as another grandson, Thorfinn Sigurdson, whose father, Sigurd Hlodvarson, was Jarl of Orkney. A third grandson, the eldest, was Duncan, subsequently to become king as Duncan I, though it is unclear whether he was at the court at the same time as Thorfinn.

As we have seen, Gillecomghain was elected to the office of mormaer of Moray on the death of his brother, but he did not enjoy it for long as he died, violently, in 1032. Macbeth then became mormaer – 12 years after his father's death.

He had a huge area under his control and moved between his great fortresses at Elgin, Nairn, Forres and Inverness administering justice, receiving dues in kind and keeping up the martial spirit of his people in case of attack from the Norse occupiers of the lands to the north of him or from the province of Atholl to the south. There were frequent disagreements between these two provinces, one (Atholl) inhabited by the descendants of the Cenél Gabhrain and the other (Moray) the home of the descendants of the Cenél Loairn.[4] The origins of the rival houses will not have been forgotten, even over so many centuries, for their bards and historians will have recited the genealogies of kings and mormaers tire-lessly at every hosting and feasting.

Macbeth's centres of power were mainly near the coast of the Moray Firth and in the lands to the south of it, and it was in the great fortress at Inverness that he spent most of his time for from there he could keep an eye not only on the Moray Firth and the mouth of the River Ness, including possible movements of enemy (Norse) shipping, but also on the Great Glen and the lands to the west of it. When we speak of fortresses of this period we must remember that they were far simpler places than the great stone buildings of later centuries; they were usually built of wood, unless no wood was available and then stone would be used; they stood on a mound of earth, natural or fabricated, with a wooden palisade and a simple arrangement of rooms within which offered little in the way of privacy to any but the lord himself and his family. The location of Macbeth's castle is in dispute; some suggest that it was originally in the Crown district at the very top of the modern city, but the site of the present castle, beside the River Ness, is the one most favoured.[5] It was razed to the ground by Malcolm Canmore, Macbeth's successor and then rebuilt by him or his son David I on its present site. It was later repaired and extended after being blown up in 1746 by the Jacobites. Being beside a river was an extra advantage from the point of view of defence and of having quick access to other areas. It is easy for us, used as we are to moving about by road, rail or air, to forget how difficult travel across country was in earlier times compared with travel by water. As we have seen the Pictish King, Brude mac Maelchon, was probably visited by Calum Cille at his fort at Torvean which also stood beside the River Ness, although a little further upstream. Both castle and fort had access to the open sea to the north and to the lochs of the Great Glen to the south.

Inverness Castle is regarded as having been a royal castle which would suggest that it was a residence of the Kings of Scots and they will certainly have stayed in it during tours of their territories, but I feel it was used on a much more permanent basis by the Mormaer of Moray who appears in the Irish records as *Righ na h-Alba* (King of Alba), thus suggesting that a mormaer was the same as a subking, the King of Scots being in Irish terms *Ard Righ* (High King).

Macbeth became Mormaer of Moray when he was about 30. He was tall with fair hair falling about his shoulders and a ruddy complexion. The way 'ruddy' is used in the *Prophecy of Berchan* suggests that it was an attribute worth having. We can imagine him walking along the river bank, on the slopes which today in the springtime are covered with daffodils and crocuses, his sword at his side, a heavy cloak of bright colours around him fastened with a gold penannular brooch, his *luchd taighe* (house carls, bodyguard) following him. The literature contains many descriptions of the dress and accoutrements of kings and great chiefs of Ireland and Scotland, although I have not found anything specifically from the 11th century. A third century Irish High King, Cormac mac Airt, wears a crimson cloak fastened at the neck with precious stones, a white shirt trimmed with gold thre!ad and golden shoes.[6] In a 15th-century praise poem an Irish chief, Tomaltach mac Diarmada from Roscommon, wears a shift of fine satin beneath his armour and carries a sword with a cross-hilt of red gold,[7] while in another praise poem, this time addressed to the Earl of Argyll (whether 4th, 5th or 6th earl is unclear but in any case from the 16th to early 17th century) the earl puts on a satin shirt 'as a charm for victory'. This shirt is of fine needlework and has a flock of birds embroidered on it in gold.[8]

There were no houses to the west of the river then; there would be cattle, probably of the small, black variety, and some arable crops on the flatter land. There must have been a river crossing of some kind - bridge, ford or ferry. 1411 is the date of the first recorded bridge - a wooden one. Before this there may have been a ferry and there was probably a ford taking one over to a point somewhere near where Abban Street is today. Much of the land around the castle today was certainly under water or in a wet, boggy condition then and there were probably no houses until some way up what is now Bridge Street.

In 1034, two years after Macbeth became Mormaer of Moray, Malcolm II was ambushed at Glamis and killed. He was in his eighties and might therefore have been expected to die of natural causes, but he was murdered by the kin or the supporters of those he himself had killed - his predecessors on the throne, Constantine III and Giric (who may have ruled jointly); Malcolm mac Boite, a grandson of Kenneth III who was also a brother of Gruoch, Macbeth's wife; and also Gillecomghain, the first husband of Gruoch. King Malcolm was lucky to avoid the attentions of his murderers for so long. In choosing his son Duncan as his *tànaiste* he abandoned the ancient Celtic practice of alternating between collaterals and followed the feudal practice of primogeniture. Had the ancient procedure been followed Duncan would have had to be chosen by election in spite of being the heir appointed by his grandfather, but it seems possible that in this case the election was waived; perhaps the unusual choice Malcolm had made caused the whole of the traditional process to be abandoned, the electors being, so to speak, in a state of shock. Duncan's seizure of the throne, if such it was, and the absence of the normal preliminaries may well have made his position unstable from the very beginning. He was in his early thirties when he was enthroned.

The introduction of primogeniture, as practiced in most of the rest of Europe, meant that the other branches of the royal kin were excluded from the kingship, perhaps for ever, instead of all having a chance at some time or other of providing the king.

Duncan did not have the attributes generally demanded of a king in Celtic lands; in particular he was a man with little military ability, unable to inspire his men in battle and with little grasp of military strategy or tactics. He began his reign disastrously by losing a series of battles with the Vikings of Orkney - a campaign immortalised in the *Orkneyinga Saga*. His cousin Thorfinn was Jarl of Orkney and, when Duncan tried to seize Caithness (a territory given to Thorfinn by Malcolm II), opposed him with a larger Viking army, drove him back and then advanced into Ross and Sutherland. According to the *Orkneyinga Saga* Thorfinn also plundered in the rest of Alba but there is nothing to confirm this in other records.

Duncan then tried to gain the upper hand by launching a war fleet against Thorfinn's ships at Deerness on the Orkney coast, but he was defeated again. In desperation he raised a huge army, drawing men from east and west and from as far south as Kintyre and also obtaining recruits from Ireland. As the mormaer of the largest province and the nearest: to Thorfinn's territory one might expect that Macbeth would have been part of this army, but his name does not figure in the records. Nor does the *Orkneyinga Saga* make any mention of him. The 'Magbiod' who appears twice in the epic and is by some identified as Macbeth, was actually killed at the battle of Skitten which took place between 995 and 1014 well before Macbeth's time. The latter's father took part in this battle and appears in the *Saga of Olaf Tryggvisson* as 'Earl Finnleik'.[9] The absence of Macbeth's name from the records suggests either that his presence in Duncan's army was taken for granted or that he withheld his support from Duncan or even actively supported Thorfinn, with whom he may well have become very friendly during the period they both spent (or may both have spent) at their grandfather's court.

The armies of Duncan and Thorfinn met at Torfnes – believed to be Tarbat Ness between the Cromarty and Dornoch Firths, although some suggest Burghead on the Moray Firth and Duncan's army, which was much larger than Thorfinn's, was defeated again.

Thorfinn does not seem to have taken as much advantage from his victory as one might expect. He could have pressed on to the south and even aimed at securing the kingship of Alba for himself by conquest, but he may not have felt strong enough for this. He already had a large land mass to control and was perhaps more interested in assuring its future and the future of his own people than in embroiling himself in a struggle for greater glory and responsibility; affairs in his own territories did not always run smoothly.

As a change, and in spite of his string of defeats in the north, Duncan then turned his attention to the south where Northumbrians had been trying to seize Cumbria, which had been given to Duncan by his grandfather. In 1039 or 1040 he besieged Durham with a large army but was defeated yet again, losing huge numbers of cavalry and infantry. Macbeth is not mentioned as taking any part in this expedition either. Was he by this time in open rebellion against Duncan or did he just think that the raid on Durham was bound to fail and that it was better not to risk the lives of his men in such an unwise and hopeless endeavour?

Whatever he was doing or thinking his position was such that Duncan may well have regarded him as a rebel by this time and, once returned from the miserable Northumbrian expedition, have tried to crush him. The war bands of the two men certainly met in Moray, either by chance or while Duncan was making one of his usual royal progresses. Duncan was mortally wounded, probably at Pitgaveny, near Elgin. He was taken to Elgin and died there on or about the 14th August 1040. He had been king for less than six years and was only about 39, not the old man portrayed in Shakespeare's play.

There was no immediate declaration of his successor as there would have been had Alba followed the new principle of primogeniture introduced by Malcolm II. The disasters of Duncan's reign would hardly have predisposed anyone to think of accepting a king without first making sure that he would come up to the desired standard and Duncan's sons were anyway very young. Macbeth had to make his claim to the throne, to gain support and to win the election. Being quick off the mark and getting to Scone before any other claimant may also have been important.

As we have already seen Macbeth was of royal blood on both his father's and his mother's side; not only this but his marriage with Gruoch and adoption of her son Lulach had ensured a further 'injection' of royal blood into his family. He was also known as a great military commander with years of experience of running a large province. He was physically attractive and without disabilities, He was well known in the fortresses and lands of the Laigh of Moray, in the smaller communities strung along the Great Glen and in the lands to the west of it, nor was he an unknown quantity in the rest of Alba and he was making his claim to a disgruntled nobility, worn down by the incompetence of Duncan's rule. His climb to power will have been supported by his wife, for Malcolm II, in his campaign to ensure that Duncan would succeed him, had alienated Gruoch by the murder of her brother Malcolm mac Boite and of her first husband, Gillecomhgain.

There is nothing in the records to suggest that there was any opposition to Macbeth's claim and he was enthroned on the Moot Hill at Scone in 1040. But discontent simmered, if in secret, in Duncan's family and his father, Crinan, the (lay) Abbot of Dunkeld, was at the centre of plotting against Macbeth. It was however not until five years after Macbeth's enthronement that Crinan felt himself strong enough to oppose him in battle. The *Annals of Tigernach* record that 'Crinan, Abbot of Dunkeld, was killed ... and many along with him, namely nine score fighting men'.[10] His defeat was followed by a further attempt, this time from Northumbria under Siward, a Dane, who had been made Earl of York by Cnut (King Canute) in 1033 and had then set out to conquer Northumbria, an aim he had achieved by 1041. His attempted invasion of Macbeth's territory in 1046 was unsuccessful. In the meantime Duncan's sons, Malcolm and Donald Bàn, had left Alba. Malcolm sought refuge in Cumbria and Donald in the Western Isles. Though only somewhere between five and 15 during this period they were to be the nucleus of constant plotting and manoeuvring during the rest of Macbeth's reign but this was of too weak a nature to have any effect. In the meantime Macbeth ruled his country wisely and justly and the richness of its harvests, undisturbed by either bad weather or marauding armies, is recognised in all accounts of his reign, even in those which, as we shall see later, were bent on discrediting him and demonstrating his unfitness to rule.

A good harvest was the hallmark of a good and righteous king in the Middle Ages, God having blessed his reign and made his land fruitful. Harvests seem to have been good throughout Macbeth's reign and the country peaceful. Things were so quiet in 1049-50 that the king was even able to make a pilgrimage to Rome. I am reminded here of Lord Curzon's story about the Amir of Afghanistan who, when faced with being given chloroform while a tooth was extracted, asked how long he would be 'out of this world' and was told 20 minutes. 'I cannot afford', he said, 'to be out of this world for twenty seconds'.[11] At a time when most of the rulers of Europe, including the King of England, were in a similar situation to the Amir, Macbeth, the King of Scots, was able to make a long pilgrimage to Rome and back without any fears as to the stability of his government. He was the only Scottish king to visit Rome and it is said that while there he scattered money like seed to the poor.

There were a further four years of peace after Macbeth's return from Rome, but in 1054 there was another invasion from Northumbria, again led by Siward. The forces of Siward and Malcolm (Duncan's son) probably rendezvoused at Dunkeld, the centre of the earlier revolt under Crinan, Duncan's father. Malcolm had sought and obtained support from the King of England, Edward the Confessor. A great battle was fought on the 27th July, the Day of the Seven

Sleepers; it is usually known as the Battle of the Seven Sleepers as its exact location is uncertain, but it is generally thought to have taken place at Dunsinane. Macbeth was routed but was able to escape to his own hills and glens. His withdrawal into Moray, beyond the Mounth, meant that Malcolm was left in possession of Scone, the heart of the kingdom. It seems likely that he had himself enthroned as king at this time, splitting Alba in two, with his half of the kingdom south of the Mounth and the other half under Macbeth to the north of it.

Macbeth remained undisturbed in his northern fastnesses for a further three years. The support he received from the people of Moray was so complete that Malcolm did not have the strength to attack him. But Macbeth was not satisfied with a partial kingship and it must have been an attempt to regain control of the rest of his kingdom that took him eastwards in 1057 towards the Dee and to Lumphanan, where he met his death in battle. He had ruled for 17 years, keeping Alba peaceful and prosperous and observing the old Celtic laws.

This is a very different Macbeth from the man to whom we are introduced in the pages of Shakespeare, based on myths and ancient stories, some originally attached to other men, and founded on a misunderstanding of our Celtic past.

The cases of murder, treachery and general mayhem at this stage of European history are so many that one might well ask why we have made such a fuss about the possible murder of Duncan by Macbeth. But this all has to do partly with the re-writing of history in favour of the victor that usually takes place when there is a change of dynasty and partly with a misunderstanding by southern (anglicised) Scots and English historians of the old Celtic laws of inheritance. During the reign of Malcolm Canmore (Malcolm III), Macbeth's successor, the southern and eastern parts of the kingdom were wrenched out of the Gaelic world and forced into a Saxon mould by their king (who had spent his formative years in England) and by his wife, the Saxon Princess Margaret Aetheling (St Margaret). She has been revered for her services to the church, but her influence on the culture of the old Gaelic kingdom is less commendable. Macbeth has been called the last of the Gaelic kings and was certainly the last Gaelic king of any consequence, for he was followed only briefly by his stepson, Lulach, who was killed in battle at Essie in Strathbogie, and when Donald Ban became king on the death of his brother Malcolm III and strove to get back to the old ways – encouraged no doubt by his stay in the western islands – his reign was short and interrupted and he was eventually destroyed by one of Margaret's sons.

We can trace the slow development of Macbeth from the great and righteous king of the 11th century to the usurper and murderer of the 16/17th century by an examination of the writings of historians during that period.

The *Prophecy of Berchain*, a contemporary piece, is the work of a number of hands and includes a praise poem by Macbeth's court poet. The poem describes Macbeth as handsome and brave and shows him as a warrior king, boldly seizing the kingship from an unworthy person (Duncan). He has brought in a prosperous reign as only a just and rightful king then could. One could, of course, object that a court poet would hardly be other than complimentary to his patron, but the inclusion of this poem in the larger work suggests that it reflects the general opinion of the time.[12]

It is when we get to the *Verse Chronicle* from the first half of the 13th century, nearly 200 years after Macbeth's death, that the situation begins to change. Macbeth is shown at times as a righteous king bringing prosperity to Alba and at other times as a usurper. A hundred years later, in the *Chronica Gentis Scotorum* written by John of Fordun, we find him described for the first time as a murderer, usurper and tyrant. Fordun accuses him of fatally wounding Duncan in secret. He introduces Macduff into his history – he is one of the victims of Macbeth's cruelty in the Shakespeare play – but neither his existence nor any of his actions as described by Fordun are supported by contemporary sources. Fordun was writing at a time when Scotland felt that its larger neighbour England despised it and it was thought essential to present it as an ancient kingdom with an unbroken line of kings (which is more than England could have said of itself). Macbeth thus ceases to be regarded as a king lawfully appointed according to Celtic practices and becomes an interloper, disturbing the tranquil process of inheritance according to feudal law. As we have seen, this 'tranquil process' had begun with Duncan, the first King of Scots to inherit according to primogeniture; 300 years later the old Celtic laws relating to kingship were entirely forgotten and a correct interpretation of what went on in the eleventh century would have been difficult if not impossible to anyone attuned to feudal usages.[13]

The supernatural element in the Macbeth story, which is such an important part of Shakespeare's play, is first introduced by Andrew of Wyntoun, writing not long after Fordun. He gives a history of Scotland from the Creation to the accession of James I (1406) in his *Orygynale Cronykil of Scotland*. Macbeth is shown to be the son of the Devil and the three weird sisters are introduced and prophesy his future successes. Wyntoun may have depended on oral traditions which are not available to us today and it is probably from these – often little more than flights of fancy though sometimes with a core of truth in them, if one can find it – that he built up his picture of Macbeth, so different from what we can create out of more securely based facts. Strangely he too does not fail to show Macbeth as a good and righteous king,[14] a view which it is hard to reconcile with his other strictures.

Hector Boece, writing in the first half of the 16th century, introduces a new character, the mythical Banquo, who is described as the 'beginner of the Stewarts in this realm', that is, the progenitor of the Stewart line. In his *Historiae Scotorum* we again find the three witches, while Gruoch appears as an ambitious and unscrupulous woman – she is not mentioned in earlier histories. It is interesting that Boece shows Macbeth as a cruel man at the time of his murder of Duncan but then as a good king, anxious for his people's welfare, passing good laws, dispensing justice and protecting the innocent. After ten years' rule however he becomes cruel again. This suggests that Boece was relying on contradictory sources and found no way of reconciling them short of contorting Macbeth's character in an unbelievable fashion.[15]

Finally we come to Ralph Holinshed from Bramcott in Warwickshire, writing half a century after Boece (he died in about 1581). His *Chronicles of England, Scotland and Ireland* published in 1577, were based largely on the *Historiae Scotorum*, but, appreciating perhaps Boece's difficulties with his sources, he presents Macbeth's suggested duality of character in a more believable way, asserting that he had a valiant but cruel nature. Gruoch he portrays as an ambitious woman with a burning desire to be queen. He too mentions Banquo and gives a long list of Scottish kings descended from him, ending with James VI.[16]

Holinshed and perhaps a translation of Boece were probably the main, if not the only sources available to William Shakespeare. It is said that he wrote his play about Macbeth in 1605 and that it was performed in the following year before James VI and Christian IV of Denmark, his brother-in-law, but many do not accept this. The play certainly reflects James's interest in both kingship and witchcraft and points to an unbroken line of kings to whom James is heir, Macbeth being the only interloper. This could not have failed to please King James – a result that the players would naturally wish to achieve.

The details of Duncan's murder were borrowed from another part of Boece's histories dealing with the death of King Duff (962-6). According to Boece, Donwald, the Captain of Forres Castle, had been persuaded by his wife to kill Duff when he was next staying in the castle. This he did while the king's guards were in a drunken sleep and, after raising the alarm, he killed the guards as though he believed that they were responsible for the murder.[17] These, of course, are exactly the circumstances surrounding Duncan's death in Shakespeare's play.

Shakespeare gives Macbeth the titles of Thane of Cawdor and of Glamis, but thanes (from the Anglo-Saxon word *thegn*) were actually not recorded in Scotland until the 13th century. Before then they bore some other name, perhaps *tighearna* (lord) or *toiseach* (leader). They were less important than mormaers, belng officials appointed by the king and responsible to him rather than to the mormaer in whose province they were active. The thanages of Glamis and Cawdor survived for much longer than the others and this might explain why these two titles became attached to Macbeth in later times.

Shakespeare cannot be blamed for giving us so distorted a picture of so great a king. He gave us history as recorded in his age. He resolved the problem which had faced Boece – how to reconcile the apparent duality of Macbeth's character – by means of the three witches and their malign influence on a man without blemish until then and by means of the harmless Gruoch, turned into a scheming and ambitious woman. He naturally used the information available to him in a way best able to create a great tragedy and probably also to please King James. Had he not been such a great poet and playwright it would be easier for us now to dismiss his picture from our minds.

In recent times most historians have come down firmly on the side of the good Macbeth, even describing him as the best of all Scottish kings. But myths are very hard to dispel and it may take a very long time before the evil Macbeth, conjured up from the works of so many historians and from so many traditional tales and twisted by Malcolm Canmore's propaganda machine, can be regarded purely as an imaginary figure.

Finally let us go back to the true story in which we left Macbeth dead on the field of Lumphanan. When his friends found his dead body their first thought will have been to carry him to Iona – Calum Cille's blessed isle – and place him in Reilig Odhrain. in the ridge of the kings close to St Oran's Chapel. Forty-eight Scottish kings, eight Norwegian kings and four Irish kings are said to lie buried there. There are doubts as to whether all these kings were really brought to Iona or whether the entries in the various annals and regnal lists recording that a king had died automatically had the formulaic words ' ... and was buried in Iona' added to them. Dean Monro, visiting Iona in the 16th century, certainly seems to have found sufficient memorial stones in Reilig Odhrain to convince him that these kings do indeed lie there.[18] It is often thought that the distances involved, for instance, from Norway or from the east of Scotland or the south of Ireland, were far too great, but with relays of bearers and by making use of the sea lanes and the lochs and rivers, these funeral journeys could easily have been accomplished. We forget the stamina of our ancestors before the advent of train and car. Did not Bach once walk 250 miles (402km) on unmade roads to hear Buxtehude play? And he was no athletic creature. Macbeth's fighting men and seamen would have thought nothing of bearing their dead king to Iona. Other traditions however have fixed Macbeth's burial in other places, all much closer to Lumphanan. If he really lies in Reilig Odhrain, and I believe he does, his friends are most likely to have carried him north and westwards from the battlefield, keeping beyond the Mounth to avoid Malcolm's territory as much as possible.

They could have gone back the way they had come, across the Spey to Inverness. If so, his final hours and days may have gone in this wise:

At the foot of Inverness Castle they placed his body in a curragh – an excellent boat for both seafaring and portage, staunch against the wild seas and of such light weight that it could easily be carried from one stretch of water to the next. Then, amidst keening and lamenting and the sad, trembling notes of the harp the rowers took up their oars and the boat slid away from the shore. They went upstream, either on the water or on foot on the bank, depending on which stretches of the River Ness were navigable, past the fort of King Brude at Torvean, past the spot where Calum Cille first saw the 'aquatic monster'. The great sail was unfurled and a wind from the north-east filled it and bore them out into the wide waters of Loch Ness – so large that it can behave like the unconstrained sea. But the men were ready for it and sailed on to the south end of the loch, to Cill Chuimein where they came ashore. They carried the curragh the few miles to quiet Loch Oich and again the few miles to Loch Lochy, where the wind took them in charge once more. Finally there were ten miles, some of portage, along the west bank of the River Lochy to Corpach (the field of bodies;). There they waited on the shore with their precious burden until a great galley received them all and bore them down Loch Linnhe, through the Corran Narrows, past the island of Lismore and round to the south-west corner of Mull. Dead calm at times delayed them and the oarsmen rowed, singing their ancient *iorram* (oar songs), and wild seas tossed them in the Sound of Lorne, but they came at last safely to Iona.

V

Alasdair Carrach

Dia 'na stiùrair an darach
Dh'fhalbh air tùs an t'siùil mhara
Seal mun tug e cheud bhoinne dhe thràghadh.

'N uair a thogadh tu tonnag
Air chuan meanmnach nan dronnag
'S iomadh gleann ris an cromadh i h-eàrrach.

Dh 'éireadh buidheann o Ruaidh leat,
Lùbadh iubhar mu'n guaillean,
Thig o bhruthaichean fuar Cham na Làirge

May God be helmsman on the boat that sailed at the turn of the tide,
a little before the first drop of its ebbing ...
When you hoisted sail on the lively sea with its little wave-ridges,
many's the trough into which she would dip her scuppers ...
A company from Glen Roy would rise with you, skilled to bend the yew
bow back to their shoulders, men that come from the cold uplands of Carn
na Lairge.

Iain Lom

AS WE HAVE already seen, it is thought by some that Malcolm Canmore had
himself enthroned at Scone after he had defeated Macbeth in 1054 at the Battle
of the Seven Sleepers. He then became, in fact but not in law, the king of half of
Alba, Macbeth continuing to rule the lands to the north and west of the Mounth.

This may or may not be true, but if it is true then this enthronement was not
accepted after Macbeth's death for it is recorded that his stepson, Lulach, was

recognised as king and remained so until a year later when he was killed in battle at Essie in Strathbogie. He was succeeded by the man who had defeated him, Malcolm Canmore, but his son Maelsnechtai retained the mormaership of Moray, as did his descendants. He too lost a battle to Malcolm Canmore and ended his days in a monastery. The mormaerdom was eventually suppressed by David I in 1130 and its lands divided amongst more biddable aspirants.

During and after David's reign a string of castle-royal, baronial or the seats of clan chiefs – were built in the Great Glen, but there was nothing in the way of monastic settlement apart from a Dominican Friary in Inverness (the Benedictine presence at Cill Chuimein only began in the 19th century). Monks needed broad fertile lands in which to build their monasteries as they depended on farming to feed themselves and to finance their activities. There was little of this kind to attract them between Inverness and Inverlochy. The castles included:

> Inverness Castle
> Caisteal Spioradan
> Urquhart Castle
> Abertarf at the south end of Loch Ness (motte and bailie)
> Keppoch Castle in Glen Spean
> Tor Castle
> Inverlochy Castle

Inverness Castle had been built by Malcolm Canmore after he had destroyed Macbeth's castle, which was probably on the same site, that is, at the top of the slope on the east bank of the River Ness (at the south-east corner of the modern main bridge). David I enlarged and improved Malcolm's castle but it was very badly damaged by the Jacobites who blew it up in 1746. It was again repaired, rebuilt and considerably extended in the 19th century.

Caisteal Spioradan (castle of ghosts), at the north end of Loch Ness, belonged to the MacLeans of Dochgarroch whose land was in this area. Nothing remains of this castle except its ghosts. The MacLeans had a feud with the Camerons of Lochiel; they executed several Camerons there and hanged their bodies from the castle walls. It is their ghosts that haunted the castle and terrified the local people.

Urquhart Castle lies half-way up Loch Ness on the west bank and on the site of a Pictish fort. This fort is one of those considered as a possible location for the court of King Brude mac Maelchon, although archeological finds do not suggest that it could have been the fort of a king. The buildings there today are the remains of the 13th century castle erected by the Durwards. It was a castle of enclosure with a curtain wall and gatehouse. It had a very stormy history being attacked by, amongst others, Highlanders, Robert Bruce, Covenanting Scots, English and particularly by the MacDonalds who frequently raided down Glen Urquhart from the west. In 1545 came the Great Raid (the last one) by MacDonalds assisted by Camerons. After this there was relative peace and a gradual decline, leaving the ruin that we see today.

Keppoch Castle was built in about 1500 by Domhnall Glas, the 6th Chief of the Keppoch (Ceapach) MacDonalds. It stood on Tom Beag, a small hillock near the confluence of the Spean and the Roy and had a moat and a drawbridge. There may have been an older castle of motte and baillie type on this site before it. Raonall Og, the 9th Chief (1554-1587), may not have found the castle comfortable enough for he built a house with panelled rooms nearby and it was in this house that the murder of the Keppoch Chief and his brother took place in the 17th century. Raonall also laid out a garden – its remains can still be seen there – and planted an orchard of pear trees which was famous all over the Highlands as Garadh nam Peuran (garden of pears). Iain Lom in his lament for the murdered Keppoch chief also deplores the trampling of this orchard after the murders, but it did at least survive until 1746 when it and the house were burnt by Cumberland. This was not, however, the first famous orchard to be planted in the Highlands for Lord Lovat brought apples and pears from the south in about 1450 and with them enlarged the old orchard of the monks of Beauly Priory.[1]

Inverlochy Castle on the east bank of the River Lochy and close to where the modern town of Fort William now stands is a 13th-century castle built by the Comyns of Badenoch. It is a rectangular building with towers at each corner and two entrances, each with a portcullis. During the Wars of Independence it was taken by Robert Bruce who brought an army up from the south, possibly through Glencoe, and took over the castle easily as those who held it were not at all enthusiastic about withstanding a battle or long siege. Two famous battles were later fought here, the first in 1431 and the second in 1645.

Alasdair Carrach (scald-headed), the 1st Chief of the Keppoch MacDonalds, was involved in the first of these battles. His father, Alasdair, Lord of Lochaber, was a brother of Donald, 2nd Lord of the Isles and had refused land in the Isles offered him by his brother in 1394 as he preferred 'the forest land in Lochaber and the lands beyond the river Lochy, Mamore and Glenspean'.[2] There has been some confusion between these two Alasdairs and it was once thought that they were one and the same person, but as Alasdair of Lochaber died between 1402 and 1406 this cannot have been the case.[3]

He was probably living at some time at Tom a' Charaich near Torlundy, but either he or his son later moved to Tor Castle.[4] Tor Castle, thought to have been originally the seat of the Thanes of Lochaber, passed through a number of hands before it ended up as the seat of the Cameron chiefs. Both Tom a' Charaich and Tor Castle are in Strath Lochy, the wide, flat bottom of the Great Glen between the foot of Ben Nevis and the smaller, softer hills that line the western bank of the Lochy and both are roughly two miles as the crow flies from Inverlochy Castle.

Alasdair Carrach's time as chief came within the period when the Lords of the Isles were struggling to protect the independence of the Lordship from the Scottish Crown and to further their claim to the earldom of Ross. He had supported Alasdair, 3rd Lord of the Isles, in a campaign against the king, had helped to sack Inverness and then played what may have been only a small part in the Battle of Harlaw in 1411.

Harlaw was one of those battles, like Sheriffmuir, where it was not clear who was the victor and both sides had a feeling that they had won. The MacDonalds – the Lords of the Isles' people – certainly celebrated it as a victory, while King James I had no doubt that he had won. Losses were heavy on both sides: the MacDonalds are said to have had more than 1000 dead.[5]

As a result of these military actions against the Crown both Alasdair Carrach and Alasdair of the Isles had been shut up in Tantallon Castle. The latter languished there for a long time, but Alasdair Carrach was soon released; his incarceration did not quieten him down however, as the king had hoped, nor did the continued imprisonment of their Lord quieten the Islesmen.

In 1431, twenty years after Harlaw, Donald Balloch of Dun Noamhaig (Dunyveg in Islay) and the Glens (of Antrim) – his Gaelic name is Domhnall Ballach (Freckled Donald) – hearing that the royal army was encamped before Inverlochy Castle, began to gather together a body of men to attack them, in the hope of forcing the king to release Alasdair of the Isles. Donald Balloch was a cousin of Alasdair Carrach: he is sometimes referred to as Alasdair's nephew but this must be the result of the erroneous belief that Alasdair Carrach and his father were one and the same person (see above). Donald was also the grandson of Good John of Islay and the son of John Tanister (Iain Mòr) who had, by his marriage to Margery Bisset, acquired title to the Glens of Antrim. Donald Balloch therefore eventually became chief of the Clan Iain Mhoir (the MacDonalds of Dun Noamhaig and the Glens). At the time of the Battle of Inverlochy he was only 18. He had come from Ireland to the island of Carna in Loch Sunart, which lies to the west of the Great Glen between Strontian and Ardnamurchan. Carna is a large island lying off Glenborrodale and nearly blocking the exits of both Loch Sunart and Loch Teacuis. He brought with him a contingent of Irish from the Glens of Antrim and called on the local chiefs to join him; MacIain of Ardnamurchan and Alan MacAlan of Moidart answered his call. They picked out 600 of the best men, embarked them in their galleys and set out for Inverskippinish, a little to the south of Inverlochy.[6]

It would be interesting to know how many galleys there were; about 20 years later Donald Balloch himself raided the islands in the Firth of Clyde and along the Renfrew coast in 180 galleys, carrying 5-6000 men, that is, about 300-330 per vessel, while in 1545 Donald Dubh (son of John, the 4th Lord of the Isles) took 180 galleys with him to Ireland to join the enemies of the Scottish crown with only 4000 men in them.[7] As the size of the galleys and the number of oars they carried differ so much it is impossible to assess the number of ships that sailed through the Sound of Mull and up past Lismore to where the waters of Loch Eil and Loch Linnhe mingle. Whatever their number they must have been a splendid sight speeding towards this great curve of land below Ben Nevis, their sails spread and banners flying from their masts.

From Inverskippinish Donald Balloch sent a message to his cousin Alasdair Carrach – a message which Alasdair must have been very glad to receive as he and 220 of his archers had stationed themselves strategically on the steep sides of Meall an t-Suidhe (the round hill of the seat), the little footstool to Ben Nevis overlooking the castle, in the hope of being able to offer some resistance to the king's army. When Donald Balloch arrived it became possible to attack on two fronts and Alasdair Carrach's archers caused such damage and demoralisation that the king's army quickly succumbed to the charge of Donald and the Islesmen.

The king's army had been led by Alasdair Stiubhart, Earl of Mar, the son of the ill-famed Wolf of Badenoch. After the battle he was on the run in Lochaber with one servant and after two days without food is said to have come across some women herding cattle. They gave him barley meal and water which they mixed in the heel of his shoe. Later, in Glen Roy, Mar and his servant were given a bed and a meal by one of the earl's supporters called O'Birein (O'Brien or

O'Byrne?). The Earl of Mar is said to have told him that if ever he was in need of help and could get to Kildrummy Castle he was to ask for hospitality from him. O'Birein, finding himself at some later time at Alford near Kildrummy Castle and in some distress, took advantage of this promise, but the guard at the castle gate would not let him in until Mar heard them arguing and came forward to welcome him. These meetings are recorded in an old song:

> 'S maith an còcaire an t-ocras,
> 'S mairg dhèanadh toilceas air biadh,
> Fuarag eòrn à s àil mo bhròige –
> Biadh a b'fheòrr a fhuair mi riamh.

> Bha mi oidche ann ad theach
> Air mhòr bèidhe 's air bheag eudaich;
> 'S ionmhainn am firean ata 'muigh,
> O Birein às a' Bhreugaich.

> Hunger is a good cook,
> woe to him who disdains food;
> barley brose from the heel of my shoe –
> the best meal I ever got.

> I was one night in your house
> on plenty food and little clothing;
> dear the man who stands outside.
> it is O'Birein from Breugach.*

*Briagach.[8]

Briagach is in upper Glen Roy on the west bank of the river and opposite to where the Coire Bothchasgaidh lets its burn down into the Roy. It has a connection with the second battle of Inverlochy, for it is here that the men of Montrose's army stopped to sharpen their swords against a curious stone with a stripe of carborundum-like substance running through its middle. They were on their way to their victory over the Campbells at Inverlochy. The stone is still there, lying quietly and largely unknown in a field of grass and rushes.

At Harlaw 20 years earlier, the Camerons had fought on the side of the Lord of the Isles, but at Inverlochy, fearing for their safety should the king win, they defected to his side, an action which naturally incensed both Donald Balloch and Alasdair Carrach. After the battle Donald Balloch ravaged the Cameron lands in revenge for their treachery. The miseries Clan Cameron suffered are reflected in the song *Piobaireachd Dhomhnaill Dhuibh* (Pibroch of Black Donald). This song is often misinterpreted; some think that Black Donald is Donald Balloch when he is actually the Cameron Chief who defected to the royal army. Or perhaps they may not realise that the Camerons were on the losing side and so understand the song as a call to arms. It goes as follows:

Piobaireachd Dhòmhnaill Dhuibh,
Piobaireachd Dhòmhnaill,
Piobaireachd Dhòmhnaill Dhuibh,
Piobaireachd Dhòmhnaill,
Piobaireachd Dhòmhnaill Dhuibh,
Piobaireachd Dhòmhnaill
Piob agus bratach
Air faich Inbhir Lòchaidh.

Chaidh an-diugh, chaidh an-diugh,
Chaidh an diugh òirnne,
Chaidh an-diugh, chaidh an-diugh
Chaidh an-diugh òirnne,
Chaidh an-diugh, chaidh an-diugh
Chaidh an-diugh òirnne –
Chaidh an-diugh, chaidh an-dè,
Chaidh a h'uile là oirnne.

Nuair ràine mi 'm baile
Cha robh faram an òil ann;
Cha robh pioban gan spreigeadh.
Cha robh caithream no ceòl ann;
Bha mo chruit fhìnealt'
Na sineadh an òrdugh,
Is lèine dhan anart
Air faram a meòirean.

The literal translation of this runs:

> Pibroch of Black Donald,
> Pibroch of Donald;
>
> Bagpipe and banner
> On the field of Inverlochy.
>
> Today went, today went,
> Today went against us.
>
> Today went, yesterday went,
> And every day went against us.
>
> When I reached home
> There was no sound of drinking;
> No pipes were striking up,
> There was neither mirth or music;
> My lovely harp
> Was laid out neatly,
> With a linen death-shroud
> Stilling her fingers' sound.[9]

This is the version that appears in Anne Lorne Gillies' *Songs of Gaelic Scotland*. She explains that the song is really a lament for a lost battle.[10] The day of battle went against them (the Camerons) and every day has gone against them since. When the singer went home there was no sign of rejoicing, no pipe music, no jollity, and his harp, which might have made music on his return, lay covered up and silent. It is one of those songs which imitate the rhythms of the pipes and are sometimes called pibroch tunes. When played briskly it could be mistaken for a call to arms but if it is played a little more slowly it has a plaintive air and its long notes throb insistently, deepening the sorrow and despair.

There are several other versions of the song. One, which is given in *Duanaire na Sracaire*, has a verse clearly indicating a Cameron defeat; it asks Lochiel where his heroes have gone.[11]

The situation is not helped by the tune, which may or may not be the original one; in either case its message can easily be altered by changes in the tempo.

Sir Walter Scott produced a version which is often called a literal translation; it is certainly not that and may have contributed to the confusion:

> Pibroch of Donuil Dhu
> Pibroch of Donuil,
> Wake thy wild voice anew,
> Summon Clan Conuil.
> Come away, come away,
> Hark to the summons!
> Come in your war array,
>   Gentles and commons.
>
> Come from deep glen
> And from mountain so rocky,
> The war-pipe and pennon
> Are at Inverlochy.
> Come every hill-plaid
> And true heart that wears one,
> Come every steel blade
> And strong hand that bears one.
>
> Fast they come, fast they come
> See how they gather,
> Wide waves the eagle plume
> Blended with heather,
> Cast your plaids, draw your blades,
> Forward each man set!
> Pibroch of Donuil Dhu
> Knell for the onset![12]

Fine verses but they have little to do with the Gaelic and can only be interpreted as a call to arms.

James I eventually began to realise that a policy of reconciliation would be more likely to achieve peace with the Islesmen and he agreed to release Alasdair of the Isles under certain conditions. To fulfil one of these Alasdair was obliged to take their lands away from the Camerons. He cannot have been too pleased with them in any case as they had deserted him at Inverlochy. He gave the land first: to MacLean of Coll – at least he tried to do so – but the Camerons defeated first MacLean of Coll and then MacLean of Lochbuie whose place was then taken by MacDonald of Lochalsh. MacDonald befriended the Camerons however; perhaps he knew their chief, Donald Dhubh, well and appreciated his qualities. So things did not turn out so badly for them in the end, largely due to the success of Donald Dubh as a military leader.[13]

Donald Balloch was, of course, in James I's bad books, but he managed to avoid capture by going to Ireland. The chief of the Ulster O'Neills, Hugh Buidhe, hoping perhaps to ingratiate himself with James (or was he trying to help Donald Balloch?), sent him Donald's head as a present, but it turned out to be someone else's head, owner unknown, so Donald was able to live happily for a long time afterwards.[14]

Alasdair of the Isles was also obliged, by one of the conditions of his release, to forfeit Alasdair Carrach's lands, most of those in Glen Spean and Glen Roy going to Malcolm MacIntosh, Captain of Clan Chattan, in 1444.[15] This caused great difficulties for Alasdair Carrach and for later Keppoch chiefs, who, having no charter, spent much of their time resisting MacIntosh's demands for the payment of feudal dues and went on holding their lands 'by the sword'.

In 1688 the Keppoch chief, Colla nam Bo (Coll of the Cows), defeated MacIntosh at the Battle of Mulroy, the last clan battle, and became the hero of the Highlands; a stone at the side of the road a little way up Glen Roy commemorates this victory. In the following year Colla brought his clansmen out in support of Bonnie Dundee and his exploits are recorded (and his soubriquet explained) in chapter IX.

VI
Blàr na Leine

True, a new mistress now I chase,
The first foe in the field;
And with a stronger faith embrace
A sword, a horse, a shield.

Yet this inconstancy is such
As you too shall adore;
I could not love thee, Dear, so much,
Loved I not Honour more.

Colonel Lovelace

JAMES FRASER OF Phopachy, who was minister of Kirkhill near Beauly in the middle of the 17th century, filled what amounted, when printed, to about seven pages on the subject of Blàr na Leine in his history of the Highlands in general and the Frasers in particular from 916 to 1674.

This battle, generally known as the Battle of the Shirts and sometimes as the Battle of Kinlochlochy, took place by the north shore of Loch Lochy in 1544 and was of particular interest to James because it had such disastrous effects on his own clan.

James was born in 1634 at Phopachy on the Beauly Firth, about half-way between Kirkhill and Inverness. His grandfather, also James, was *fear an tigh* (house steward) to Lord Lovat and acquired a wadset of the lands of Phopachy in 1599. Our James eventually inherited these. He was educated at Inverness grammar school and went in 1651 to King's College, Aberdeen, where he took his MA in 1655. In 1657 during the Interregnum, when Scotland was under the heel of Cromwell, he set off on the grand tour, having obtained a pass from the colonel of the English garrison at Inverness and later from General Monk in Edinburgh. During the tour, which took him through England, France, Germany, Italy and the Low Countries, he passed himself off as a Roman Catholic whenever this was to his advantage and saw the Pope and seven cardinals celebrating mass in Rome. He even served in the papal guard for nine months and in the Low Countries saw the future Charles II and James VII and II, then in exile there. One wonders what Cromwell would have said about this.

Apparently quite unaffected by his junketings with the Church of Rome – a very tolerant attitude for his time – he returned home and settled down as Episcopalian minister of Kirkhill, a parish formed by amalgamating Wardlaw and Fernua. Although this was a difficult time for Episcopalians, whose ministers were constantly in fear of being replaced by Presbyterians, the moves against James's particular parish seem to have been only mild and he remained minister there until his death.

Parish duties cannot have been too demanding, for he left behind him more than 53 manuscripts, including an Irish (Gaelic) dictionary, a book on place-names and the book on Highland history which was itself originally twice the length of the volume published by the Scottish History Society in 1905. This amounts to 524 pages and bears the title *Chronicles of the Frasers. The Wardlaw Manuscript entitled 'Polichronicon seu policratica temporum, or, The True Genealogy of the Frasers' 916-1674*. Fortunately it is generally known as the Wardlaw Manuscript.[1]

He began this work in 1666 and dedicated it in 1699 to Simon, Lord Lovat, who had only very recently assumed this title; he is generally known today as Lord Lovat of the '45.

The immediate cause of Blàr na Leine was a quarrel over who should be chief of the Clanranald MacDonalds. Their main stronghold was Castle Tioram in Moidart on the west coast but the repercussions of the quarrel were felt as far away as the Great Glen.

When Alasdair mac Ailein mhic Ruairidh, 7th Chief of Clanranald, died in about 1529 two possible candidates for the chiefship were his half-brother, Ranald Gallda, and his natural son, generally referred to as John of Moidart or Iain Muideartach; he had no legitimate sons. Iain was very popular with his clansmen who showed no interest in appointing anyone else of the *dearbh fine* (the true kindred) to the vacant chiefship. He therefore became the 8th Chief. He was still chief in 1540 when James V set off on his circumnavigation of the Highlands. There had been several attempts in the west to restore the Lordship of the Isles which had been forfeited in 1493. James's expedition was aimed at crushing this movement.

He set off from Leith in the spring of 1540. There were 12 ships, well supplied with artillery, but the king's ship was very luxuriously appointed; he was obviously determined to show off his power and prestige to the western chiefs. He had musicians on board who played for him during meals and he ate off gold plate. He paced the deck in the May sunshine or rested under a canopy, drinking and talking to his courtiers as the ships passed Fife and St Andrews and crossed the Firth of Tay to Arbroath and Aberdeen, round Kinnaird Head and through the Moray Firth, sailing up the shores of Caithness to Orkney and Cape Wrath. So far it had been like a royal progress, an opportunity to show himself as a rich and cultured monarch.

He hoped perhaps to send ahead the message that it would be better to support an elevated personage like himself with his Renaissance castles and houses, his great court and resplendent courtiers, his ancient stronghold on a rock in Edinburgh, rather than cling to the concept of some petty lord holding sway in a simple little castle on a tiny island in a minor loch on the Isle of Islay, stepping along a causeway, sometimes under water, to an even smaller island to meet his counsellors and discuss the future of his scattered lands, for so he would have thought of that great kingdom, half-Norse, half-Gaelic, which had ruled the west since the days of Somerled. But after rounding Cape Wrath the atmosphere changed. The expedition was no longer a mere propaganda exercise but became more threatening, more warlike when the western isles were reached and the King began arresting the more recalcitrant of the chiefs, including Alexander MacLeod of Dunvegan and Iain Muideartach. The ships visited Lewis, Harris and the Uists, followed by Skye, Coll, Tiree and Mull, the coast of Argyll, Kintyre, Arran and Bute. At last, in mid-August, they reached Dumbarton where the captured chiefs were put ashore and despatched to prison. The king returned home the way he had come.

Two years later, in December 1542, he died, leaving his crown to his infant daughter, Mary, Queen of Scots. The Earl of Arran, who was acting as Regent, released the captive chiefs in the following year.

During Iain Muideartach's absence in prison his place as Captain of Clanranald had been taken by Ranald Gallda. He was the son of Alan, the 4th Chief, by a second marriage to the daughter of Thomas, Lord Lovat, and was therefore not only an uncle of Iain Muideartach but also a nephew of Hugh, the Lord Lovat who fought at Blàr na Leine. He had been fostered by the Lovats and his claim to act as chief in Iain Muirdeartach's absence was supported by them.

James Fraser calls him 'a polisht youth'[2] but he may not have been as young as this would suggest; his rather complicated relationship to the Clanranald chiefs makes it difficult to assess his age, particularly as we have few of their dates of birth.

He had not been popular with his clansmen during his period as chief. The soubriquet Gallda (foreign, unable to speak Gaelic) already suggests some antipathy to him because of his upbringing amongst the Frasers, and Gregory tells us that they also disliked his 'parsimonious disposition',[3] which suggests that there was very little feasting or music or poetry at Castle Tioram during his time. They were also resentful that it was with Fraser support that he had insinuated himself into Iain Muideartach's shoes. When the latter was released from prison they therefore immediately acknowledged him as Chief and obliged Ranald Gallda to seek refuge with his uncle, Lovat.

Once Iain Muideartach had settled himself again in Castle Tioram his men promptly overran Abertarf and Stratherrick in the Great Glen – lands belonging to Lovat – and raided in Glen Urquhart and Glenmoriston, giving signs of intending to stay there. In response George Gordon, Earl of Huntly, who was acting as the King's lieutenant in the north, gathered a force which included Lovat and Ranald Gallda. They began to move southwards against Clanranald, whereupon Iain retreated towards his western fastnesses and Huntly marched down the Great Glen as far as Inverlochy, making punitive expeditions against MacDonald of Keppoch and the Camerons on the way. Then, finding himself unable to bring the Clanranald MacDonalds to battle in the Great Glen and probably not wanting to venture any further into the territories of the western clans and the wild country of Moidart, he turned his force round and marched back the way he had come.

According to the Wardlaw MS Lovat ' ... entered his nephew, Ranald Mackdonel, into the peaceable possession of Mudard ... ',[4] while Gregory tells us that Huntly's force went as far as Inverlochy and put Ranald Gallda in possession of Moidart without opposition.[5] One could hardly be in peaceful possession of Moidart without also holding Castle Tioram and only a total misunderstanding of the geography of the Highlands could enable anyone to believe it possible to seize this castle – far away on the western seaboard and in very hostile territory – without leaving the Great Glen.

Castle Tioram (or Caisteal Tioram, to give it its correct Gaelic name) is one of the most romantically situated castles in the western Highlands, which is saying a great deal. To reach it from Acharacle – the nearest settlement – one must cross the River Shiel and follow a narrow track on the right bank ending at a small sandy bay. On the northern side of this bay is the castle itself, perched on a hillock of grass and rocks and surrounded at high tide by the salt water of Loch Moidart, with the wooded island of Shona rising behind it. At low tide a causeway from mainland to castle is revealed and explains the castle's name, which in English is 'dry castle'. Castle Tioram is not only beautifully situated but also easily defensible, if reasonably well garrisoned. Any hostile force approaching it by land would have to negotiate the narrow track beside the river with its twists and turns and ups and downs and, having arrived at the causeway, might be faced by a high tide which would leave it exposed to fire from the castle until the tide turned. By sea there is only one place where a ship might anchor without being seen, and then only in the dark, for though she might remain unnoticed for a time once tied up under the cliff to the north west, her approach would be noted in daylight or moonlight as soon as she entered Loch Moidart.

In any case Ranald Gallda was still with Huntly when the latter marched back up the Great Glen and it is therefore hard to think of his reported replacement in Castle Tioram as anything more than wishful thinking on the part of Huntly (or on the part of James Fraser).

The Wardlaw manuscript, not surprisingly, gives all the credit for the Great Glen expedition to Lovat and makes him the prime mover in the creation of an army to combat the MacDonalds and their allies, saying:

> George Gordon, Earle of Huntly, is highly incensed at this, that any should be employed but himselfe in such an undertaking and honourable expedition, being Kock off the North; and therefore contrived all the malicious methods imaginable against Lovat ... [6]

Fraser does not say what these methods were and other writers are silent on the matter.

Lovat's quickest way home from Inverlochy was to keep straight on up the Great Glen towards Inverness. He must have felt he had a reasonable chance of getting through the country of the Glengarry MacDonalds beside Loch Oich and once he reached Cill Chuimein (Fort Augustus) he would be on his own land up the east side of Loch Ness. Huntly and the Laird of Grant, however, intended to turn east out of the Great Glen. Some writers, MacDonald of Castleton and Gregory, for instance, send them along Glen Spean and then either up Glen Roy or through the Braes of Lochaber,[7] but neither of these ways were of more than local interest at that time. The main highway from west to east brought travellers from the west over the ford at what we now call Gairlochy, north-east up Glen Fintaig and so into Glen Gloy.

Gloy comes from the Gaelic *glaoidh* meaning glue or sticky, though why the glen should have been described in this way I do not know. Could it be anything to do with the nature of the soil? The inventor of that delightful and rather liquid glue with which as a child I used joyfully to stick paper chains together at Christmas must have had some knowledge of Gaelic and/or the Highlands to call his product 'Gloy'.

Huntly was not at all happy at letting Lovat go on up the Great Glen and begged him to turn off to the east with him, but Lovat was not prepared to be frightened off a route that would take him home so much more quickly. James Fraser of Foynes, 'a headstrong man', also dissuaded him from accepting an offer from the Laird of Grant and the MacIntoshes to accompany him, saying it would look like cowardice.[8] Accordingly they separated at the Water of Gloy and Lovat with Ranald Gallda and Grant of Glenmoriston[9] went on up the east bank of Loch Lochy. The hills on the west side of the loch go down very steeply towards the water, but they do leave a small flat margin between themselves and the loch and it was along this narrow track that Lovat's party, after passing Letterfinlay, saw marching a large contingent of MacDonalds, subsequently assessed at about 600 men, whereas Lovat had only 300 to 400. The MacDonalds were divided into seven groups, each carrying its own banner. Six of these groups were provided by Alasdair of Glengarry, Alan of Morar, Angus of Knoydart, Ranald of Keppoch, Alasdair MacIain of Ardnamurchan (all belonging to Clan Donald) and Ewen Cameron of Lochiel. The seventh was composed of Iain Muideartach's men, but whether Iain was with them or not is unclear.[10] It seems generally to be assumed that he was, but on the other hand, given the other six contingents, only a relatively small number of Iain's men would be needed to make the total force up to 600 and he would be unwise to leave Castle Tioram ungarrisoned and his territories generally without his overall direction. His name is not specifically mentioned in reports of the subsequent battle and he certainly was not a casualty, nor do any descriptions of the action include any accounts of his exploits during it, which would certainly suggest that he was not there.

It was obvious to Lovat that his force and the MacDonald force were bound to meet at the head of Loch Lochy and he knew that he had missed the last chance of taking avoiding action. He therefore halted, held a council of war, heard mass from his own chaplain and gave his men what James Fraser calls 'a short harrang' (about 300 words as reported by Fraser). But with the MacDonalds progressing swiftly up the other side of the loch it seems doubtful whether there would have been time for all this.[11]

In his speech Lord Lovat declared that he would ' ... rather chuse a noble death than survive a disaster and enjoy my life, tho opulent and secure, after the admission of so foul a fact as a base retreat' and he referred the event ' ... to Almighty God, for the battle is the Lord's, who can save with few as many'.[12] The constant belief of commanders that the Lord is on their side and their subsequent acceptance of the fact that He had obviously not been, always amazes me.

The battle began as soon as the two forces met at the head of Loch Lochy. Although they stood initially on firm ground there they had marshy ground just to the south of them which eventually became their battle area.

James Fraser calls the battle Blàr leine or Blàr na Leine or Field of Shirts, so-called, he says, because they fought in their shirts.[13] Blàr na Leine however is a singular and would have to be altered to Blàr nan Leine to give a plural. In the opinion of many Gaelic scholars the word *leine* should really be *leana*, meaning not a shirt but a marshy place, which is precisely the sort of place on which much of the battle was fought. In any case to call this encounter 'Battle of the Shirts' suggests that casting one's plaid before battle was an unusual event, whereas it was common practice in Highland warfare except in really cold weather. In that case the plaid could easily be arranged so that it did not impede the wearer when fighting. But this was a hot July day and the battle area lay in the full rays of the sun when at its highest and hottest and as it declined towards the west after noon. Another possibility is that they removed their tunics as well as their plaids, but this would only apply to the gentlemen of the clan. A further point to be considered is that Highlanders may then still have been wearing chain mail. Redshanks (Highland mercenary soldiers fighting in Ireland) were observed by the English to be so accoutred and Fraser himself also speaks of 'such as boar armour, head pieces and coats of mail'.[14]

Topographical details at this end of the loch have been altered by time and by the construction of the Caledonian Canal during which the level of Loch Lochy was raised several feet. Before this time there was very flat, low-lying and marshy terrain here in which much of the battle took place. From the battlefield, which encompasses an area now known as Laggan Locks, as the locks at the beginning of the stretch of canal from Loch Lochy to Loch Oich begin here, there is a view of the whole of Loch Lochy right down to Gairlochy at its southern edge and often even further, in a straight line, to the soft hills of Ardgour. It is one of the points from which the straightness of this ancient rift can best be appreciated. Nearby on the west bank is the burial place of the Glengarry chiefs, the old grave-yard of Kilfinnan, consecrated to St Finnan, who is also remembered at Eilean Fhianain, the Green Isle, in Loch Shiel.

Some accounts of the battle state that it began with a shower of arrows shot from a distance, but others (including the Wardlaw MS), say nothing of this. All however agree that the chief weapons used were two-handed swords and Lochaber axes (James Fraser calls them Dence axes). These were both ancient weapons. The two-handed sword would be eclipsed in less than a century by the basket-hilted claymore. The Lochaber axe would meet a similar fate; it was a terrifying weapon – a long shaft with a fiendish sharp blade or axeshaped device at one end and in addition a hook that could be used by the foot-soldier to pull his mounted oppo-nent from his horse.

They fought, as James Fraser says, 'more like lyons than men'. It was 'the most unparalleled batle that story records; I never read, never heard of such anoth-er'.[15] When the fighting was at its fiercest Lord Lovat was appalled to see his eld-est son, Simon, the Master of Lovat, arriving with about a dozen companions. He had expressly told him to remain at home and look after things there; should he die he did not want his heir to be killed too, but Simon's stepmother had taunt-ed him with the observation that ' ... the old men were fighting in the fields and young men loitering at home with their wives'.[16] She could not, of course, have known anything about Blàr na Leine, as it was too far away, but she must have expected that some such encounter was likely. Her words were too much for the young man and, gathering some of his friends together, he set off down the Great Glen in the hopes of reaching his father before any major conflict began. His arrival 'dampt and dispirited' Lovat,[17] but each one of the new recruits fought as well as ten men, although this was not enough to alter the course of the battle. Eventually the combatants ran down into the loch – perhaps because the battle site was too encumbered with bodies to give them foothold – and fought there, slashing at each other with their dirks, ' .... and in that Loch they fought so that the stream from the lake run blood for many days'.[18] It would not by any means be the only stream near a battlefield to do this, but the slaughter was neverthe-less particularly horrific. Many of the dead were found afterwards lying together, MacDonald and Fraser, clasping each other in a last furious embrace in the shal-low water. There are no reliable casualty figures and most reports suggest that each side was reduced to single numbers though these vary. James Fraser thought that his clan had won and believed that the MacDonalds ' .. chuse the floure of their numerous clan to fight this battle, and lost it both in credit, conduct and slaughter ... ',[19] while Buchanan's *Historia* records that ' ... the Frasers, being fewer in number, were overcome and all slain to a man ... '.[20] Nearly all Lovat's 80 gentlemen were said to have been killed. Neither Lord Lovat himself, nor the Master of Lovat, nor Ranald Gallda survived; their bodies were retrieved from the field and buried at Beauly Priory. Lord Lovat was aged 55 and his son Simon was probably in his early twenties.

With Hugh, Lord Lovat and his eldest son, Simon, both dead, the title descended to the second son, Alexander, a boy of 17. Since anyone who might have acted as tutor to him had probably been killed in the battle the estates were managed by Hugh Lovat's widow, Janet, ' .... which she did well and wisely' according to James Fraser.[21] This contradicts his earlier opinion that Janet had taunted Simon in the hope that he would be killed, thus making way for one of her own sons, for she seems to have protected the interests of Alexander, who, like the dead Simon, was also her stepson.

The Wardlaw MS says nothing of the fate of the gentlemen of Clan Donald, although Ranald Mòr of Keppoch must have come safely out of the battle for he was executed two years later. Of Iain Muideartach there is no word, presumably because he was not there, as already suggested.

The MacDonalds, of course, thought that they had won and there were cer-tainly enough of them left to continue their support of the new Lord of the Isles, Donald Dubh. When Huntly again entered the Great Glen and carried out fur-ther punitive raids on anyone he might think deserved it there was no shortage of Clan Donald men to respond by raiding Urquhart Castle in the following year.

In the Great Raid of 1545 the plunder taken by the MacDonalds and Camerons was:

> 2000 cattle
> 383 horses
> 3000 sheep

2000 goats
122 pigs
64 geese
12 feather beds with bolsters, blankets and sheets
brewing vats
roasting spits
pots and pans
a chest containing £300
guns, gunpowder and stands of armour
iron gates
tables and other furniture
three large boats

This was the last raid from the west that the castle had to withstand. After it life in Glen Urquhart gradually became more peaceful and the castle began to decline in importance in the following century.[22]

Ewen, the 13th Chief of Clan Cameron and Ranald Mòr, the 7th Chief of Keppoch, were both involved in all the risings associated with attempts to resurrect the Lordship of the Isles, but their participation in the raid on Urquhart Castle after Blàr na Leine was the final straw for the authorities and they were arrested and beheaded in 1546. Ewen, who had been chief for 66 years (and there is no word of his being a minor when he succeeded),[23] must by then have been in his eighties. Iain Muideartach avoided sharing their fate by retreating to the west. He remained Chief of the Clanranald MacDonalds until his death in 1584.

The Frasers slowly regained their military strength due to a great extent to the roughly 80 Fraser widows who thoughtfully produced boys within the next few months. In the last period of James Fraser's life, under the famous (or infamous) Simon Fraser, Lord Lovat of the '45, the clan flourished until Simon, who had spent his life trying always to be on the winning side, at last made a mistake and joined the Jacobites. Given the ruthless and indiscriminate nature of the revenge taken by the Duke of Cumberland after Culloden however, they may not have fared much worse than those loyal to the Hanoverians.

VII
Montrose

Queen and Huntress, chaste and fair,
Now the sun is laid to sleep,
Seated in thy silver chair
State in wonted manner keep:
Hesperus entreats thy light,
Goddess excellently bright.

Ben Jonson

ONE NIGHT AT the end of January 1645, when the Great Glen lay in winter's grip and the hills to either side were covered with veils and drifts of snow, there was movement and laughter on a slope to the south of Loch Ness as the flames of camp fires leapt up towards the bright moon. The army encamped there was formed principally of Gaels from the Highlands and Ireland, with a small admixture of Lowlanders. They had returned from a winter expedition into Argyll and, had their commander been Julius Caesar, would several weeks earlier have retired into winter quarters, but their leader could not spare the time to indulge in such idleness, whatever the weather.

That leader, who was to become to his contemporaries a 'matchless heroe'[1] and was to bring fame to the Great Glen itself because of his exploits there, was James Graham, 1st Marquis of Montrose. He had inherited the earldom of Montrose from his father, the 4th earl, in 1626 when he was only 14. Eighteen years later, in June 1644, he was created Marquis by Charles I. There are many portraits of him, in particular the famous one by Honthorst painted in 1649 in Holland for Elizabeth, Queen of Bohemia, but the one which for me best expresses his style and character is that attributed to Dobson and probably painted in Oxford in the summer of 1644. Dobson could get beyond the conventions of the court painters and find the real man and his portraits of Charles I have a touching human quality which is absent from those of Van Dyck, splendid as they are.

In the Dobson portrait, which can be seen in the National Portrait Gallery in Edinburgh, Montrose wears dark armour with a wide, white collar. His eyes are dark brown (though some report them as grey) and his brown hair with a tinge of auburn in it is dressed with a fringe and long curls in the Cavalier style. His head is very slightly turned towards the viewer and his expression is thoughtful yet alert, perhaps even a little wary – a spring at rest, waiting to be released – altogether a great contrast to the rather sad, quiescent figure in the Honthorst portrait.

Although it is chiefly for his military achievements that he is remembered, he was also a statesman, to the limited extent allowed to him by his circumstances, and a poet and in his poetry he sometimes uses the vocabulary of statecraft:

> My dear and only love, I pray
> This noble world of thee
> Be governed by no other sway
> But purest monarchie.
> For if Confusion have a part,
> Which vertuous souls abhore,
> And hold a Synod in thy heart,
> I'll never love thee more.
>
> Like Alexander I will reign,
> And I will reign alone.
> My thoughts shall evermore disdain
> A rival on my throne.
> He either fears his fate too much
> Or his deserts are small
> That puts it not unto the touch,
> To win or lose it all.
>
> Or in the empire of my heart,
> Where I shall solely be,
> Another do pretend a part
> And dares to vie with me,
> Or if Committees thou erect
> And go on such a score,
> I'll sing and laugh at thy neglect
> And never love thee more.[2]

Is he addressing his mistress here ... or his country?

Since the events described in the last chapter there had been huge changes in both Scotland and England. The two Crowns were now united under Charles I, the great-grandson of James V of Scots, and Charles was in the middle of a Civil War between Crown and English Parliament, a war which also had its repercussions in Scotland, fuelled by the King's attempt, some years earlier, to force an English-style prayer book on the Scottish Kirk. Montrose had himself signed the National Covenant protesting against the King's action but had later been repelled by the extreme bigotry developing amongst the Covenanters and had not signed the much more stringent Solemn League and Covenant issued in 1641. He had also been attracted by the personality of the King when he met him at Oxford. Abandoning any sympathies he might have had with the Covenanters' cause he raised an army in support of the King.

On that cold January night near Loch Ness he was bringing this army away from Inveraray, the stronghold of the Chief of Clan Campbell and Marquis of Argyll (MacCailein Mòr), a leading figure amongst the Covenanters. They had arrived in Inveraray just before Christmas, intent on destroying Campbell power in the Highlands. This was an unexpected twist to Montrose's plans and he had been very unenthusiastic about it at first.

He was 32 and had won three battles against the Covenanting army – Tippermuir, Aberdeen and Fyvie; he then hoped to go into the Lowlands for the winter, where it would be easier to obtain supplies for his army, and eventually to join the King who, after the defeat of Prince Rupert at Marston Moor, had seen the fortunes of war slip away from him.

The Gaels, whether Irish or Scots, who made up almost his entire army viewed the situation from a rather different angle. The Stewart kings had on the whole attacked Gaelic culture and the autonomy of the clan chiefs, but Charles, though a remote figure, had shown little sign of doing so and was therefore more appealing, even if for rather negative reasons. They wished him well but could not forget their own politics, in particular the undue power and aggression of Campbell chiefs, who had ravaged their lands and killed their people – not that they themselves had been entirely innocent in this respect – and had sometimes resorted to devious legal processes to extend their power – *Tha sgriob ghiar peann gearra/Cumail dian air MacCailein* (The sharp stroke of short pens protects Argyll), as the great 17th-century Gaelic bard, Iain Lom, tells us.[3]

What this Gaelic army wanted was to raid into Campbell lands and crush the power of 'King Campbell'. When they heard that Montrose wanted them to march out of the Highlands, to embroil themselves in fighting in a strange countryside far from their native glens, to make it impossible for them to return home at intervals to leave their battle spoils or to help with sowing and harvest, they were appalled. This was the way the clansmen had always fought and Montrose was always to be unsure of the number of men he had at his disposal at any particular time. He knew in this instance that if he insisted on moving south there would be massive desertions. On the other hand, if he agreed to go into Argyll's territory in the middle of winter the whole army might be lost. These lands were regarded both by the Campbells themselves and by outsiders as impenetrable. 'It's a far cry to Lochow [Loch Awe]' was the old saying, and it would be an even further cry in deep snow when the passes, even if they could find them, were blocked and food scarce and every man's hand turned against them.

At this juncture Montrose's army amounted to about 3000 men which included between 1000 and 1100 from the north of Ireland led by Alasdair MacColla, 800 men Alasdair had recruited in the west of Scotland after the Battle of Fyvie, plus the Atholl Stewarts and the clans of the Great Glen – Keppoch and Glengarry MacDonalds and some Camerons. They were probably right in thinking that no true and lasting victory was possible unless they had first crushed the traditional enemies of Clan Donald. Montrose found himself obliged to fall in with their plan and, as it turned out, the winter expedition into Campbell country was enormously successful.

The celebrated Alasdair MacColla leading the Irishmen raised at the behest of his kinsman, the Marquis of Antrim, was, like Montrose, in his thirties at the time. I wish there was more to be said about his appearance; there are no portraits of him and we only know that he had dark hair and was seven-foot tall (a measure that we do not need to believe precisely). The highly improbable traditional stories about his strength do suggest however that he was a person of great presence, powerful and with a commanding air. He was said in his youth to have eaten a toad, which seems to have been a commendable thing to do if one was to turn out to be a hero. Montrose himself and Viscount (Bonnie) Dundee were both credited (if that is an appropriate word) with doing so. A great many of his men were Ulster MacDonalds or MacDonnells while the rest came from Irish families bound to the MacDonnells by blood or friendship. At that time the ties between Ireland and Gaelic Scotland were very close. Alasdair's famous kinsman Somhairle Buidhe (Sorley Boy), who had established MacDonald power in the

Glens of Antrim at the end of the previous century, only needed to light a beacon fire at Ballycastle on the north Irish coast and the fighting men of Kintyre would row their swift galleys across to help him within a few hours.

Alasdair himself, whose fuller Gaelic name was Alasdair mac Cholla Chiotaich (Alasdair son of Coll the Left-handed) was the son of Colla Ciotach MacDonald of Colonsay, best known to non-Gaelic speakers as Colkitto, a name that has often been incorrectly applied to his son. Colla Ciotach had been engaged in endless fighting, much of it directed against the Campbells, who, amongst other acts calculated to infuriate MacDonald chiefs and clansmen, had seized Colonsay, forcing Colla to become a fugitive. He and two of his sons were eventually captured by Argyll. In bringing his men from Ireland Alasdair's object was not only to support the king but even more to reduce the power of the Campbells and to release his father and brothers from captivity. As second-in-command he brought with him Manus O'Cahan, the son of the Giolla Dubh MacCathan who was a foster brother of the Marquis of Antrim.[4] Alasdair and Manus had been associated in military exploits for some years, the O'Cahans being the Irish family most closely tied to the MacDonnells.

Alasdair has had a bad press in non-Gaelic circles, being often described as a strong man of little brain with no thought beyond killing, who would have been nothing without the leadership of Montrose. This view has, I hope, been dismissed by the masterly picture of him presented by David Stevenson.[5] He was a brave and successful soldier and his Irish contingent was the core of Montrose's army. He developed a tactic which he first used in Ireland at the Battle of the Laney in 1642; it became famous as the Highland Charge and was used successfully by Highland armies for the next 100 years. Montrose could not have won his long string of victories without Alasdair.

Argyll was quietly spending the winter at Inveraray Castle when he was told that Montrose was only a few miles away. He laughed at first and could not believe it, but when the news was confirmed he at once got into a boat with his family and was taken down Loch Fyne, gone, as he explained, to recruit a force to help withstand the Royalists. Though this could be regarded as a reasonable action, considering his importance to the Covenanting cause, it can hardly have been reassuring to his clansmen to be deserted by their chief at such a critical time. Tradition, after all, required the chief and his nearest kinsmen to stand in the front line of battle, leading and protecting the *clann*, the children, behind them.

> Irresolute and well-nigh beside himself with dread, he scram-
> bled into a fishing-boat and saved himself by flight, abandon-
> ing his friends, clansmen, and the whole of his country to
> fate and the mercy of the enemy.[6]

These are the words of Wishart, Montrose's chaplain, who missed most of the
campaign because he was a prisoner of the Covenanters and took a great deal of
his information about it from Montrose himself when they were together in
Holland afterwards. Could this therefore represent what Montrose himself
thought of Argyll at this juncture?

There is little agreement about the number of people killed during this raid.
Some claim that everyone the men of Montrose's army met was slaughtered,
whilst others believe that booty was the most important thing and that few
Campbells lost their lives. MacMhuirich gives 895 as the number killed.[7]
Montrose's army certainly emerged from MacCailein's lands loaded down with
every conceivable kind of arms, furniture, clothing, food, not to mention the
great herds of cattle that they drove away.

They had reached Inveraray just before Christmas and left on the 14th
January, going up Glen Aray towards Dalmally and through the Pass of Brander
to the shores of Loch Etive, which they crossed. The crossing in small boats took
two nights of brilliant moonlight and the day that lay between them. They then
moved on through Appin, collecting a party of Stewart recruits on the way and
emerged on the south shore of Loch Leven, possibly meeting MacIan of Glencoe
at the foot of Meal Mòr near the entrance to the glen. It is likely that MacIan led
them up the glen as far as Altnafeadh and so over the hills where we today
encounter the Devil's Staircase (later built as part of one of Wade's military roads
and now part of the West Highland Way). This took them to Kinlochleven from
which the shortest way into the Great Glen was through the Mamore hills via the
Lairig Mòr to Lochan Lunn Da Bhra and so to what is now the Upper
Auchintore Road which leads to the roundabout at the south end of Fort
William. Inverlochy was then only a mile (1.6km) away to the north.

There is certainly some evidence for this route as far as the south shore of
Loch Leven, but after that we find a very wild selection of alternatives in the lit-
erature. Maps showing Montrose's route are nearly all similar to that given by
John Buchan in his life of Montrose,[8] which shows the royalist army going up the
Devil's Staircase from Altnafeadh to Kinlochleven and then continuing north-

eastwards up the east side of Loch Treig into Glen Spean and then down Glen Spean to its junction with the Great Glen ten miles (16km) north of Inverlochy. This completely ignores the track from Kinlochleven to Fort William, described above, which is only ten to 15 miles (16-24km) long, as opposed to three to four times this distance along the Loch Treig route. It is nevertheless this latter route which is usually the one shown in maps of the campaign even when the accompanying text tells us something different, or even when the writer speaks of Montrose resting for a day or two at Inverlochy, which he would have by-passed had he gone by Loch Treig.

Having walked from Altnafeadh in Glencoe to Kinlochleven and from Kinlochleven through the Mamores to Fort William, I feel certain that this is the way they went. Buchan does suggest it as a possible route although for some strange reason he favours the long slog by Loch Treig. There seems to be a general obsession with Loch Treig although there was never a major track there until the railway came. The railway must have a mesmerising effect for the problem crops up again with reference to the first Jacobite Rising (1689) when Viscount Dundee came up from Loch Rannoch to Glen Spean. In the literature he is regularly sent to the east of Loch Treig instead of along the well-worn and much shorter route through the Lairig Leacach.[9]

Contemporary writers like Wishart and Father Macbreck[10] wisely gloss over the journey from Loch Leven to Lochaber, for neither of them was present. Father Macbreck's information came from a priest who was there but was very probably unfamiliar with the territory.

When they reached Inverlochy they found the castle empty and were able to camp comfortably within and without it, surrounded no doubt by pots and pans, swords and axes, statues and ornaments, lengths of silk and velvet, in fact all the multifarious bits of booty they had removed from MacCailein Mòr and his people, though what happened to the vast herds of cattle I do not know. They must have been left somewhere in safe hands to be collected later.

Old paintings show Inverlochy Castle in the midst of a wild and beautiful countryside with grass and heather round it and rugged hills behind, but today, although the rugged hills are still the same, the castle itself is close to a complex of industrial buildings and railway marshalling yards. Much work has been done on it in recent years however and perhaps eventually these unsympathetic objects can be removed and we shall have the castle again as it used to be. It was built in the 13th century by the Comyns of Badenoch but their power was destroyed by

Bruce in 1308 and the castle passed into other hands, including those of the Gordons of Huntly. It has a round tower at each corner enclosing a rectangular courtyard and its two entrances – opposite to one another – each has a portcullis. Even now with its more modern encumbrances it is a peaceful, idyllic spot on a sunny afternoon, with the green, clipped grass round it, the River Lochy running past and the ancient coloured stones glowing softly in its walls.

From it the clansmen could see on one side the lower slopes of Ben Nevis but were too close under the great hill to be aware of its ultimate summit. Snow lay in the corries and the folds of the slopes and at night the moon, as bright as when they had crossed Loch Etive, picked out the contours of every rock and the bare, twisted branches of every tree. On the other side of them was the River Lochy and beyond it the long narrow outline of Loch Eil leading to the west.

But it was northwards they were bound when they broke camp. A hostile army commanded by the Earl of Seaforth waited for them somewhere beyond Loch Ness and they needed to engage with it and defeat it before they could continue with the rest of their campaign.

In the blessed interval of rest at Inverlochy the priests who had come with the Irish and those accompanying the Catholic clans had built altars from the branches of trees and had celebrated Mass and heard confessions there;[11] these altars must now be abandoned and the chalices and candles packed away.

They set out along a broad track to the east of the river, the foothills of Ben Nevis on their right and on their left a slope and a wide strath between them and the water. When they reached the River Spean, rushing down from the east towards the Lochy with an ever louder roar and boring deeper and deeper into the hillside, they probably kept to its west bank for a little and crossed it by a ford at Inch, to the north of where Highbridge was later built as part of Wade's military road. They were then at the edge of the great plain of Mucomir (the plain of the confluence) that lies between Gairlochy to the west and Stronaba to the east. (It was here that 44 years later Viscount Dundee, a collateral of Montrose, would gather his Highland army to support James VII and II.) Now they no longer had the river to the west of them but Loch Lochy itself with the tall hills sweeping down close to its western shore and near its further end the ancient burial ground dedicated to St Finnan. They passed to the east the entry to the great cleft of Glen Gloy – going up to join the Corrieyairack Pass. The bulk of the march to the head of Loch Lochy had still to be accomplished and then there was only a mile or two (1.6-3.2km) over flat land to Loch Oich, four miles (6.4km) long and

220yd/201m wide – a miniature compared with the great sheets of water to the south and north of it. It has a quiet, intimate quality which makes one feel always peacefully alone there, where the steep banks to the east fill the still water with green and the tall trees on the western bank leave little place for the sky.

There was only the length of Loch Oich plus another two miles (3.2km) to Loch Ness, but before they went as far as this Montrose drew his men up on the Leitir nan Lub (the slope of the [river] bends), roughly parallel to the present-day straight section of tarmacadam road known by many as Montrose's Mile. Their camp fires flickered all that night between Aberchalder and Loch Uanagan

On the following day Montrose got all his main supporters to sign a Band declaring their willingness to unite against Argyll and the Covenant. Most of the 53 signatures which appear on it were appended there in the church dedicated to St Cummen which stood a little to the south of Loch Ness, near the burial ground still in use today in Cill Chuimein (Fort Augustus). The list of signatories is headed by Montrose himself and his 14-year-old son, John, Lord Graham, who accompanied him on this campaign, largely because he would not otherwise have been safe from capture by the forces of the Covenant. The signatures that follow include those of Alasdair MacColla and the Earl of Airlie, the MacDonald chiefs of Glengarry, Clanranald and Keppoch, Stewart of Appin, MacLean of Duart and MacLean of Lochbuie. Spaces must have been left in the document, for later on the names of people who were not present were added, for instance Lord George Gordon and Nathaniel Gordon and, strange to relate, the Earl of Seaforth who later found it politic to cease his hostility to Montrose for a time.

During this pause in the march many of the clansmen took the opportunity of going home to leave their booty and see that all was well with their families, which was normal practice with a Highland army. So many of them left, with the intention of rejoining later, that Montrose found he was left with only 1500-2000 men, instead of the original 3000. Assuming that none of the Irish had left, as they could not go home, there would only have been about 500-900 Highlanders. The clan chiefs will have been there, but most of them with a reduced force.

At this point Fate, in the shape of Iain Lom, the bard of the Keppoch MacDonalds, arrived at the camp with news that Argyll had returned far more speedily than expected and had gathered a Campbell army, supported by lowland troops, which was now waiting at Inverlochy. Montrose was thus caught between Seaforth in the north and Argyll in the south. He questioned Iain Lom very closely, not at first being quite sure whether he could trust him. In the end he decided that he must deal with Argyll first but that with his depleted numbers the only chance of defeating him lay in introducing an element of surprise and mystery into the proceedings. Had he turned back to Inverlochy by the way he had come Argyll would have known exactly what he was doing. Instead he took advice on alternative routes and then set out up the track beside the River Tarff, drawing his army after him from its camp on the Leitir nan Lub, but leaving a small body to keep an eye on the main highway and deal with any scouts sent out by either hostile commander, Seaforth or Argyll.

They passed over the natural feature known as Glun Cùl Eachaidh (the knee of Culachy), which Iain Lom mentions in his poem on the Battle of Inverlochy,[12] thus surely indicating that he was himself present on the march. After following the direction of the Corrieyairack for a short while they turned south and went through the Aberchalder Forest into Glen Buck, over Carn Dearg and down by Glen Turret into Glen Roy. Here they made use where they could of the three parallel roads which line Glen Roy; they are sometimes as much as 22 yards (20m) wide though often interrupted by slippages or other forms of erosion and are the result of glaciers melting and freezing at different levels at the end of the last Ice Age. At the head of the glen near where the Roy and the Turret meet stands the shattered trunk of an ancient tree, believed to be the one on which Alasdair MacColla intended to hang Iain Lom if his information turned out to be incorrect. Fortunately for the welfare of 17th-century Gaelic poetry it did not.

At Achavady (Achadh a' Mhadaidh, the field of the wolf) about half-way down Glen Roy they turned westwards, away from the river and behind Bohuntine Hill, to avoid marauding Campbells thought to be setting fire to the houses in Bohuntine village. This deviation brought them down somewhere near Inverroy, which may have been the original junction of the Spean and Roy or may mark the end of the flood plain between it and Bunroy, the present confluence. Crossing the Spean at Dalnabea, upstream of the modern Spean Bridge and to the east of the junction of Spean and Cour, they went up the Cour to Leanachan and then, keeping to the lower ridges of Ben Nevis, finally reached the slopes of Meall an t-Suidhe (the round hill of the seat), the small hill lying at the foot of the Ben and overlooking Inverlochy.

When they began their march from Cill Chuimein the air was biting and at first the moon shone as brightly and as piercingly as when they were crossing Loch Etive the week before. They stumbled through drifts of snow and over ice-capped rocks, their only food the little oatmeal they had in their sporrans or tied in the corner of their plaids which they mixed with water and ate from the blades of their sgian dubh. No other sustenance was to be expected in this desolate stretch of hills with scarcely a habitation in it, where the deer with difficulty sought some living green amongst the pinched grasses and the frozen heather.

They are thought to have bivouacked briefly at Achavady and in his dispatch to the king Montrose says that four miles (6.4km) from Inverlochy they waited from 5-8pm to allow the rest of the army to catch up.[13] This may have been at Dalnabea where they crossed the Spean, although it is more like eight miles from Inverlochy as the crow flies, but it may have seemed less to him because the going was easier and they had had a good rest first. Shortly before Achavady they had paused at Briagach (Breagh Achadh – fine field) on the west bank of the river and opposite Coire Both Chàsgaidh or Coire Bohaskey on today's OS maps, (Both = a bothy, Chàsgaidh – meaning is uncertain). There, in a field on the slope between the lowest parallel road and the river there is a greyish-white boulder with a deep incision across the middle of it. Some, at least, of Montrose's men are thought to have sharpened their swords on it in readiness for the coming battle.[14] It is a small boulder and rather like a sandwich in that the incised stripe, the 'filling', seems to be of a quite different type of rock from that of the 'bread' on either side of it. It has the same effect as carborundum on any metal blade applied to it. We do not know whether the army came upon it by chance, or whether, which is more likely, it was already well known to the MacDonalds living in Glen Roy.

The march had begun on the morning of Friday, the 31st January; it was to take them 36 hours and cover nearly 40 miles (64km). The freezing weather which had accompanied them for about the first day and night gave way to a period of heavy rain which turned rivers into roaring torrents and little trickles into fast-flowing burns. The rough tracks, from being slippery with ice became sticky and slippery with mud, but by the time they reached Meall an t-Suidhe the weather had changed again and the moon again shone through the frosty air, chilling the clansmen in their rain-sodden plaids. They could see below them the camp fires of Argyll's army, the men clustered round them in comparative comfort.

The Royalist army dared light no fires lest they betray their presence or their numbers to their enemies, who suspected there was some force or other on the slopes above them but thought it was only a raiding party which they could easily dislodge in the morning or a portion of Montrose's army under one of his commanders. So there was not much to worry them, they thought, and their chief was with them, as he had returned with the Lowland troops he had recruited after leaving Inveraray Castle so precipitately. The night passed slowly; painfully slowly for the shivering men on Meall an t'Suidhe with aching limbs and empty stomachs. There was occasional skirmishing between the two armies but still not enough to reveal to the Campbells that anything remarkable awaited them up there in the shadows, only partially and fleetingly invaded by the light of the moon.

At length, as dawn began to break, Montrose ordered the trumpets to sound to salute the unfurling of the Royal Standard and the noise, echoing amongst the rocks, told the men waiting near Inverlochy Castle that it was no raiding party they had to deal with. These were the trumpets blown before a king and their presence there revealed that the king's captain-general himself stood on the slopes above them.

It was the 2nd February, Candlemas Day and the Feast of the Purification of the Virgin Mary. Irish priests went up and down the lines celebrating mass and blessing the swords of the combatants. Alasdair mac Colla went to Iain Lom, who had drawn apart a little from the others, and said: 'Iain, will you go with us?' and offered him a sword. But Iain, the bard of his clan, asked who would record the feats of arms of Clan Donald if he were killed, adding, 'Cathaichibh sibh-se is innsedh mise'. (The fighting is for you and the telling of it for me). He withdrew to a nearby rock where he had a good view of the battlefield.

It had been decided that the Marquis of Argyll, the Campbell Chief, who had injured his shoulder a few days before in a fall from his horse, should play no part in the coming battle. His galley, An Dubh Linnseach (the black-sailed), waited at anchor in Loch Linnhe and at some time before morning light he had gone aboard, leaving Campbell of Auchinbreck – luaidh nam ban a Cinn-tire (the darling of the women of Kintyre)[15] – to lead his army. Once again we have to say that his life was very important to the covenanting cause – a prime consideration in Lowland terms – but to his clansmen his departure meant that once again they had been deserted by their chief in the hour of their greatest need. Even Willcock in his life of Argyll does not wholly exonerate him from blame for deserting them.[16]

One story about Argyll and his galley tells how Cameron of Lochiel (Ailean, the 16th Chief), now well into his eighties, had come down to Inverlochy with some of his men – according to one version led by his son John who been dead for ten years! It seems to me that Ailean may have been paying a courtesy call on

Argyll rather than bringing recruits for a battle, as, although he only had to come from Tor Castle, a mile or so to the north beside the River Lochy, it would have taken some time to gather the men together for a battle which in any case they did not know was about to happen. Be that as it may, Ailean, seeing that Argyll was about to go aboard his galley, said to him: *'Theid mi fein leat, ach cha gheall mi gun theid mo dhaoine leat'* (I will go with you but I cannot promise that my men will go with you). He then went on board the galley with Argyll, leaving his men on the Braes of Corpach uncertain what they should do.[17] It seems that they did not join Montrose then – they were on the wrong side of the river in any case – but did present themselves to him as recruits after the battle.

To understand this situation better it should be remembered that at this time Ailean's grandson, Eoghann Dubh, who eventually became the next chief, was a ward of Argyll's and that Argyll had been helpful (though no doubt with an eye to possible advantages to himself) in the very sticky financial and territorial difficulties in which Ailean had found himself. Ailean's friendly relations with Argyll had perhaps upset many of his clansmen and, though there were certainly Camerons in Montrose's army, they all lived on the east side of the Great Glen, that is, furthest away from the seat of their chief and therefore perhaps less under his control.

Montrose's dispatch to the King says that the two armies met a little after the sun came up ' ... the prime of the Campbells giving the first onset, as men that deserved to fight in a better cause'.[18]

There were about 3000 men in Argyll's army and about 1500 in Montrose's. Alasdair MacColla and Manus O'Cahan led the Irish on the right and left wings respectively of the royal army with Montrose in the centre leading the vanguard of Highlanders – Clanranald, Keppoch, Glengarry and Glencoe, MacLeans, Athollmen and Appin Stewarts; he had an Irish reserve behind him. Facing them was Auchinbreck in the centre with the main body of the Campbells, his two wings made up of Lowlanders stiffened with an admixture of Campbells.

According to Montrose his men ' ... came immediately to dint of sword after their first firing'. This describes the tactic introduced by Alasdair which became famous as the Highland Charge and in which clansmen ran towards the enemy holding their fire until they had almost reached them and then fired once, abandoned their muskets and plunged into the opposing ranks with their broadswords.[19]

The fighting did not last long. The Lowlanders crumped almost at once but the Campbells fought on bravely and suffered terrible casualties. Patrick Gordon[20] says that Auchinbreck was killed with 40 Campbell barons and 1700 of the army. These numbers equal the whole of Montrose's army of which 200 were wounded and four killed, one being Sir Thomas Ogilvie, son of the Earl of Airlie, who died a few days later, greatly lamented.

Meanwhile Iain Lom, from his vantage point on the braes overlooking Inverlochy, was enjoying the battle and preparing the rousing lines that would describe it:

> *Dhìrich mi moch madainn Dòmhnaich*
> *Gu bràigh Caisteil Inbhir Lòchaidh;*
> *Chunnaic mi 'n t'arm dol an òrdugh;*
> *'S bha buaidh a' bhlàir le Clann Dòmhnaill.*

Early on Sunday morning I climbed the brae above the castle of Inverlochy. I saw the army arraying for battle, and victory on the field was with Clan Donald.

He praises the exploits of Iain Muideartach:

> *Iain Mhùideartaich nan seól solleir,*
> *Sheòladh an cuan ri là doilleir ...*

John of Moidart of the bright sails, who would sail the seas on a dark day ...

and:

> *Alasdair mhic Cholla ghasda,*
> *Làmh dheas a sgoitadh nan caisteal ...*

Alasdair, son of handsome Coll, expert at breaking castles asunder ...

He delights in wounds and death meted out to the Campbells and is particularly pleased to see Auchinbreck's body stretched out on the ground. Even the women of Argyll, who have lost their fathers, brothers and husbands in the battle get no pity from him:

> Sgrios oirbh mas truagh learn bhur càramh,
> 'G éisdeachd anshocair bhur pàisdean,
> Caoidh a'phannail bh'anns an àraich,
> Donnalaich bhan Earra-Ghàidheal.

> Perdition take you if I feel pity for your plight as I listen to the
> distress of your children, lamenting the company which was
> in the battlefield, the wailing of the women of Argyll.

He was a great poet though a vindictive man, but above all he was a member of the great Clan Donald and in this poem Montrose, the King's captain-general, is not even mentioned. All the glory goes to Clan Donald:

> Hi rim hó ro hó ro leatha,
> Chaidh an latha le Clann Dòmhnaill.

> Hi rim hó ro hó ro leatha,
> Clan Donald won the day.[21]

Many survivors tried to save their lives by taking to the water and some were seen swimming in the River Nevis where it runs into the Lochy. Others swam out into the loch in the hope of being taken on board their chief's galley, but she unfurled her black sails when the Campbell banner was seen to fall; she sped away down the loch and did not wait for them.

Montrose spared 50 Lowlanders who had taken refuge in the castle. He would no doubt gladly have given quarter to the Campbells and did indeed claim to have saved a few,[22] but it was impossible to calm the battle fury of his own army and Alasdair's men chased many of the fugitives as far as Lochan Lùnn Dà Bhra, eight miles or more down the Lairig Mar on the track to Kinlochleven, while in the other direction, at Tom a'Bhrataich (the hillock of the standard), the Campbells tried to make a last stand.

By the time darkness fell and the moon got up that night Inverlochy Castle and the land around it were filled with exhausted men, returned at last from chasing – and frequently killing – the fugitives from the field of battle. They had left Cill Chuimein early on the morning of the Friday, had struggled for 36 hours or more with little, if any, food, over hills, rocks and rivers, through ice and thick snow and rushing torrents on the top of the world, had waited in the frost and darkness for about eight hours on the slopes of Ben Nevis, had rushed down into the bottom of the glen to drive their enemies into the arms of death or into the embrace of loch or river, which meant much the same thing, chasing them for miles over rough hard ground and now, on the Sunday evening, having made their way back to the scene of their triumphs, they can scarcely have had enough strength left to do anything but throw themselves on the ground and sleep.

Even food can have had little appeal to them, so tired were they. The moon, as bright as it had been the night before, lit up the walls and towers of the castle and cast silvery lights into the river while the men of the royal army slept, scarcely distinguishable from that other army lying only a short way off, even more still and more silent than they. They had several nights of rest there before Montrose led them back up the Great Glen to Cill Chuimein where they took the track on the east side of Loch Ness and, having emerged near Inverness, turned away to the east to more triumphs.

Five years later Montrose appeared again, briefly, in the Great Glen. In the intervening years he had won victories at Auldearn, Alford, and Kilsyth and had the whole of Scotland at his feet, but at Philiphaugh he was taken by surprise by a Covenanting army under David Leslie and suffered a bad defeat. He managed to get away and had begun to gather a new army when the King, who was trying to come to some agreement with the Covenanters, ordered him to disband and go abroad.

He made his final appearance in Inverness in May 1650, a year after the execution of the King. He had landed in Caithness with a small force of 1500 men, mostly Orcadians, and set up his headquarters in Thurso. He was subsequently surprised in Carbisdale, his army scattered and many of them killed. He managed to get away and at last found refuge – or so he believed – in Ardvreck Castle on Loch Assynt with the MacLeods of Assynt. Neil MacLeod was away but his wife took Montrose in. Either then or later he was confined in the dungeon and word of his presence was sent to Neil at Dunbeath and to General Leslie at Tain. Soldiers were sent to Ardvreck and they took Montrose prisoner. How far Neil MacLeod himself was involved in this arrest remains unclear. Montrose was led in what was intended to be a humiliating journey down to Edinburgh. It became a triumphant procession.

As he and his captors approached Inverness his progress was observed and recorded by the 16-year-old James Fraser of Phopachy who later became Minister of Kirkhill. He has already been introduced in the chapter on Blàr na Leine. The Frasers were not supporters of Montrose but James could not restrain his enthusiasm for him.

It was usual at that time for important people to be welcomed by the local nobility and gentry when entering a town and escorted through it with appropriate hospitality. This courtesy was not lacking for Montrose. The whole countryside came flocking to greet him and to accompany him into Inverness and his Covenanter guards permitted this, perhaps as a matter of course, perhaps because they were conscious of the uproar that might result if they refused.

Montrose, who was feverish from wounds that had not been treated, asked for a drink and the cortège stopped west of the town at the Fuaran Allt Ionnlaid (Well of the Cleansing Burn). This well was situated between Clachnaharry and Muirtown, opposite the old Toll House but has been lost during the course of road-building works. It is believed to have been blessed by St Columba and the monks of Muirtown monastery used it as a supply of holy water which did not need to be further consecrated. It also had healing properties.

James Fraser introduces us to the scene in the following words:

> We are now to set doun the fatall preludium and parrad of one of the noblest and gallantest generalls this age saw in Brittain, whose unexampled atchievements might frame a history; were its volume farr biggar than mine, it would yet be disproportional to the due praise of this matchless heroe.

He describes Montrose sitting upon a 'little shelty horse' with rags and straw as a saddle, his feet fastened under the belly of the horse with ropes; he was wrapped in an old ragged dark red plaid. A musketeer walked on either side and behind him came on foot the other prisoners taken at Carbisdale.

As they stopped at the well a crowd of people from the town came to have a look at him and, which was much more to his liking, two ministers came to talk to him, one of them being John Annand whom he knew well. At the town cross there was a table with a cloth upon it presided over by the magistrates. They offered him wine but he would only take it mixed with water. The other prisoners, Fraser recalls, all drank heartily. As they left Inverness on its eastern side the provost, Duncan Forbes of Culloden, saying goodbye added: 'My Lord, I am sorry for your circumstance', to which Montrose replied: 'I am sorry for being the object of your pitty'.[23]

So he left Inverness and the Great Glen saw him no more. He spent the night at Castle Stuart near the Moray coast. In the days that followed he was brought to Edinburgh where, without a proper trial, he was condemned to death by hanging and quartering. But ten years later, after the Restoration of Charles II, his bones were gathered together and given a splendid state funeral in St Giles's Cathedral where they lie now in a marble tomb.

VIII
Sir Ewen Cameron of Lochiel

Ipsa vel indomitum frons aspera terreat hostem,
Obtutusque ferox, ater et color oris Iberi,
Ardentesque oculi, barba et mystace reflexa
Cornua seu lunae ...

His very look, so fierce, might fright the boldest foe.
His savage glance and the swarthy hue of his Spanish countenance,
his flashing eyes, his beard and moustache curled
as the moon's horn ....

James Philip, *The Grameid.*

IN THE SEVENTEENTH century the Cameron lands lay mostly to the west of the Great Glen and within the embrace of Loch Eil and Loch Lochy, but also including that magical region around Loch Arkaig and the two glens of Dessary and Pean which point away from it towards the western sea and the lands of MacDonald of Clanranald. To the north was MacDonald of Glengarry and to the east MacDonald of Keppoch with a small wedge of MacMartins inserted like a buffer state between. The MacMartins were so closely allied to the Camerons that they often bore that name rather than their own. Further south and east were more Camerons in and at the mouth of Glen Nevis and along the shore of Loch Linnhe, and below them across Loch Leven lay the harshly beautiful Glen Coe where MacDonalds snatched their sustenance as best they could from the few areas of useful soil and from their great ability in cattle raiding, in which pursuit the Camerons themselves were not far behind them.

Hills great and small surrounded the Camerons, the greatest of them all, Ben Nevis, stood just across the flat strath of the Great Glen, while to the north Ben Tee and her sister peaks guarded Glen Garry and to the south the wild tops of Glen Coe stood like armed sentinels beyond the shining waters of Loch Leven.

Eòghann Dubh mac Iain mhic Ailein mhic Dhomhnaill Dhuibhe (Dark-haired Ewen son of John son of Alan son of dark-haired Donald), the 17th Chief of the Clan Cameron, had never met Montrose or Alasdair MacColla, nor did he know anything about them or their cause until his late teens. His father had died when he was six, at which time his grandfather, Ailean, was 73. Until the age of 12 he was looked after by his foster-father, MacMartin of Letterfinlay, and by his uncle, Cameron of Fassfern. This was not because his grandfather was such an old man; it was a custom for the sons of chiefs to spend their early years with other members of the clan or indeed with members of associated clans. This helped to create strong alliances and chiefs were often found to have closer ties with their foster-brothers than with members of their own family – a not surprising result of their being brought up together.

When Ewen was 12 years old however his life changed. His mother had been the daughter of Campbell of Glenfalloch (later of Glenorchy) and this brought Ewen's family to some extent into the orbit of Clan Campbell and even of the Marquis of Argyll himself, MacCailein Mòr, Montrose's great enemy. Argyll had been helpful to Ailean in his multifarious financial difficulties, or, as many would say, he had successfully lured the old chief into the elaborate web of legal processes by means of which the Campbells were able to extend and consolidate their power in the Highlands. Both views have some truth in them.

Argyll was of the opinion that Ewen was not receiving as good a grounding as he would need to have behind him when he became Chief and he therefore persuaded his grandfather and guardians to entrust the education of the young boy to him. This they were rather reluctant to do at first but it was finally agreed and Ewen went to live with MacCalein Mòr at Inveraray Castle. It has to be admitted, whatever one may think of the Marquis, that he did his best with his young charge; he gave him a good education and a loving home, in fact Ewen became a great favourite. But he cannot have learnt much about current affairs, for he knew little of the great political movements of his time, of the civil wars in Scotland and England and of the aspirations of the various political and ecclesiastical parties. All this was to change however because of a chance encounter.

After the Battle of Philiphaugh in 1645, in which Montrose suffered a serious defeat, his supporters were rounded up and two of them, Sir Robert Spottiswoode and William Murray, the brother of the Earl of Tullibardine, were imprisoned, awaiting sentence of death, in St Andrews. Ewen happened to be in the town with his guardian and, hearing of the two men's plight, visited them in their prison without Argyll's knowledge. He was amazed to hear their stories of Montrose's wars and greatly impressed with their courage and by all they had to tell him. He was obliged to be present at their execution on the following day and later on expressed his feelings to his guardian.[1] It would seem that from this time on his life at Inveraray became distasteful to him. Without having any desire to break the bonds naturally formed between himself and Argyll, he nevertheless longed to play his part on the other side of the political divide about which he had up to then known next to nothing.

When his grandfather, Ailean, died in 1647 Ewen, his father being already dead, became chief and was determined to get back to Lochaber and to influence the politics and direct the exploits of his clan. Argyll did not want to lose him; he was fond of the young man, although one cannot avoid the thought that he might have considered it politic to keep the Chief of the Camerons as it were in his own pocket. The gentlemen of Clan Cameron however eventually managed to persuade him to let Ewen go and he returned joyfully to Tor Castle.

Tor Castle stands on the west bank of the River Lochy only a few miles north of the present town of Fort William. The river there is in the process of performing a great loop and change of level and the castle is on a high knoll which on one side overlooks a dark and deep pool of water. This pool empties abruptly into a waterfall towards the south and is fed from the north by very turbulent water fighting its way round rocks and the trunks of great trees. The castle itself, or whatever stood on its site, is believed to have belonged to the Thanes of Lochaber and thus supposedly at one time to Shakespeare's mythical Banquo. It is not by any means a large castle and one should not imagine it as anything like Caernarvon or even Inverlochy; it is a tower house or keep, now in ruins and in the process of disappearing within the arms of exuberant vegetation. It was rebuilt in the 14th century and at that time may have belonged to the MacIntoshes. The Camerons seized it in 1380 and strengthened it again at the beginning of the 16th century as a defence against the MacDonalds of Keppoch.

Further up the river is a beautiful avenue which may once have been part of an approach road to the castle; it is known as Banquo's Walk and is about a quarter-of-a-mile (400m) long. Underfoot are wild flowers amidst soft grass and moss, while beeches, oaks, sycamores and birch trees line its sides, letting the sunlight or the wandering mist through between their branches. A fine place for a Thane of Lochaber to walk, pondering his affairs of state, although I suppose that if it was then a highway to the castle it would hardly have been so still and solitary as it is today. The peak of Ben Nevis stands above it to the south-east and it is from this side of the glen, the west side, that the great hills can best be appreciated rather than from the modern main road which clings to the glen's eastern edge.

Ewen, whom we must now call Lochiel, became Chief of Clan Cameron two years before the English Civil War culminated in the execution of Charles I. The Scots were not happy that a King of Scots had been tried and executed without any reference to them and their great dissatisfaction expressed itself in a some-what confused movement in which royalists and Covenanters tried to move for-ward together to thwart the aims of the English Commonwealth. Cromwell, hav-ing disposed of the king, turned his military attention to Scotland, while the Scots brought the young exiled son of the king back from the Continent and crowned him King of Scots at Scone. He led a Scots army against Commonwealth troops but was finally defeated at the Battle of Worcester in 1651 and had to seek safety abroad again after hiding in priest's holes and in an oak tree in the English countryside.

In the years that followed Cromwell's men were engaged in combating the Earl of Glencairn's Rising in support of the king. It was a curious upheaval in which there were no battles of sufficient consequence to be given a name but many skirmishes, mostly inconclusive. It lasted for two to three years and one of the most constant of the Earl of Glencairn's adherents was Lochiel – at least if the Memoirs written by his grandson, Drummond of Balhaldy, are to be believed. He writes of his grandfather that ' ... he was always the first that offered himself in any dangerous piece of service' adding that in these exploits he 'gained great glory and reputation. His greatest fault was an excess of forwardness'.[2] Those involved in the Rising included the MacDonalds of Sleat, of Keppoch and of Glengarry, along with Fraser of Foyers and Lochiel himself, of course, but people seemed to join and leave and join again quite inconsequentially – except Argyll who steadfastly supported Cromwell.

One episode which gives us a taste of the general state of confusion concerns the movement of English troops down the Great Glen from Inverness. Lochiel heard that his own country was likely to be in danger from them and he arranged a meeting with Glengarry and Keppoch near Aberchalder, which lies at the north-ern end of Loch Oich just where today the main road from the south swings round to the east across the top of the loch and over both the River Oich and the Caledonian Canal. Glengarry did not turn up. When a party of English soldiers was seen coming down the glen Lochiel was amazed to see Glengarry in their midst talking in a friendly way to their commander. Lochiel made some pithy remarks to Keppoch about the folly of trusting a MacDonald and Keppoch went off with his men in high dudgeon. Lochiel wanted to attack the troops but was advised by other gentlemen of the clan that this would not be a good idea. The English soldiers marched past Aberchalder and on as far as Inverlochy and then turned round and marched back to Inverness. One supposes it was all just a show of strength, a reminder from Cromwell that he was in charge.[3]

Glengarry afterwards explained that ' ... the sudden advance of the enemy having disconcerted their measures, he judged it wiser to submitt, and embrace the offers of peace than to expose his country to rapine and plunder ... '. This sensible (or self-seeking) decision was not one likely to appeal to the young and hot-headed Cameron Chief and it caused ' ... such a dryness between the two chiefs that they were never thereafter sincerely reconciled'. Glengarry is believed already to have submitted to one of Cromwell's generals but he had promised to join the Camerons and Keppoch MacDonalds as he felt his own country might be in danger.[4]

Lochiel, making his way back to Lochaber during a lull in the Rising, was horrified to find that he had arrived just too late to stop General Monk's soldiers from establishing a fort a little south of Inverlochy, the fort around which the town of Maryburgh developed, eventually to be called Fort William. These soldiers had arrived by sea, sailing up Loch Linnhe, whereas it was expected that they would come from the north. They swiftly cut down a great deal of timber from which to fabricate defences and Lochiel found that they had not only destroyed many of his best trees but were also in the process of shooting his game, both furred and feathered.[5]

On the following day he went down to have a look at the new fort from the opposite side of the river and decided that it would be difficult to attack it, so he withdrew three miles to the west along the north bank of Loch Eil to the woods of Achdalieu which are roughly half way between Corpach and Fassfern. From this vantage point he was able to see two ships, full of soldiers, sailing from the fort towards the place where his men were hidden. There were 140 on board plus officers and workmen with axes and other equipment. Lochiel was sure he would be able to deal with them although they were far greater in number, but the older and more sober men amongst his followers felt that they should wait until more clansmen could be brought up, for these English soldiers were hardened veterans and could not be disposed of so easily. Lochiel, however, as might be expected from what we have heard of him, brushed these objections aside and an attack on the insurgents began. It was during the fighting that followed that Lochiel very nearly lost his life at the hands of an Englishman of exceptional size and weight who manoeuvred him into the bed of a narrow stream and, having trapped the chief beneath him so that he had no room to get at his weapon, was about to stab him when Lochiel managed to raise the upper part of his body a little and take a bite out of his opponent's throat. The Englishman bled profusely – perhaps from the jugular vein – and Lochiel was able to get away.[6]

After terrible fighting the Camerons were triumphant and found that they had killed 138 of their enemy, that is, almost the entire force they had taken on. They themselves lost only five men, one of these being a foster-brother of Lochiel who had thrown himself in front of his chief on seeing an English officer taking aim at him.[7]

The governor of the fort was appalled when the mangled bodies of his men were brought back to him, with arms and legs sliced off and heads cut in half. He could not understand how men of average size, which the Camerons were, could find the strength to give such blows, for he did not know that when a Highlander uses his sword 'he draws it with great address the whole length of the blade, whereas an unskilfull person takes in no more of it than the breadth of the place where he hits'.[8]

The Glencairn Rising came to an end during 1655 but Lochiel still felt resentful about the Cromwellian milieu in which he found himself. Most other chiefs and local magnates had already submitted but some time was to pass before the Cameron Chief could be persuaded that it would be in his best interests to follow suit. When he did reach this stage he was determined to obtain the best conditions of surrender possible. To this end he 'kidnapped' three English officers along with Lieutenant Colonel Duncan Campbell – the Campbells, as already noted, supported the English – and imprisoned them on the island in Loch Arkaig. Here they were kept in tolerable comfort considering the smallness and wildness of the island and Lochiel did his best to be the perfect host, arranging feasts and shooting parties and forays into deer forests for them. In his conversations with his captives he first gave them the impression that he had no intention of giving up the struggle against Cromwell, but this attitude he gradually tempered as though his mind had been changed by his conversations with them. He finally expressed a desire to submit, but only if he were given good terms. Argyll's help was obtained in settling the terms and at last it was agreed that the

Camerons, provided that they kept the peace, should be allowed to keep their arms and should not have to take an oath to the Protector, Cromwell, whose name was not to appear in the agreement.[9] In spite of what Lochiel's grandson says about keeping Cromwell's name out of the affair, we find that the 'Articles of the Agreement' were described as being between ' ... his Highness the Lord Protector of England, Scotland and Ireland and Ewen Cameron, Laird of Loughyell, alias Macon Aldowy [MacDhomhnuill Dhuibh]'.[10]

One day in May 1655 Lochiel went down the Great Glen to the fort superbly dressed and armed to the teeth. With him he brought as large a 'tail' as he could manage, that is, at least a piper, a bard and/or *seanachaidh* (historian), a banner-man (*fear brataich*), a treasurer (*fear sporain*) I perhaps a swordbearer (*gille mòr*), and others perhaps, like the *gille cas fliuch* (wet foot servant) who carried the chief over streams. There would certainly also have been a party of fighting men (*luchd taighe*). Behind these came the gentlemen of the clan and the clansmen and with them the four captives from the Loch Arkaig island, now at liberty. They halted in front of the fort. The pipers blew and the banners waved in the breeze and the governor brought out his men and lined them up outside. Then at a sign from their chief the Camerons laid down their arms, held in the name of the king, and took them up again in the name of the state. This ceremony was followed by a feast during which Lochiel and the governor were careful to keep the two groups apart:, lest they should remember earlier bloody encounters.[11]

It is very likely that Lochiel retained an ardent desire to rise again in support of the king – to begin with at any rate – and no doubt he would have done this had any circumstances arisen that would have released him from his promises. Having lived for a long time in Ireland it is very hard for me to find anything good to say about Cromwell, but I have to admit that, as Lochiel himself eventually admitted, hateful as it was to be subject to Cromwell, it did nevertheless have certain material advantages. One of these lay in a further article of the agreement which relieved Lochiel from paying any past feu duties owed to the Chief of the MacIntoshes.

MacIntosh had for a long time laid claim to Cameron lands. This arose partly from changes in the laws and customs of land tenure in the Highlands. Under the old Celtic laws which obtained during the period of rule of the Lords of the Isles the land did not belong to the chief – he merely organised and protected it on behalf of his clansmen. The Lordship of the Isles, which covered the western islands and the western seaboard and highlands, had been forfeited in 1493 to the King of Scots. Since that time feudal practices, which had already been gnawing at the edges of the Gaelic lands for some time, advanced further. The charters of the Lords of the Isles were declared null and void but the king could, if he wished, grant Crown charters in their place. This is what happened in the case of the MacIntoshes, but when they later moved to the east, leaving their lands in Lochaber, the Camerons moved into the empty space. They held their land 'by the sword' instead of 'by parchment', that is, the parchment on which a charter was written. The sword was the only weapon they had to resist MacIntosh's demand for his feu duties and to defend themselves against his right to eject them from their territory if they did not pay up. Lochiel was being constantly chivvied by MacIntosh for payment of past dues, one of the financial problems which had beset his grandfather. The cancelling of this debt under the agreement he had now made with the state was therefore extremely welcome and the presence of government troops in the Great Glen meant that he was no longer harried by MacIntosh or other predatory magnates.

The presence of the fort therefore became more of a blessing than an incubus. Its benign influence was however interrupted by the downfall of the Cromwellian State in 1660, the year of the Restoration of the Stewart kings in the person of Charles II (already King of Scots, it will be remembered). All the restrictions imposed by Cromwell's government were lifted and Highlanders could once again move about the country wherever they liked. The king had all the military paraphernalia of the Commonwealth dismantled and this included the fort at Inverlochy. Lochiel, like his neighbours, was glad to say goodbye to the alien forces in the glen, but with the removal of the garrison there he soon found himself once again at the mercy of MacIntosh who in 1662 obtained permission to remove Lochiel's clansmen from their lands. Nothing came of this, however. In May 1665 there was a meeting at Kilvean, south of Inverness, to settle the matter. Lochiel and his 300 supporters were camped at Tomnahurich while MacIntosh with 500 men were on the other side of the River Ness. The Wardlaw Manuscript describes the scene as follows:

> Earth, water, aire, rebounded at the sound of bagpipes
> Martial musick. At the sound of a trumpet the meeting sits,
> at some distance I and my Lord Bishop of Moray and the
> Laird of Alter,* as arbitrators and trenchmen, passed betwixt
> them, and at last, the 3d day, being Thursday, maters were

brought to an accommodation and agreement, that it pre-
vented litigation and cost in law. This was a noble sight of gal-
lant gentlemen and the clergy in decent grave garbs.[12]

*Altyre, east of Darnaway

All this having come to nothing MacIntosh lost patience altogether and later
appeared with 1500 men on the north bank of the River Arkaig, where he faced
Lochiel and his clansmen spread out along the opposite bank. The future Earl of
Breadalbane, Iain Glas, who was a kinsman of Lochiel's on his mother's side,
arrived with 300 men, stating that he would support whichever side was first
attacked. He was right in believing that this was the best way of preventing blood-
shed for MacIntosh already found himself in a difficult position because of
Lochiel's clever manoeuvring of his clansmen around Loch Arkaig. We do not
know exactly what this was but the intention may have been to draw MacIntosh's
men up the glen and trap them there. Iain Glas's intervention was the last straw
for MacIntosh and an agreement was finally reached. There were later difficulties
with MacIntosh however, some relating to the sum of money Lochiel had to pay
as part of this agreement, but he never gave in and his clansmen were never ejected from their lands until after the 1745 Rising, 80 years later.[13]

Some time between 1655 and 1660 Lochiel moved from Tor Castle. He had
been annoyed by soldiers from the fort wandering up the east bank of the river
and observing whatever he was doing and felt he would be more comfortable if
he moved out of their reach. He had a house built for himself at Achnacarry
which lies near the east end of Loch Arkaig and on the south bank of the River
Arkaig about a mile from where it empties into Loch Lochy. Here amidst beautiful woods and rocks and sounding waterfalls, in a setting which Scott would have
regarded as ideal for any Highland chief, he was quite out of reach of the fort and
could build a more commodious house which was reported to have been 'all built
of Fir-planks, the handsomest of that kind in Britain'.[14] Unfortunately we cannot
give any judgement on these splendid wooden planks as this house was burnt by
the Duke of Cumberland's troops after the Battle of Culloden in 1746 and only
one gable wall, which is of stone, can still be seen not far from the larger stone
house which eventually took its place.

Lochiel was knighted in 1662 for his services to the king and his portrait, by
an unknown artist, which hangs in Achnacarry House, probably dates from about

this time. He was in his early thirties then. He is shown in armour with a full white cravat at his throat, masses of thick, dark, shoulder-length hair, bright eyes and a thin dark moustache, curling slightly at the ends; but above all such an impression of vitality that he seems about to jump out of the picture frame. As his grandson says of him:

> He was of the largest size; his bones big, his countenance
> fresh and smooth, and he had a certain air of greatness about
> him, which struck the beholders with awe and respect.[15]

In 1663 the Great Glen was buzzing with reports of what was going on in Glen Spean, a side glen branching off to the east about ten miles (16km) north of the present Fort William. It did not directly affect Lochiel but he cannot have failed to have discussed it exhaustively with his other neighbours.

The 12th Chief of the MacDonalds of Keppoch, Domhnall Glas had died and was succeeded by his son Alasdair Mac Dhomhnaill Glais. Alasdair and his brother Ranald were being educated abroad and the Clan's affairs were managed in the young chief's absence by his uncle, Alasdair Buidhe, the Tutor of Keppoch. When the chief and his brother returned Alasdair Buidhe retired to his own house at Bohuntine in Glen Roy. The new chief set in motion a period of 'improvement', his ideas based perhaps on what he had learnt while abroad about the best ways of governing men. They were not in line with the more democratic methods which applied in Highland clans where the chief was expected to take counsel with the gentlemen of the clan and where he could be removed if his character or methods were not acceptable. The Chief of Keppoch therefore became very unpopular, especially when he punished Alasdair Ruadh of Inverlair for obtaining a lease of his lands direct from the Marquis of Huntly without his permission. Inverlair is further up Glen Spean than Keppoch and near the west bank of Loch Treig, which is said to be inhabited by a water kelpie whose roars echo in the surrounding hills. The chief led a party of 60 followers to Inverlair's house, where they forced an entrance, destroyed and removed furniture, pulled down part of the house, burnt the timber and drove off a large number of cattle, sheep and horses. The place became uninhabitable and Inverlair and his family had to seek refuge elsewhere. He complained to the Privy Council but the chief did not respond to the charges they brought against him. Unrest grew within the clan and at last it was decided that he must be removed.[16]

On the 25th September 1663 the chief and his brother Ranald were visited in their castle at Keppoch by two of the sons of Alasdair Buidhe and seven of the MacDonalds of Inverlair. The Inverlair MacDonalds were of the Sìol Dùghaill (the seed of Dugald), and their ancestor, Dùghall Ruadh of Sunart, had settled in Brae Lochaber in the middle of the 16th century. With the friends and henchmen who accompanied them there may have been as many as 30 people involved in the attack. They burst into the house, probably finding the brothers in their bedroom, and killed them both with frenzied dagger strokes.[17] Our old friend the bard of Keppoch, Iain Lom, who brought warning that the Campbells were gathering at Inverlochy to Montrose, lamented:

> B'iad mo ghràdh na cuirp chùbhraidh
> Anns 'm bu dlùth cur nan sgian,
> 'S iad 'nan sineadh air ùrlar
> 'N seòmar ùir gan cur sìos,
> Fo chosaibh Shìol Dùghaill,
> Luchd spùilleadh nan cliabh;
> Dh'fhàg àlach nam biodag
> Mar sgàile ruidil ur bian.

> Beloved by me were the fragrant bodies in whom the stabs of knives were close and many, as they lay stretched on the ground and were being prepared for burial in an earthen chamber, beneath the feet of Sìol Dùghaill, the spoilers of breasts; the set of dirks gave your skins the appearance of a sieve.[18]

Iain was a kinsman of the murdered men. He was descended from Iain Aluinn (Handsome John), the 4th chief, who held that title only for one brief year. He had been deposed by the clan because he had handed over a clansman, Domhnall Ruadh Beag mac Gille Mhantaich, a renowned cattle lifter, to MacIntosh. This he had done on the understanding that Domhnaill's blood would not be shed. MacIntosh got round this condition by hanging him.[19]

Iain prepared the bodies of the chief and his brother for burial. In a poem he deplores the destruction of the chief's house, where harp music is no longer heard, and of its gardens where cattle trample round the pear trees.[20] Yet he was the only person who did so; not a single other voice was raised in protest. In a later poem he reveals the identity of the murderers:

'S ann air madainn Di-h-aoine
Rinn na mèirlich do reubadh:
Dà mhac brathair t'athar,
Gum bu sgrathail leam féin sud,
Agus seachd de Shiol Dùghaill
Luchd a spùilleadh nan ceudan.

It was on a Friday morning
that you were murdered by the robbers;
By two sons of your uncle,
horrible indeed do I deem that deed;
And seven of the Seed of Dugald,
despoilers of hundreds.[21]

Iain looks forward to the time when the deaths will be revenged:

Ach thig Sir Seumas nam bratach,
'S bheir e mech dhuinn ur n-éirig;
Agus Aonghas o Gharaidh,
Leomhann faramach gleusda.

But Sir James of the Banners* will come,
and will exact your blood-price for us;
And Angus from Garry,
a roaring unerring lion is he.[22]

* MacDonald of Sleat

But the MacDonald Chiefs did not stir and Angus from Garry (Glengarry) turned out to be anything but a roaring lion in this instance. He had been created Lord MacDonell and Aros by Charles II in 1660 for his help in Glencairn's Rising. Lochiel had not thought very highly of his much-vaunted loyalty at that time, as we have seen. He now claimed to be the High Chief of Clan Donald but he showed no sign of enquiring into the death of a fellow Clan Donald chief, nor was there any stirring amongst the Keppoch clansmen. They appeared to be well satisfied with what had been done. Iain Lom alone stood firm and incurred the wrath of the clan for his determination to avenge the death of the brothers. He was attacked and his house damaged. He was obliged to seek safety in Kintail. From there he approached Sir James MacDonald of Sleat and when nearly two years had elapsed he finally persuaded him to organise an expedition to Glen Spean to kill the murderers. He was to act as guide and the leader was to be a fellow poet, An Ciaran Mabach (the lisping, or stammering, dark one), the brother of Sleat. Sir James obtained a Royal Commission of fire and sword against the murderers in July 1665 and in September of that year 50 men under the command of An Ciaran Mabach set out from Uist. Led by Iain Lom they approached the house of Inverlair, now again fit to live in, and killed Inverlair and the other six members of the Sìol Dùghaill. Alasdair Buidhe's two sons were not there; he himself had in the meantime become chief of the clan without the slightest opposition.[23]

According to tradition Iain cut off the heads of the seven dead men and strung them on a rope of heather by their hair. He was taking them to Invergarry as a reproach, it is thought, to Glengarry for having taken no action himself. Glengarry had been unwilling to do anything to displease Alasdair Buidhe, who had provided a good number of clansmen for Glencairn's Rising. On the way to Invergarry with his gruesome burden Iain stopped at a well beside Loch Oich and washed some of the blood from the heads – to tidy them up a little, one supposes, before laying them before Glengarry. This well is now covered by a stone monument placed there in 1812 by Alasdair Ranaldson, the eccentric 17th Chief of Glengarry. The monument wrongly describes the deaths as being ' ... inflicted by the orders of the Lord M'Donell and Aross [sic] ... ' and dates them in the 16th instead of the 17th century. The heads were sent to Edinburgh but only five of them seem to have arrived there.

Iain describes how they were boiled to remove the flesh before being affixed to the gallows between Edinburgh and Leith.[24] The hillock near Inverlair Farm was examined in 1818 and seven headless bodies were discovered.

There are several imponderables in the story of the Keppoch murder. The total silence and satisfaction of the clan seem reasonably well explained, but after the murder where were the 60 people who had accompanied the Chief of Keppoch when he attacked and spoiled the house and land of the Inverlair family? Were these clansmen? I suppose they must have been, but perhaps they felt themselves to be such a minority in Glen Spean and Glen Roy that it was best to keep their heads down. Why were the other MacDonald Chiefs so reluctant even to protest? Sleat himself took two years to make up his mind. Chiefs had been deposed before, indeed it was accepted that a man could not hold that position if he were mentally or physically incompetent or cruel and despotic. Why then did Alasdair mac Dhomhnaill Glais have to die? And even more why did his brother have to die too?

The injuries done to MacDonald of Inverlair must have been so great and Alasdair's interference in the life of the clan so serious and so undesirable that no other fate could be contemplated.

Twenty-three years later on the 4th August 1688 Colla mac 'ic Raonuill, the 16th Chief of Keppoch, and the grandson of Alasdair Buidhe, led his clansmen at the Battle of Mulroy, the last clan battle. Mulroy is the hill rising behind the Catholic Church at Roy Bridge in Glen Spean. A cairn commemorating the battle stands to the right of the road a little way up Glen Roy. Colla's opponent was the Chief of the MacIntoshes, seeking once again to squeeze feudal dues out of the Keppoch MacDonalds who had had the same difficulties with MacIntosh as Lochiel. On this occasion MacIntosh had brought a company of regular troops with him to bolster his clansmen and make his victory certain. But Colla won hands down and was the toast of the Highlands for some time afterwards.[25] He had sought help from several other nearby clans, including the MacDonalds of Glencoe and the MacMartin Camerons. Lochiel was away from home at the time and knew nothing of what was going on, but the authorities still regarded him as responsible for the MacMartins and he was very nearly thrust into prison. He heard that a warrant was out for his arrest and he therefore visited the Tolbooth in Edinburgh, the last place where his enemies would be likely to look for him. He must have known that the chief clerk there was a Cameron who would – and did – get him safely out of the town and so back to Lochaber. No government officer would dare to arrest him there![26]

Only seven months later in March 1689, Ewen received a letter from King James asking him to be ready for a call to arms. Charles II had died in 1685 and his brother James VII and II was king. James had become a Catholic and although what he really wanted was religious toleration for all, the English were afraid that he would try to make England a Catholic country again. It was also felt that many of the top posts then filled by Protestants would go to Catholics.

These fears were increased when James's wife produced a male heir. The Protestant William of Orange, the Stadholder of Holland, was therefore invited to come to England; his wife, Mary, was James's daughter. He came with enthusiasm and a large force of foreign, chiefly Dutch troops (ironically many of them were Catholics) and soon became king himself. James had been obliged to seek safety in France. The desire of the Protestant English for a Protestant king arose perhaps more for economic/prestige reasons than for religious ones.

In response to King James' letter Lochiel visited all the chiefs living near him and wrote to many others. They arranged a rendezvous near his house in May for all the loyal clans. Lochiel may well have felt that this was to be the high point in his life, something that would make up for his inability to help Montrose and that would also crush any reservations other clans had in relation to his collaboration with Cromwell's officers during the last few years of the Commonwealth.

The next perhaps most exciting period of his life must wait until the next chapter.

IX
Bonnie Dundee

Bella Caledonios civiliaque arma per agros Instructasque acies, variisque horrentia signis Agmina, et horriferae canimus certamina pugnae, Magnanimumque Ducem, pulso pro Rege cientem Arma, acresque viros, ipsumque in saeva ruentem Vulnera, terribilemque in belli pulvere Gramum Ingentemque heroem animis armisque potentem, Pangimus et saeclis Mavortia facta futuris.

We sing the Scottish wars and civil strife, the lines of battle, and ranks bristling with many standards, the encounters of a horrid contest. And we sing the noble Leader, calling brave men to arms for an exiled King, and himself rushing to meet cruel wounds. We sing the Graham, the great Hero, terrible in the dust of battle, mighty in spirit and in arms. We tell of warlike deeds for times to come.

James Philip, *The Grameid*

GAIRLOCHY LIES BESIDE the Caledonian Canal about ten miles (16km) out of Fort William. There is a bridge there over the canal carrying a minor road and swinging back to allow the passage of canal traffic. This bridge is a little south of the point where the River Lochy once left its parent loch. The engineers building the canal were faced with a problem here – they had to get both the canal and the river through the same narrow gap. They solved the problem by re-routing the river a little to the east and allowing the canal to run for a short distance in its bed. As a result of this the River Lochy joins the River Spean to the east of their natural confluence. This deviation, along with the three or four houses built at Gairlochy, has slightly changed the topography of this part of the Great Glen, but not so much that we cannot be aware of the great area of flat ground available there. A little to the east of Gairlochy and on a slightly higher level is the old MacMartin burial ground and beyond it a vast field of grass, daisies and sheep, with a patch of forestry behind it from which the land slopes up gently towards Stronaba on the A82. Until the canal was built there was no interruption to the relatively level ground and although it is now intersected by the re-routed River Lochy, the break is scarcely noticeable from most viewpoints.

In the 17th century there were no grass, daisies or sheep here and maybe no trees either and instead the area was covered with heather, which is surprising, as one would expect it to have been used for the grazing of cattle, since it must be the largest area of level ground anywhere in the glen.

We know that this land was covered with heather because James Philip of Almerieclose tells us so in a long Latin poem he wrote about a gathering there in 1689.[1] This poem is known as *The Grameid*. Philip was a kinsman of John Graham of Claverhouse, Viscount Dundee, the hero of this epic and one of the few who did not desert James VII and II when he was deposed in 1688. As we have described in the previous chapter James, who had become a Catholic during the reign of his brother, Charles II, was wrongly suspected of wanting to force Catholicism upon England when what he really wished to achieve was religious toleration for all. William of Orange, Stadholder of Holland, was regarded as the Protestant champion who would save the country from Rome. He responded to an invitation from the 'Immortal Seven' – a group of lords plus the Bishop of London – by arriving at Brixham on the 5th November 1688 with a large force of men and quickly attracting many English magnates to his cause. James was compelled to seek refuge in France. William and his wife Mary, the daughter of James, eventually became joint sovereigns. James could never forget the anguish of being rejected by his own flesh and blood as well as by his subjects.

William was first accepted as king by the English; the Scots had still to make up their minds. When a Convention in Edinburgh in March 1689 finally came down on the side of William several of its members, led by Dundee, left the city and headed north, to Stirling and, in the Viscount's case, to Dudhope Castle, his home on the slopes above the town of Dundee and looking over the Firth of Tay. A period of uncertainty followed as Dundee had no instructions from James and did not at first know whether he should organise resistance to William or not. In the meantime he was declared an outlaw at the Mercat Cross in Edinburgh. In April he raised his standard on Dundee Law above his castle of Dudhope and departed for the Highlands where he could expect to raise most of the army needed for his bid to regain the throne for James.

Dundee was a kinsman of James Graham, 1st Marquis of Montrose; they came from collateral branches of the great Graham family but in 1650, when Montrose was executed, Dundee was only a child, living in the Tower of Glenogilvie amongst the Sidlaw hills; the stories he was told of Montrose caused him to regard this kinsman as a hero he longed to emulate.

In 1689 he was 41 and his son (and only child) had been born in April of that year, five years after his marriage to Jean Cochrane. With his grey eyes, quiet yet alert, his thick dark hair flowing over his shoulders in curls and ringlets and his tranquil yet commanding air, he certainly deserved to be called 'Bonnie' although this word was not, as far as we can see, attached to him at that time; Walter Scott may have been the first to add it to his name. Nor was he ever known as Iain Dubh nan Cath (Dark John of the Battles) by his Highland soldiers. This name, which we almost always meet in any accounts of him written in English, is never mentioned in any Gaelic writings of his time. I suspect he has been confused with Iain Ruadh nan Cath, the red-haired 2nd Duke of Argyll, who was active in the continental wars not long after the 1st Jacobite Rising.

Earlier in his career Dundee had been Captain and then Colonel of a troop of horse employed in policing areas in the south-west of Scotland which were disturbed by covenanting agitators who disagreed with Charles II's religious policy. Charles had decided to establish a non-presbyterian form of religion in Scotland (he once said that Presbyterianism was no religion for gentlemen), but he did not wish to force the Scots to accept anything they did not want if he could help it, so although there were to be bishops there were no prayerbooks, surplices, confirmation or altars. The more extreme and fanatical of the Covenanters could not be appeased by this however. They stirred up their followers to commit such crimes as the murder of the Archbishop of St Andrews and the killing or wounding of the king's officers and to deny 'the authority of Charles Stuart and all authority depending on him'. The country was on the brink of civil war. Acting as a policeman was not the sort of military career Dundee had hoped to have – very far from the honour and glory which had accrued to Montrose – but he did his best for the King while at the same time trying to protect the small people who had become involved in violence. His policy was to punish the ringleaders but let the rank and file go quietly home. This approach was showing signs of producing good results, but he was taken away from this work and affairs in south-west Scotland did not go very well afterwards. Unfortunately most of the cases of death or imprisonment reported at this time have been attributed to him although he had no justiciary powers and was often not even in the neighbourhood when an arrest was made.

The two best-known portraits of him are the beautiful pencil drawing by an unknown artist after David Paton, which is to be found in the National Portrait Gallery in Edinburgh and the painting by Kneller which hangs in the drawing room of Glamis Castle.

After 1678 he spent more time as courtier and politician than as soldier. These new duties brought him into close contact with the king and with his brother James, Duke of York, the future James VII and II.

The Great Glen first set eyes on him in early May 1689 when, during a recruiting drive in the eastern Highlands, he arrived at Inverness, having heard that Highlanders were gathering there. They turned out to be a party of MacDonalds and Camerons led by Coll MacDonald (Colla mac 'ic Raonuill – Coll son of the son of Ranald) the 16th Chief of Keppoch. They had been plundering the lands of MacIntosh of MacIntosh against whom Coll had a, to some extent, legitimate complaint. MacIntosh held a charter to Coll's lands and was constantly trying to extract feudal dues from him. Coll and his ancestors however had held these lands for generations 'by the sword' and re:garded them as their own.

Difficulties like this had quite often arisen in the Highlands when the King of Scots rewarded some ally or courtier by making a grant of lands to him without considering the situation of the people living there. The gap between the cultures of the Highlands and the Lowlands which began to appear as early as the eleventh century during the reign of Malcolm Canmore, who was brought up at the English court, and his Saxon wife, Margaret, had never been closed and the two parts of the country were in many respects even more divided in the 17th century than they had been in Malcolm Canmore's reign. Some years before this confrontation at Inverness Coll had gone there in the hope of meeting MacIntosh and resolving their differences, but had been thrown into gaol on MacIntosh's instructions. He remained in prison for three months and was then released but only after he had petitioned central government.

In 1688 MacIntosh entered Coll's territory in Brae Lochaber (Glen Spean) and was defeated by Coll at the Battle of Mulroy, the last clan battle. This victory made Coll the hero of the Highlands. It did not however save him from further attack, this time by government troops, who burnt his crops and houses. He was obliged to raid to feed his people. Although MacIntosh was technically in the right. having a charter to these lands, Dundee appreciated Coll's difficulties and he smoothed things over for him with the Inverness councillors, who at the time were shut up in Coll's tent guarded by an impressively armed body of MacDonalds until they paid a ransom, so quite a lot of smoothing would have been necessary.

Having settled matters for the time being Dundee tried to persuade Coll to join him in attacking the forces of General Hugh Mackay, William of Orange's Commander in the Highlands, which were building up to the east of Inverness, but Coll made the excuse that he could not use the Camerons in his raiding party for that purpose without first having the permission of the Cameron Chief. In fact he was probably more anxious to get home as soon as he could with the booty they had lifted from MacIntosh. After a few more days near Inverness Dundee rode down the Great Glen as far as Invergarry, thus avoiding Mackay's men who were advancing to Inverness from the east and were too many for him to take on. Finding no-one there he turned back along the seven miles (11.2km) to Cill Chuimein (Fort Augustus), and went over to the eastern Highlands via the Corrieyairack Pass.

He was seen in the Great Glen for the second time on the 18th May. He had been in touch with Cameron of Lochiel and had arranged to rendezvous with him somewhere near his house at Achnacarry. Lochiel had been busy encouraging other Highland chiefs to join in the proposed Rising in favour of James. Dundee had ridden westwards from his home in Glenogilvie with about a hundred supporters. They included David Graham, his brother, Lord Dunfermline with a party of Gordons, Halyburton of Pitcur and Fullarton of Fullarton, both near neighbours, Graham of Balquapple and Graham of Duntrune, both cousins of his, John Grant of Ballindalloch who had defied his chief, Grant of Grant, to come out with Dundee, James Philip of Almerieclose, his standard bearer and kinsman and many other neighbours and friends. They rode towards the Moor of Rannoch which they crossed on the ancient track which runs from Loch Eigheach to Corrour and from Corrour up the Lairig Leacach (Pass of the Flagstones) to Corriechoillie in Glen Spean. Spring was late in the west Highlands and the weather was appalling; it was more like a journey in the depths of a hard winter than a pleasant excursion amidst the flowers of May. They reached Glen Spean after about three days of struggling through ice and snow, sleeping in the open and finding their hair and clothes frozen to the ground when they awoke. Near Loch Ossian they lost many of their horses in the bog, for thin ice obscured the treacherous stretches of spongy marsh sucking at the heels of their beasts, They toiled up the Lairig Leacach to the final ridge and dropped down thankfully into Glen Spean where they spent another comfortless night, though it was not quite as cold. James Philip declared that their journey had been worse than that of Hannibal when crossing the Alps – but we must allow for some poetic licence.[2]

On the following morning Lochiel came to welcome them. He and Dundee had not met before and met now at last somewhere between the mouth of Glen Spean and the confluence of the Lochy and Spean rivers, two strong and charismatic personalities coming together for the first time. The huge area of more or less level ground described above would become their camp. In his poem Philip calls it Dalcomera, which is a latinised form of the Gaelic placename Dal na Comair (the Plain of the Confluence); its modern name is Mucomir. Dundee himself was installed in a house belonging to Lochiel at Strone on the north bank of the River Lochy and about five miles from the camp. But he probably only used it when writing his long letters to the king and to his actual or potential recruits. Most of his time will have been spent with his Highland army.

The Lowlanders Dundee had brought with him – or at least their leaders – may have used the house at Strone or another house at Moy two to three miles nearer the camp, as sleeping quarters. They were not used to Highland bivouacs and the prospect of sleeping in the heather wrapped in a plaid that had been wrung out in water to keep out the wind will not have appealed to them. There is no mention of tents anywhere in the literature, apart from the one in which Coll MacDonald imprisoned the Inverness councillors and Lochiel is reported to have kicked away the stone which his son John was using as a pillow and rebuked him for being so degenerate! There are several references in *The Grameid* to complaints about bad conditions by those who had come from Angus:

> Under the miserable hardships of this barren land secret complaints arise among the companions of the Graham, but he himself neither hunger nor cold nor tempest affect, strong in his devotion to his King ... He frets only against the delays of war.[3]

They were to be there until the last week in July, with only one short foray to the east. There were many comings and goings during these weeks. Some of the chiefs had their own domestic problems to deal with while those who came from the islands had to adjust their movements to suit wind and wave and there were in any case not enough cattle in Lochaber to feed them all.

Dundee himself was waiting for more recruits to join him from Scotland and also for the arrival of Irish troops promised him by King James, who was gathering an army in Ireland. There was little movement on these two fronts for the replies to his letters written to potential supporters were very few and James's Irish army was stuck outside the walls of Derry and could not leave until that city had fallen. These delays meant that there was much coming and going at the camp. The chiefs who lived nearby in the Great Glen took their men home, where they remained, prepared to respond instantly to a call to arms. In *The Grameid* Philip tells us that Dundee held a review at the camp on the 25th May, a week after he had arrived, but the clans he describes as being present could not all have been there at that time. He may have felt that it was more effective, dramatically speaking, to introduce them at one go and it enabled him to give a more stirring and flamboyant description of their arrival.

He shows us the clansmen marching onto the field behind their chiefs, banners flying and pipes playing. In this great amphitheatre amidst the high hills and the rushing rivers the sound of the pipes rose into the clear air and filled all the lofty spaces in the glen with their music. Each piper fingrered his chanter with the greatest skill he could muster, hoping, at this gathering in support of the king, to be called the King of Pipers. The great MacCrimmon family, hereditary pipers to MacLeod of MacLeod, was not represented as Iain Breac, the 18th chief, had failed to respond to Dundee's invitation to join him, but one of the Rankins, (Clan mhic Fhraing – children of the son of Frang or Francis) must have been there in the tail of either MacLean of Duart or MacLean of Coll. The first Rankin appointed to Duart is thought to have developed his skills in Ireland and to have founded a piping school in Mull long before the MacCrimmons established their famous school in Skye. The Rankins transferred to MacLean of Coll when the Duart chiefs got into financial difficulties and it was Neil Rankin who played regularly at dinner when Boswell and Dr Johnson were entertained by the Laird of Coll in 1773.[4]

When Ewen Cameron of Lochiel rode onto the field, wearing the great belted plaid and a tri-coloured tunic trimmed with gold lace, he brought with him his son John, father of the Gentle Lochiel of the '45, and also his son-in-law, Alexander Drummond of Balhaldy. Alexander had two sons one of whom became a famous Jacobite spy in the 1740s; the other, John, wrote the *Memoirs of Sir Ewen Cameron of Locheill, Chief of the Clan Cameron.*[5] The Balhaldys were really MacGregors but this clan had been proscribed by James VI and I and its members were forbidden to use their name or to carry arms. They had been brought low largely by the machinations of the Campbells and the Colquhouns of Luss and having lost their lands could only exist by fighting and raiding on a large scale, which made them very unpopular.

A contingent of the MacGregors of Glengyle led by their chief, Domhnall Glas also accompanied the Camerons. He brought some of his sons with him, probably including the famous Rob Roy who is regarded either as a brigand or as the heroic saviour of his clan, depending on one's point of view.

The MacMartins of Letterfinlay also followed Lochiel. Being few in number and their lands marching with those of the Camerons, they had attached themselves to the larger clan. This was a situation which often arose, a smaller clan or group joining a larger one for reasons of propinquity and the need for protection. Duncan MacMartin of Letterfinlay had been Ewen Cameron's foster father and it was his great-grandson, Martainn Og, who led the MacMartins onto the field as his father was too old to do so. He was tall and dark – ' ... his dark locks hang around his face and cover his cheeks and his eyes shine like the stars, while his neck rivals the white flowers'. Quite a remarkable person! He must also have been decidedly overweight as the earth is said to have groaned beneath him.[6]

Clan Donald turned out in force for this Rising. Forty years earlier MacDonald of Sleat (Seumas Mòr) had not at first been too enthusiastic about joining Alasdair MacColla when the latter was raising troops for Montrose, but his son Domhnall Gorm (Blue-eyed Donald) did not hesitate to respond to Dundee's call. The other branches of the clan to rise were Glengarry and Keppoch, both from the Great Glen, Glencoe, lying to the south of it and Clanranald, whose lands lay on the western seaboard and in Benbecula and South Uist; there were also small parties from Colonsay, Islay, Jura and Kintyre and we must not forget Rathlin, the large island off the north coast of Ireland which was such a good source for gallowglasses or Redshanks;[7] many of Alasdair MacColla's men had come from there.

Two hundred Stewarts of Appin had joined, led by the Tutor of Appin. There were MacLeans from all points of the compass; Duart and Lochbuie on Mull, Ardgour, Coll, Islay, Jura, Otter and Torloisk; of MacLeods only those from Raasay came, MacLeod of MacLeod preferring to remain neutral. Seven hundred MacLeods had died fighting for Charles II at Worcester and it was believed that he had never expressed his gratitude for this sacrifice, consequently the

MacLeods became, and remained, unwilling to fight for the Stuarts again.

In addition to these contributions from the larger clans there were MacAlisters, MacLachlans and Lamonts from Kintyre, MacNeills from Barra, and MacNachtons from Dunderawe and we must not forget the hundred or so supporters Dundee had brought with him from Glenogilvie.[8]

The chiefs with whom we are mainly concerned as they lived in the Great Glen are: Cameron of Lochiel, who has already had a chapter entirely to himself, Coll MacDonald of Keppoch, Alasdair MacDonell of Glengarry, Fraser of Foyers, Fraser of Culduthel, Grant of Glenmoriston and the Glen Urquhart Grants of Sheuglie and of Corrimony.

Coll MacDonald of Keppoch was the grandson of Alasdair Buidhe, the 14th Chief of Keppoch, who is suspected of being involved in some way in the Keppoch murder, but whatever the rights and wrongs of this tragedy it seems to have been forgotten by Coll's time. Coll was, of course, the man we have already met at Inverness outside a tent in which he had shut the Inverness Councillors, their predicament being solved by the arrival of Dundee. All this would suggest that Coll was little more than a brigand and so he has often been presented by Lowlanders. James Philip, for instance says he was ' ... a man whom love of plunder would impell to any crime'.[9] But they do not take account of his many difficulties. Continually harassed over feu duties by MacIntosh of MacIntosh, who had him shut up in gaol in Inverness, obliged to fight a battle (which he won) against this magnate and then finding his crops and his houses burnt by the same enemy, the animals driven off and his people starving and without shelter, what could he do but seek redress by seizing as many sheep and cattle as he could from MacIntosh and by demanding money from the town which had treated him so unkindly? Dundee seems to have had some sympathy with him, although at the same time he found his outbursts rather inconvenient. For instance, Coll later burnt Dunachton, which belonged to MacIntosh, claiming that it was right to do so as the latter was an enemy of King James. Dundee, however, was anxious to avoid all unnecessary burning and rapine because they might turn the local populations against James. But however aggravating Coll's addiction to plundering may have been, he could certainly be relied upon to find cattle to feed Dundee's army when nobody else could. He came to be known as *Colla nam Bo* – Coll of the cows.

The Glengarry MacDonalds (or MacDonells) were led by Alasdair Dubh mac Raonuill mhic Dhomhnuill (Dark-haired Alasdair son of Ranald son of Donald), the acting chief (his father was an old man). He was tall and dark and at the review wore a cloak 'shining with gold'.[10] He is celebrated in a poem written by Silis na Ceapaich, the sister of Coll of the Cows. According to her he was the leader in wisdom and council, handsome and generous, an excellent warrior and the darling of beautiful women.[11] Drummond of Balhaldy in his memoirs of his grandfather, Sir Ewen Cameron, shows Alasdair as a more politic and evasive character, unreliable where his own interests were involved; to sum up he ' .... was possessed of a great many shining qualitys, blended with a few vices, which, like patches on a beautiful face, seemed to give a greater éclat to his character'.[12]

Hugh Fraser of Lovat hesitated about turning out in this Rising, in fact the Frasers of Lovat did not support the Jacobites at all until half way through the '45 when Simon Fraser of Lovat, having spent his life trying always to be on the winning side, finally made a mistake and came 'out' on the Jacobite side, losing his head as a result. But two lesser Frasers were with Dundee – Fraser of Culduthel from near Inverness and Fraser of Foyers whose lands lay around the great waterfall which tumbles down into Loch Ness on the eastern side. The east bank of Loch Ness was all Fraser land and a favourite place of rest and refreshment to Simon Lovat of the '45.

In joining the Jacobites the Grants of Glenmoriston and Glen Urquhart defied their High Chief, Grant of Grant, whose lands lay to the east of the Great Glen, round about the River Spey. They were to do the same in the other two Risings. Ian Grant (young Glenmoriston) was known after this first Rising as Iain a' Chreagain (John of the Rock) because he was obliged to live in a fort he built on the Crocan Darach beside Bhlaraidh to avoid the attentions of government soldiers. Being few in number the Glenmoriston and Glen Urquhart Grants fought under the banner of MacDonald of Glengarry.

Dundee moved amongst them over the heather, on horseback, accompanied by our poet, James Philip, carrying the royal standard. The clansmen all wore saffron shirts reaching down to the knee and over them the *féileadh mòr* (the great belted plaid), a width of tartan, 12 yards or more long, the lower half loosely pleated at the back and the upper half pinned to the left shoulder and arranged down the back in graceful folds. They were armed with *claidheamh mòr* and *biodag* (basket-hilted sword and dirk), their heads covered with a blue bonnet roughly resembling the modern beret in shape.

The site of Dundee's Gathering is only 230-330ft (70-100m) above sea level, yet Philip speaks of it as 'Dalcomera ardua' (high Dalcomera). This may perhaps be because there is a ridge to the east of it which obscures the lower portions of Ben Nevis and Aonach Mòr, making them seem lower than they are and so giving a feeling of height to this great plain. Dundee and his supporters were to spend nine weeks here, feeling the influence of these great hills and watching the mists and the clouds form and reform around them. Dundee particularly will have looked towards them at night when he sat in the house at Strone, alone but for someone to mend the fire, writing and writing, pausing from time to time to rest for a few minutes with his head propped up on his hands, at times seeing the bright stars and the moon lighting up each rock but making of each corrie a pool of darkness, at times watching the slanting rain or the hills retreating into the mist until all the world seemed a flat plain within a silvery wall.

He wrote above all to the king or to Melfort, his secretary of state, listing the people who supported him and describing the difficulties they faced while the whole campaign was on hold, waiting for the king to come or at least send part of his army. He described his own difficulties with lack of money, ammunition and supplies. He had little satisfaction from Melfort who replied after long delays, if at all, and may well have withheld Dundee's letters from the king for reasons best known to himself.

Dundee carried on a long correspondence, most of which can only be inferred from a single surviving letter, with John Campbell, Earl of Breadalbane, Iain Glas, 'as cunning as a fox, wise as a serpent, but as slippery as an eel',[13] whom he really seems to have thought might join him. Breadalbane was next in importance in the great Clan Campbell to the Duke of Argyll, who favoured William of Orange's government and was the enemy of the other clans of the west. But Dundee may have hoped to get help from Breadalbane in spite of this because Breadalbane was jealous of Argyll and would gladly have supplanted him as the most powerful man in the clan.

Other letters, certainly many more than those which have survived, were written in the hope of securing more recruits to his army. His most extended correspondence within this category was with Duncan MacPherson of Cluny. Cluny was in a rather unfortunate situation at the time. He was sympathetic to the Jacobite cause; his father, Ewen Og, had brought 300 of the clan to join Alasdair MacColla when the latter was recruiting for Montrose. Cluny's problem was that up to the time of James's flight to France he had been doing his best to keep on good terms with his neighbours so as to prevent future inter-clan feuds. The MacPherson chiefs had always been friendly with Grant of Grant who, as we have seen, unlike the Grants of the Great Glen, supported William's government. Cluny, moreover, had just married his daughter to Sir Hugh Campbell of Cawdor. This not only connected him very recently with an enemy house but had also upset his clansmen, as they believed he would entail the chieftaincy onto Cawdor since he had no son himself. This meant that Dundee was asking him to raise a regiment from amongst discontented clansmen. On the 19th May, the day after arriving in Lochaber, Dundee sat down in the house at Strone and wrote his first letter to Cluny, in which he flatters him by suggesting that a man of such known honour will hardly hold back from supporting the king, then tries to persuade him that his help will greatly enhance his fortunes in the future and finally assures him that there is no need to fear for the safety of Protestantism under James's rule. There were other letters to Cluny, becoming more and more insistent, even threatening, as the time passed. But Cluny still hesitated and the last letter he received was written by Dundee from Blair Castle shortly after he arrived there on the 26th July, the day before the Battle of Killiecrankie. Cluny did at last join the Highland army but it was not until two days after the battle.

MacLeod of MacLeod did not move, as we have described above and did not reply to a letter from Dundee, nor did Lord Murray, the eldest son of the Marquis of Atholl. Although the Marquis himself had originally agreed to join Dundee he had then been overtaken by an attack of cold feet and had retired to Bath to drink the waters. His son, whom he had left in charge of Blair Castle, was married to a severely Presbyterian wife and, being without the support of his father, he may well have thought it politic to keep away from Dundee. But the Atholl clansmen, led by Patrick Stewart of Ballechin, Atholl's agent, took over Blair Castle and held it for King James.

All the hours Dundee stole from sleep writing his letters brought very meagre results and the army gathering at Dalcomera had few prospects of increasing unless the king were at last able to bring his troops out of Ireland. Meanwhile the clansmen had little to do but to think of their next meal and to practice and perfect their use of *claidheamh mòr* and *biodag* – the weapons they had learnt to wield during their boyhood. Only the oldest of them however will have used them in anything more than a local skirmish as there had been no major battles during the Cromwellian period – Cromwell had kept the Highlands full enough of English soldiers to make sure of that – or during the reign of Charles II. It seemed to Dundee, who had learnt the art of soldiering in the Continental wars, that they needed to be properly trained since, as far as he could see, they had absolutely no idea of drill and seemed likely to approach an enemy in a very haphazard manner which would be of little danger to a well-trained army. Lochiel however quickly explained to him the Highlanders' traditional way of fighting.

First, the men should be divided into clan regiments so that they would be fighting under their own, well known chief and members of the chief's family; this helped to give them confidence and stability and also introduced a competitive spirit, for they would make even greater exertions if they saw another clan doing better than themselves.

Second, there was no question of the chief or his officers directing the battle from the rear; the chief always stood in the front line with his closest kin around him and his absence, for whatever reason, had a dispiriting effect on his clansmen.

The third consideration was the Highlanders' method of attack. For centuries they had always hoped to begin a battle by achieving *cothrom a' bhràighe* (the advantage of the slope), that is, they had endeavoured to dispose themselves on a hillside overlooking their enemy so that their speed of approach and the weight of their attack were increased. This method, which was, after all, a very basic one with nothing much to distinguish it from any other unsophisticated method of warfare, had been further developed in Ireland by Alasdair MacColla. He had used a refined version at the battle of the Laney in 1642 during Phelim O'Neill's Rising. The two modifications he had introduced were to use firearms as well as swords and to arrange his men in small, tight groups. They began their charge, fired once when they were fairly near their enemy, threw down their muskets and continued with their charge, running within the protection of the smoke they had produced by their fusillade. Although the small groups of men did not, of course, present a continuous line of attack to their enemies, each group flung itself on the opposing line of troops with much greater weight, not only destroying the men actually opposite to them but also throwing the rest of the enemy line into confusion.

This was the method Alasdair imported into Scotland and with it he won all the battles he fought for Montrose against the Covenanters. It has come to be known as the Highland Charge. Dundee saw its advantages and understood that introducing the battlefield tactics he had learnt in Europe into Highland warfare would only confuse the clansmen. He abandoned any idea of re-training, although he may have used some drills to help the clansmen hold their fire until they were close to their enemy and abandon their muskets after firing them.

James Philip certainly claims that he did so, for he says in *The Grameid*:

> For him there is no pampering of himself, no sluggish ease or
> luxury, no listless sleep, but practising for the battle, he
> reviews his troops, and turns out his foaming squadrons on
> the plain. He deploys his compact columns, and wheels them
> again into formation, displaying the image of the future bat-
> tle on the heavy and dusty plain. Mounted on horseback, he
> teaches the toilsome task of Mars, and how to meet the fire
> of the enemy and the heavy charge of swift cavalry, and how
> to charge by horse and foot.[14]

This would have required a continuous effort on Dundee's part for the composi-
tion of the forces at Dalcomera altered from day to day.

The MacMartins and the Camerons, apart from those from the western end
of Loch Arkaig and the glens beyond it, were his most constant companions. The
other Great Glen chiefs had taken their men home to relieve the food situation.
Most of the island clans did not arrive until early June and then MacLean of
Lochbuie was sent back to Mull with prisoners Dundee had taken in Perth, while
the Sleat MacDonalds returned to Skye in the vain hope of persuading the
MacKinnons and MacLeod of MacLeod to rise. An attempt was also made to
wrest Kintyre from the hands of the Campbells and many of the MacLeans were
involved in this, but with little success.

Dundee had ordered his supporters to rendezvous in Lochaber on the 28th or
29th July and it was earlier in this month that King James said goodbye to the
Irish contingent he was at last sending to Dundee under the command of
Brigadier-General Alexander Cannon and Colonel James Purcell. The latter does
not seem to have been a kinsman of the great English composer, Henry Purcell –
certainly not a close one – although Henry's eldest brother, Edward, was in King
James' Irish army at some time.

Dundee rode down to Inverlochy on the 14th July to make arrangements for
receiving the Irish troops. They did not, however, reach the Corran Narrows until
the 20th and it took a long time to bring them all across from Ardgour over that
swiftly flowing tide which sweeps all craft out of their desired course. They were
however only 300 Irish, poorly clad and poorly armed, but all the king could
spare, for the siege of Derry was not yet at an end. Dundee had been hoping for

five to six thousand but ' ... the brave Lord Dundee was not to be discouraged by accidents of this nature'.[15]

On the 17th July the Sleat MacDonalds arrived on the mainland, probably somewhere near Mallaig. Their chief, Domhnall Gorm (Blue-eyed Donald) had to return to Skye almost at once as he was taken ill, but his men remained, under the command of his son, Domhnall Gorm Og (Young Blue-eyed Donald). They marched via Loch Eil to Dalcomera, arriving there on Friday the 19th. With them was a party of Keppoch MacDonalds who had accompanied their chief, *Colla nam Bo*, to Skye as he had been appointed Lieutenant-Colonel to the Sleat chief. (It is not clear to me how he could have fulfilled the duties of this command while leading his own clan). They also had with them the Keppoch bard, Iain Lom, whom we met in chapter VII. He was born at the latest in 1624 and was a descendant of the 4th Keppoch Chief, Iain Aluinn, who had been deposed as he was found to be unfit to lead the clan. The precise meaning of 'Lom' in this context is debatable as it means a great many things, for example, bare, bleak, lean, miserly, satirical, cutting, smooth; 'satirical' seems a likely translation.

Iain was in his twenties when he hurried up the Great Glen to Cill Chuimein to warn Montrose of Argyll's presence at Inverlochy and in his forties when he avenged the murder of the 13th Keppoch Chief and his brother. Another 19 years later he comes to the fore again, greatly to the relief of the historian, at the very point at which James Philip's epic poem, *The Grameid*, ends, or rather at the very point at which he stopped making a fair copy of it. After his description of the King's farewell to his Irish troops there are several blank pages, headed and numbered, ready to take the next part of the work, so it is reasonable to suppose that he intended to continue, indeed had already continued but had not got as far as making a fair copy of the last section. I cannot think that he did not finish it as he had yet to tell us of the Battle of Killiecrankie the most important event in the life of his hero. Perhaps the rough draft will turn up one day, tucked into a dusty book in some forgotten library.

Iain wrote two songs celebrating the first Jacobite Rising – *Oran air Feachd Righ Seumas* (A Song to King James's Army) and *Cath Raon Ruairidh* (The Battle of Rory's Upland Field), known to non-Gaelic speakers as the Battle of Killiecrankie.

He had a long life. His last poem was written in 1707 when he was at least 83; it was a protest against the Union of the Parliaments. The date of his death is likely to have been 1710 when he was in his late eighties.

In his *Oran air Feachd Righ Seumas* he details the route and timing of the
march of the Sleat MacDonalds from the mainland (probably somewhere near
Mallaig) to the camp at Dalcomera which they reached on Friday the 21st July.
They stayed there for three days – ' ... for the day before Sunday and two days after
it' as Iain explains.[16]

The camp was then broken up hurriedly because news was received that
Mackay was coming north in the hope of capturing Blair Castle, a move which
Dundee needed to prevent at all costs as Blair was pivotal to any commander
wanting to control movements between the south and the north of Scotland. He
knew that they must move at once, that it was impossible to wait until the rendezvous date he had set, even though this meant that they must risk going with
only part of the army. Matters were so urgent that Lochiel had to leave with only
those clansmen living around Achnacarry and on the east bank of the Lochy. The
rest of them, from the western end of Loch Arkaig and the glens beyond, were
gathered up and brought on later by his son John and did not arrive at Blair until
the battle of Killiecrankie was over. The Glencoe MacDonalds and the Keppoch
MacDonalds were away, probably gathering more cattle, and came eventually on
the 28th, as originally arranged, but of course too late. The MacGregors were also
absent; they may have been with the Glendessary Camerons and so too far away
to leave with Lochiel himself. The 300 Irish had eventually managed to get across
the Corran Narrows; they were too late to join the camp at Dalcomera, but they
caught the army up, possibly somewhere near the entrance to Glen Gloy.

Dalcomera was on an ancient highway between the western and the eastern
Highlands. Anyone standing today on the camp site or on the road above it that
follows the west bank of the River Lochy can see the jaws of Glen Gloy a little way
off to the north-east. Travellers from the west would cross the Lochy via the ford
near Mucomir (Dalcomera) and then go north-east to Glenfintaig Lodge beside
the modern A82 and so into Glen Gloy which would take them, via the upper
reaches of the River Roy, to the Corrieyairack at Melgarve.

James Philip's epic is cut off before this hurried march began and Iain Lom
says little about it apart from 'We set out in very stately order till we reached the
head of Glen Roy ... '.[17] We can only imagine their departure, Dundee probably
going ahead with the cavalry – only about 40 in number by this time and including his closest friends – the clansmen following in their swift loping stride which
could bring them across miles of rough country in a single day. The banners flut-
tered and the pipes sent up their shrill, searching notes into the dome of the sky.

The Great Glen lay deserted, the heather, crushed under so many feet, made ready to rise again and show its late summer flowers. Dundee had but the shortest of times to bid goodbye to this place where he had paused to gather strength, where he had come to know his clansmen and their commanders. His thoughts now rushed ahead to the east where he would win a great victory over his enemy, would create the right conditions for the further success of the Rising but at the same time end all the hopes of his friends by his death in battle.

X
The Military Roads

The Grampians, like ramparts, stood between two ages, one of paper, one of steel; on either side were peoples foreign to each other. Since roads had been in Scotland they had reached to Stirling, but at Stirling they had stopped, and on the castle rock the sentinel at nightfall saw the mists go down upon a distant land of bens and glens on which a cannon or carriage wheel had never yet intruded

...

> *Now was the furrow being made ... on which to drive the Gael like bridled oxen ...*

Neil Munro

WHEN THE SOUND and fury of the Battle of Killiecrankie was over and he had seen his leader, Viscount Dundee, laid below the flagstones of St Bride's, Sir Ewen Cameron set out for home, taking his wounded with him. Dundee's army had swelled to five thousand by a day or two after the battle; according to Lochiel's son-in-law, Drummond of Balhaldy, the new recruits included 500 Camerons brought in by Lochiel's son John who had been too far away to get to Blair in time for the battle; 200 Stewarts of Appin; some MacGregors command-ed by MacGregor of Roro; 250 MacPhersons (Cluny had at last managed to resolve his problems, stirred up perhaps by Dundee's last message to him from Blair Castle); 250 MacDonalds of Keppoch and of Glencoe and all the men of Atholl. But, as Balhaldy records:

> ... so soon as Dundee's death was generally known, the scene changed, and all those mighty preparations, and that univer-sall spirit of Jacobitism, vanished into nothing.[1]

The new commander, Brigadier-General Alexander Cannon, was useless as leader of a Highland army, indeed perhaps of any army. The Jacobite army soon suffered defeat in spite of its greatly increased numbers and the Rising was virtu-ally over, although there were continuing alarms and excursions and some of the chiefs, including Lochiel, tried to get it going again.

The government was by no means satisfied with the state of the Highlands and in 1691 the Highland chiefs were required to take an oath of allegiance to King William. The 1st January 1692 was the last day on which this could be done. The consequences if it were not done would be dire. The Jacobite chiefs would not sign until they had received permission from King James and they wrote to him asking for his approval and assuring him that should his situation alter and make it possible for him to send them the troops and arms he had intended to send before his campaign in Ireland failed they would not forget him. The King's reply was delayed and did not arrive very long before the final possible date. Lochiel was only just in time to take the oath. The MacDonalds of Glencoe were not so lucky as their chief had made a mistake about the official before whom he had to appear. He went first to Colonel Hill, Governor of Fort William, but Hill had to send him on to Inveraray, giving him a letter of explanation to take with him. MacDonald was delayed on his way there by heavy snow and then found that Campbell of Ardkinglas, who was to adminster the oath, was away. By the time he returned it was several days after the date set, but he promised to forward Hill's letter and his own recommendation to the Sheriff-Clerk of Argyll, although he could not guarantee what their reception would be. Contrary to what MacDonald of Glencoe was expecting these documents were ignored. The mas-sacre which took place within that glen on the flat stretches of green beside the rushing river was not, of course, the result of a feud between Campbells and MacDonalds, as is still often the popular belief, but was backed by a decree signed by King William and carried out by a regiment of his army which happened to be commanded by a Campbell and contain a minority of Campbells in its ranks. All Highlanders, not just the Jacobite clans, were horrified by these killings. Lochiel ordered all his clansmen to turn out any government soldiers who had been quar-tered on them.[2] The government, nervous about the reaction to the massacre from all quarters of Britain, withdrew its troops from Jacobite areas and tightly restricted the movements of the Fort William garrison.

Lochiel was to live for another 27 years, dying in 1719 at the age of 90, but his son John bore most of the burden of managing the clan during the latter years and of taking part in the 1715 Jacobite Rising. One morning at the end of December 1715 Lochiel told his wife to make the house ready for a great celebration because their king was coming. She thought he was out of his mind but did her best to do as he asked, not wanting to upset him and made Achnacarry as welcoming as she could for so important a visitor. Later they heard that the king had landed at Peterhead on that very day. But he was not to stay for long; the weather at sea was against him and the Rising was almost over before he was to able to play any part in it.

The Earl of Mar had held his tinchal (hunting party) on the Braes of Mar on the 26th August 1715. In the Great Glen MacDonald of Glengarry raised his men and the Glenmoriston Grants joined him. They marched to meet General Gordon of Achintoul in Glenorchy, attacking Inverlochy Castle, in which there were soldiers from Fort William, on the way. These were the only actions that took place in the Great Glen during the '15. On the 13th November however 300 Camerons of Lochiel and 460 MacDonalds of Glengarry (this figure probably includes Glenmoriston Grants) from the Great Glen fought in the Battle of Sheriffmuir. The argument over who actually won it, if anyone, has been going on ever since; the last time I visited Inveraray Castle they were claiming it as a Campbell victory. MacDonald of Keppoch was also 'out'; he was on his way to join Mar but, finding his path blocked by a larger force led by Fraser of Lovat, he was obliged to turn back and did not join the main Jacobite army until after Sheriffmuir.

When the Rising and all its trials, executions and imprisonments were at an end the government began to turn its mind to the question of what should be done to keep the Highlands quiet in the future. Nothing much happened for a time but the abortive rising of 1719 in Glenshiel resulted in the building of a fort at Cill Chuimein (Fort Augustus) and of barracks at Bernera (Glenelg), Ruthven (near Kingussie) and Inversnaid (Loch Lomond). But even so there was no real movement towards dealing with the problem until 1724 when Simon Fraser of Lovat, who had been very upset at the standing down of the Highland companies, particularly his own, wrote a letter to George I giving his views on the state of the Highlands.

He believed that the Highland companies should be re-established; they had been formed after the 1689 Rising and disbanded in 1717 because they were thought to be a waste of money. He also thought that there was little point in building barracks when the country was so rough and wild that regular soldiers found the marches they had to make from one to the next too difficult, used as they were to the smoother and flatter highways of the south. Lovat's letter seems to have had an immediate effect for General Wade was sent to Scotland in the same year to see whether what Lovat had said was correct and, if so, what should be done about it. He reported back later that year.

George Wade was born in Ireland, in Co Westmeath, in 1673. He joined the army in 1690 and had risen to the rank of Major-General by the time he arrived in Scotland. He was made a full General in 1739 and in the following year left Scotland, handing over his work there to Major William Caulfeild. Wade became a Privy Councillor in 1743 and a Field Marshal in 1744. His contribution to the Hanoverian cause in 1746 was not a distinguished one as he failed to intercept Prince Charles Edward's army on its way down to Derby. He was however in his seventies at the time and died two years later at the age of 75. He was buried in Westminster Abbey. He never married but had four natural children. Being an Irishman he had a very hospitable nature and was a great conversationalist. He gave the soldiers working on his roads – he called them 'my Highwaymen' – occasional 'treats', such as an ox roast, when they had completed a particular piece of their road and let them brew their own liquor. Unfortunately this ran him into difficulties with the excisemen but it was eventually agreed that the conditions of work were exceptional so the 'illegal brewing' continued. He entertained passing travellers in the houses built for him to use when inspecting the work on the roads; there was certainly one of these on the Great Glen road near Foyers, known as the General's Hut. A map that belonged to him places it somewhere between Foyers and Inverfarigaig and it may have been near the Fraser burial ground which lies between the present road and the loch and near the entrance to Boleskine House. In the early 20th century Boleskine House was occupied for a time by the 'wizard' Aleister Crowley of whom very unsavoury stories are told; he is believed to have celebrated a Black Mass there and the head of Lord Lovat, executed after the '45, was said to roll down the corridors after dark. That side of Loch Ness was all Fraser country then and Simon Fraser of Lovat, the owner of the head, made frequent visits there as it was an area of which he was particularly fond. Dr Johnson visited the General's Hut in the 1770s during his tour in the Highlands with James Boswell; he says it is ' ... so called because it was the temporary abode of Wade when he superintended the works upon the road. It is now a house of entertainment for passengers, and we found it not ill stocked with provisions'.[3]

Wade's report revealed his alarming conclusion that more than half the men capable of bearing arms in the Highlands had Jacobite sympathies and that the difficulties brought about by this state of affairs had beeen compounded by the lack of roads and bridges. He agreed with Lord Lovat that the Highland companies should be reintroduced. He also thought that a string of forts down the Great Glen was essential to the proper patrolling of the country as it was a route of such importance to communications, particularly troop movements. There was already a fort at the south end of the glen (Fort William) and a small one at Cill Chuimein but he thought there ought to be one at Inverness and a larger one at Cill Chuimein, which he regarded as 'the most centrical part of the Highlands'.[4] The absence of decent roads on either side of Loch Ness meant that the easiest way to provision the fort at Cill Chuimein was to have a ship on Loch Ness that could move soldiers and supplies between Cill Chuimein and Inverness. Finally be declared himself in favour of a new and stricter Disarming Act; the earlier one had been a failure as Highlanders had bought old unusable arms from Holland, had virtuously handed these in and had hidden their own arms, in good, even pristine condition, in the thatch of their houses.

Almost at once Wade was made Commander-in-Chief North Britain and in the spring of the following year he asked for six Highland companies to be recruited, three of 60 men each and three of 30 men each. He also wanted two regiments to garrison forts and barracks and money to pay for the building of a boat on Loch Ness and for the construction of forts at Cill Chuimein and Inverness. The existing roads, such as they were, would need to be mended. These roads and tracks, some of which had been in existence for a very long time, were used mainly by travellers on foot or on horseback and by drovers or reivers. The drovers complained bitterly whenever the new roads built by Wade or later by Caulfeild coincided with the tracks they had been using for generations to move their cattle. They thought the new gravelled surfaces hurt the hooves of the cattle or interfered with their grazing and the stances where they had been used to rest, although the road builders declared that the cattle did more damage to the new roads than the new roads ever did to the cattle.

Once all Wade's requests had been agreed he set out for Scotland and reached Inverness on the 10th August 1725 after a long journey disrupted by riots in Glasgow and contrary winds between Leith and Angus.

Without losing any time he implemented the new Disarming Act which the government had passed and nearly 3000 arms were handed in, but whether they were in any better condition than the ones given up under the old Act is doubtful.

Wade then turned his mind to fort building at Inverness and Cill Chuimein and to the new ship that was to be constructed to sail between these two places. This would not be the first ship built for this purpose, for Cromwell had had one as part of his system for controlling the Highlands during the Commonwealth. An amusing contemporary discussion upon this new ship declares:

> ... and here it is, in these slippery streams, that an English ship, by curious invention, was haled over the mountains to this solitary Lough; brought hither on purpose to reclaim the Highlander.[5]

and goes on to explain that the ship was built on the coast and a regiment of soldiers then hauled her over rollers into the loch, in other words ' ... she relinquished the brinish ocean to float in the slippery arms of Ness'. She was known as the *Highland Galley*. The Rev James Fraser of Phopachy reported that they:

> ... carried a bark driven uppon rollers of wood to the Lochend of Ness, and then enlarged it into a statly friggot, to sail with provision from the one end of the loch to the other; one Mr Church governour, and Lieutenant Orton captain of this friggot, and 60 men aboard of her to land upon expeditions where they pleased. I happened myself, with the Laird of Strachin, near Portclaire, to be invited aboard by Orton, when we were gentily treated.[6]

On her first trip the galley was decorated with flags and firing her guns, and people appeared everywhere on the hillsides to see her.[7] She was used until the early 1800s to supply Cill Chuimein and after that to move materials for the canal. She too was known as the Highland Galley and, when orders were given for her construction, work also began on the strengthening of Fort William and the building of a new fort at Cill Chuimein; this would eventually be called Fort Augustus.

The old barracks at Cill Chuimein had been built in 1716. As Wade's agent Burt says, 'I need not tell you upon what occasion'.[8] In 1729 it was named Fort Augustus after the young William Augustus, Duke of Cumberland, a son of George II. The new name was gradually applied to the village that grew up around it and so the old name honouring St Cummen disappeared, but not entirely and we may retrieve it yet. It occupied a site roughly where the present Lovat Arms stands, that is, some distance from the loch, but Wade put up another building close to the loch and the intention was to connect it to the older fort and make the whole structure the main fort in the Great Glen. Another idea was to build a town round it larger than Inverness; this idea seems to have arisen because there was some dissatisfaction with two or three of the Inverness councillors at the time,[9] but this came to nothing. Although the new building was finished by 1742 the connection between the two parts was never made and some of the Jacobite forces, on their return from invading England, began a siege of the new part of the fort on the 3rd March 1746 and bombarded it from the older part, having first ejected its occupants by a simple assault. The besieging force was led by Lt-Col Walter Stapleton commanding the Irish Picquets, plus the Ecossais Royal and Cameron and MacDonald clansmen from Lochaber. In only two days they were successful and the governor surrendered. The fort was used in a damaged state to house prisoners taken after the end of the '45 Rising and was also intended as accommodation for William Augustus, Duke of Cumberland and some of his staff officers, but it was felt to be too uncomfortable to house so august a person and the soldiers built a 'bower' for him from the branches of trees. In 1747 the fort was rebuilt and a garrison was retained there until 1854 when the military abandoned it. In 1867 Lord Lovat acquired it and presented it to the Benedictines who built an Abbey on the site. Very little of either part of the original fort remains.

Fort William was built in 1650 by Oliver Cromwell. In 1660 at the Restoration it was 'slighted' but was rebuilt after the accession of William and Mary in 1688. Between the 20th March and the 3rd April 1746 it was besieged by the same Jacobite forces that had taken Fort Augustus, but they had to abandon the siege when they were ordered to proceed to Inverness and join the rest of the army there. The fort was abandoned by the military in 1855 and subsequently came into the ownership of the West Highland Railway Company, who blew it up. Only a few fragments remain.

In Wade's time Fort George was on the site of the present castle at Inverness. There had been a castle there from the eleventh century, if not before. The new Fort George which we see today is on the Moray coast and well away from Inverness. It was begun in 1746, the old fort having been blown up by the Jacobites, and was finished in 1769. George II was determined to create a substantial base from which to combat any further attacks and it certainly is substantial and is, in fact, the largest fortified structure in Britain and perhaps in Europe, but it has never been used for the purpose for which it was built.

Lord Lovat had already pointed out how useless it was to build forts and barracks when the terrain made it so difficult for soldiers to get from one to the next and Wade must have realised, during his preliminary work, that it was not enough to mend the existing roads; new ones would have to be made. Why this was so necessary can be deduced from the experiences of Captain Edmund Burt, General Wade's agent. He set out on a journey of inspection, he does not say where but it is likely to have been somewhere in or near the Great Glen and possibly near Inverness. He took with him a servant and a guide along with some 'cold provisions' and oats for his horse as he would not find anywhere to eat until the end of the first day. After about four miles he came to a river and found there a ferry boat, very much patched with small bits of board. The ferryman told him it was 60 years old at least. As with most ferries a horse could not be taken on board and had to be swum through the water at the stern of the boat, its head held up out of the water by the bridle. Sometimes the horse would get tired of swimming and would turn over on its side and have to be hauled along.

For some miles after getting over the river Burt struggled with very stony and uneven tracks which at one point became a bog that was two feet (0.6m) deep. After this they reached another river, not a wide one, but with a very rocky and steep descent to the water and an even worse climb up the other side. Further on they came upon a stretch of bog much worse than the one they had encountered before. Burt went over it on foot and the horses were led carefully across, trying to avoid the most treacherous parts. Burt's own horse got across safely, but was very frightened and trembling by the time it reached the other side. The pack horse however sank right down, but luckily struck a layer of rock and was able, eventually, to struggle out, panting and shaking with fear. Burt points out the difference between his own horses – English horses – and the little Highland garrons when they sink into a bog. The former shake and struggle so much that they make their position worse, whereas the latter just stand quietly until they are helped out. Burt himself, wearing high-heeled boots, found it very uncomfortable leaping from tuft to tuft to avoid the most dangerous places and very time-consuming too, but his guide, who wore flat brogues, managed it all quite easily. What annoyed Burt most throughout his journey was that his companions *would* refer to the track they were following as 'a road'. After another session of struggling with large stones and rocks while getting up a hill they found yet another river before them and the village where they were to spend the night was on the opposite bank. The river was not wide however and the horses were very clever at making their way between the slippery stones and rocks on the river bed. Having got to the other bank Burt stopped to observe a party of six men and one woman; they were preparing to wade through the water. They formed into a line each with their arms over their neighbour's shoulders, the largest and strongest of them standing at the end which would first have to withstand the force of the current. Sometimes one or other of them would miss his footing amongst the slippery stones and the whole line would tremble and change countenance.

> I believe no painter ever remarked such strong impressions of fear and hope on a human face, with so many and sudden successions of those two opposite passions, as I observed among those poor people; ... [10]

He had to have a new guide next day as the first one did not know the country ahead of them, but unfortunately this new man spoke no English. The day before them was notable mainly for their finding themselves on a very narrow ledge with a steep rocky ascent on one side and a precipice on the other. The precipice was, according to Burt, 'twice as high ... as the cross of St Paul's is from Ludgate Hill'. They got past this somehow and, in correcting a mistake by the guide (who feared Burt was going to shoot him for it, so dreadful was his picture of the English), also managed to ease themselves out of a stony corner leading to another precipice; the horses had to be brought out of it backwards. However they reached their goal that night and went on hopefully on the following day, the last one, encountering little more than snow piling up into thick drifts and fearful winds that almost swept them off their feet.[11]

If these adventures were reported to Wade, which they almost certainly were as the journey had been undertaken for inspection purposes, it is not very surprising that he decided it would be better to make new roads, if this were possible, rather than try to 'mend' the old ones.

The Great Glen was the most important line of communication in the Highlands. All parts of the Highlands, to the east and to the west, could be reached, if with difficulty, from this immense groove, so it is not surprising that Wade, as his first essay in road building, decided on a road from Inverness to Fort William which would link the three forts along the glen and help communications generally in the Highlands. Once the money for this was made available he mapped out the line from Cill Chuimein to Fort William and began work on it in the summer of 1725. It was to run to the east of Loch Lochy and of Loch Oich, unlike the modern A82 which goes to the east of Loch Lochy but to the west of Loch Oich. This section was completed by the end of that year, that is, by the end of October; road work always stopped at this time as the weather was not suitable after that date. The main difficulties here were, firstly, the bridge across the Spean, Highbridge, which was not completed until 1736. (Low Bridge is the Wade bridge crossing the Gloy Burn between Glenfintaig Lodge and Lower Glenfintaig Farm). The second difficulty was the section of the road passing Loch Oich, where the rocks projected over the loch in places and were so steep and uneven that 'the passenger was obliged to creep on his hands and knees'.[12] Before the road was built many travellers had preferred to find some way on the west side of the loch, even though this involved crossing the River Garry.

In the following year the road was continued all the way up to Inverness. On the Loch Ness section Wade took the road away from the loch and over high ground to the east of Foyers, but it was found very unsatisfactory in the winter and in 1732 he realigned the whole section between Foyers and Dores, bringing the road back to the loch side and making four new bridges. They had difficulties in the Black Rock area at the edge of the loch where they found coarse black marble and the miners had to hang ' ... by ropes from the precipice over the water ... to bore the stone, in order to blow away a necessary part from the face of it'. A wall was built up on the loch side at points where the precipice below was too horrifying.[13] This lower road eventually became the B862 and was the main route to Inverness until the early 1800s when a road on the west side of the loch was completed.

Both Wade and his successor Caulfeild were inclined to leave bridge-building until after a road was finished. In the meantime they depended on fords but in most cases these were so likely to be obstructed by stones brought down by floods that bridges were usually found to be a necessity.

Work on these new Highland roads was confined to the weeks from the beginning of April to the end of October to avoid the worst of the weather and parties of between 300 and 500 soldiers were used. These were all unskilled men, and civilian masons, blacksmiths and carpenters were therefore also needed when making bridges, traverses and cross-drains. The roads were on average 16-ft wide (4.9m) but particular features of the ground made it necessary sometimes to reduce their width. They would follow a straight line as far as possible but traverses or zigzags had to be made on steep portions, as, for instance, on the steeper parts of the Corrieyairack Pass on the Dalwhinnie to Cill Chuimein road where there are 18 traverses and on sections such as the Devil's Staircase above Altnafeadh on the Stirling to Fort William road, where there is a series of zigzags. Marking stones were placed at the edge of high-level roads as guides to travellers in mist or snow. Every ten miles (16km) a camp was established and these camps eventually turned into what were known as 'kingshouses', that is, inns to provide shelter and food for travellers. Perhaps the most famous of these is Kingshouse of Glencoe which lies on the edge of Rannoch Moor and at the foot of the Buachaille Etive Mòr. In his book *The New Road* Neil Munro imagines it as a lively place, full of drovers and tinkers and music and full of drink and food as well.[14] But he places his story in 1733 and the Stirling to Fort William road was built between 1748 and 1753, the inn itself coming into being beside it in about 1760. It developed presumably from a camp for the soldiers/road builders, although it is not impossible that some sort of inn may have been on the site earlier.[15] Dorothy Wordsworth who stayed there with her brother William in 1803 gives a most unattractive picture of it:

> The house looked respectable from a distance – a large square building, cased in blue slates to defend it from storms, but when we came close to it the outside forewarned us of the poverty and misery within. Scarce a blade of grass could be seen growing upon the open ground ... there was no enclosure for a cow, no appropriated ground but a small plot like a church yard, in which were a few starveling dwarfish potatoes.

The house was crammed with 'drovers, carriers, horsemen and travellers' all wanting their supper and only one woman to provide it. She had no eggs, milk, potatoes or bread and they finally made their meal off a shoulder of mutton from which it was difficult to scrape any meat. They found the sheets on their beds wringing wet and it took them until bedtime to dry them as the peats on the fire were wet too and would not burn properly.[16] Though the food does sound horrid I cannot say that the wet sheets impress me very much as examples of unusual phenomena, having several times encountered them in Co Donegal; there it seemed better just to let them be, as this did at least keep the dampness quiet, whereas an electric blanket produced clouds of steam in which a good night's sleep seemed a somewhat hazardous adventure. Even in those good old days before the advent of central heating and electric blankets and before the original building developed into a design-award-winning hotel I found the sheets at Kingshouse remarkably dry and the food delightful, especially the porridge and the curds and cream, so the anxieties expressed about how to provide food for an unknown number of travellers in a remote region with very poor soil in the 1760s to 1800s must have produced some good results. In 1802 Thomas Telford wrote:

> A very important Consideration also is the erecting and maintaining of proper Inns upon the roads. Several of the Houses which were built by the government upon the Military Roads are striking instances of the necessity there is of giving the people who are to keep the Inns something else to depend on besides what arises from supplying Travellers; there should be some land attached to the House.[17]

though he may have been thinking more of the income of the innkeeper than of providing better food for the guests.

On the Great Glen road, in addition to the kingshouse at Foyers/Inverfarigaig, there was one at Whitebridge, now an hotel, and also one at Letterfinlay which later became a drovers' inn. Many fugitives from Culloden found a brief refuge there. It lies on the east side of the A82, part-way along a straight, treeless length of road beside Loch Lochy.[18] It was originally much further from the loch than it is now, as the level of the loch was raised when the canal was built.

Wade managed to persuade the government to pay soldiers working on the Highland roads an extra sum in addition to their normal army pay. Subalterns received 2s.6d extra per day, sergeants 1s, corporals 8d and privates 6d. Captains did not receive any extra money as they had nothing to do with the road work, serving merely as administrators and keeping military discipline.[19]

Before work could begin on a road the route had to be surveyed, maps drawn and the line of the road marked on the ground, huts had to be built to accommodate the soldiers and the necessary equipment provided, from spades upwards, including such items as a forge for the civilian blacksmith.

The foundations were then dug and any big boulders broken up (with gun-powder if necessary) and lowered into the dug trench. Smaller stones were then broken up, packed on top and covered with gravel to a depth of two feet (0.6m). The gravel was beaten down with shovels and by the passage of wheeled vehicles and of human feet. Where there was a bog it had to be dug down to rock level and filled in with gravel. If no loose stones were available timber was used instead with gravel over it. The constant presence of moisture made the wood as hard as iron – a phenomenon which can be observed in bog oak. Marking stones were put at the sides of the road where necessary and milestones also had to be set up. The gravel top remained rather unstable, even after all the pressures applied to it and usually had to be replaced every year. The earth that had been removed to create the trench was piled up to provide a bank on each side and beyond these banks on each side a drain was cut to take away surplus water and prevent erosion. Underground drains or culverts were sometimes needed but there is no mention of them in the records until the Fort Augustus to Bernera road was built – it was begun in 1755 after Wade had retired.

James Boswell came along the Great Glen road in 1773 with his friend Dr Samuel Johnson, whom he had persuaded to make a visit to the Highlands. On the 30th August they hired three horses in Inverness, one for each of them and one for Boswell's man Joseph Ritter who was from Bohemia and over six feet tall, 'a fine stately figure'; he could speak several languages. They took a fourth horse as well to carry the baggage. They also had two Highlanders to walk beside them and serve as guides. The horses belonged to these Highlanders who would take them back from Bernera. Johnson says that the road 'was so hard and level that we had little care to hold the bridle' and they rode along happily, admiring the views of the loch for about four miles (6.4km), when they came to a house lying beside the road – they must have been somewhere near Dores at the time.

Finlay J MacDonald in his book further illuminating Johnson's account has a story that the predecessor of the woman who lived in this house had been murdered by one of Cumberland's officers when she tried to stop him raping her daughter. This was by no means a rare event during Cumberland's time at Fort Augustus, but as there is no certain trace of the house in question the story cannot be linked with any certainty to this particular one. They went into the house, a typical blackhouse with the living quarters at one end and livestock (goats in this case) at the other behind a wattle screen. Dr Johnson expressed a desire to know what the bedroom was like and when one of the guides translated this to the woman of the house she replied, with some emotion, that she was afraid they wanted to go to bed with her. Boswell was inclined to interpret this as coquetry but it is quite likely to have been a genuine sign of fear, bearing in mind the situation of only 25 to 30 years earlier, whether MacDonald's story is true or not. Johnson was too polite or too sensitive to go into the bedroom but Boswell went in and had a good look round. In joking about it afterwards Boswell suggested it was Johnson who had alarmed the woman, to which Johnson replied:

> No, sir, she'll say, 'There came a wicked young fellow, a wild dog, who I believe would have ravished me, had there not been with him a grave old gentleman, who repressed him: but when he gets out of the sight of his tutor, I'll warrant you he'll spare no woman he meets, young or old'. 'No, sir,' [Boswell replied], 'she'll say, "There was a terrible ruffian who would have forced me, had it not been for a civil decent young man who, I take it, was an angel sent from heaven to protect me".'

Any difficulty was resolved by the woman asking them all to sit down and take a dram; so after the whisky and a good chat the two travellers and their companions went on, leaving a gift of money behind them and with the woman's prayers in Gaelic ringing in their ears.

They stopped further on and dined at the General's Hut, between Inverfarigaig and Foyers, and then hurried on to Fort Augustus, as it was getting late. General Trapaud, the deputy-governor of the fort, was waiting for them at the gate and they spent a pleasant evening with him and his wife, eating a good supper, in fact, as Boswell puts it 'with all the conveniences of civilized life in the midst of rude mountains'.[20]

While making the Great Glen road the idea of a complete road network in the Highlands must have developed in Wade's mind and of the other roads he and Caulfeild built three were of particular interest to the Great Glen. These were the road from Dalwhinnie over the Corrieyairack Pass to Fort Augustus – this was begun in 1731; the Fort Augustus to Bernera road on which work did not commence until 1755; and the Stirling-Glencoe-Fort William road begun in 1748.

In 1730 Wade decided to tackle the building of the road from Dalwhinnie to Fort Augustus which would connect the Great Glen with the Central Highlands and ultimately with Ruthven barracks. He obtained a grant of £3000 for this in 1731. The road was to be 28 miles long (45km). Its most exciting section was the last 15 miles (24km) at the Fort Augustus end where the road builders had to get their road over the Corrieyairack Pass,[21] which in places reaches a height of more than 2500 feet (762m). Eighteen traverses were needed over the highest portions, so it was a project requiring considerable engineering skills. Captain Burt thought the finished road was smoother than Highgate Hill.

They had begun in April 1731. The weather turned wet at the end of the summer and it rained more or less continuously for six weeks. The soldiers were very tired of being shut up in their camp, particularly as they did not receive their extra pay if they were not actually working. Wade had hoped to complete the work in the year he had begun it for, although there were unusual difficulties to be overcome, 28 miles (45km) was, comparatively speaking, a short distance to cover. In a letter to Lord Islay in October Wade was still unsure how quick their progress would be, but they did get the road finished by the end of that month, otherwise the whole project would have had to be shelved until the next year. That would have meant applying for a further grant to cover the extra expense involved. Wade did not forget to provide his 'Highwaymen' with an ox roast to celebrate the successful conclusion of the work. This was held at the bridge over the Allt Lagan a' Bhainne (the burn of the milky dell, from the rich milk given by the cattle which grazed there). It lies to the south of Culachy House and the soldiers called it Snugborough. Wade had 500 soldiers working for him by that time; they were formed into six divisions and each division had its own fire and ox, not to mention plenty of drink. Whether this drink was brought in or 'home-brewed' is not revealed. They certainly deserved every mouthful of the feast after such a hard struggle with the elements. It cannot have been pleasant working at the top of the pass, often in fierce winds or in mist or drizzle.

The road was used throughout the 18th century as a military road but after the Laggan to Spean Bridge road was built in 1818 the Melgarve to Fort Augustus section of the Wade road was no longer repaired, apart from the bridges, which were maintained to make the journey easier for cattle. So it became a drove road again and remained so until the end of the 19th century.[22] Today it is still used by walkers or horses and was, unfortunately, sometimes invaded by 4x4s until a few years ago when a particularly heavy flood broke up the final portion of the road at Fort Augustus so badly that there is now no chance of wheeled vehicles getting through. It remains a haven for the mountain hare, for blackcock and ptarmigan, curlew and red deer and if you stop to listen to the skylarks you may find their song interrupted by the music of a ghostly piper, if those 4x4s did not frighten him away.

In 1740 Wade left Scotland; he had built 250 miles (402km) of road and 40 bridges. He handed his work over to Major William Caulfeild whom he had first employed in 1732. Caulfeild was also an Irishman, a son of the 1st Viscount Charlemont whose descendant by the end of the 18th century was James, 4th Viscount and 1st Earl of Charlemont. He was a patriot leader and elected Commander-in-Chief of the Volunteers in 1780. The Volunteers were a part-time military force raised in 1778-9 to help keep law and order. They later campaigned for legislative independence for Ireland and Charlemont became less radical once this had been achieved. He therefore survived the horrors associated with the suppression of the 1798 rising and, as he died in the following year, was spared the knowledge that the Irish Parliament would vote itself out of office by the Act of Union of 1800.

William Caulfeild however does not appear to have meddled in politics, except in a military sense – he was quartermaster to Sir John Cope (of 'Hey, Johnny Cope' fame) during the '45 – and he remained in charge of Highland roads until his death in 1767. The military roads in the Highlands are usually spoken of as 'Wade roads' but Caulfeild was actually responsible for 800-900 miles (1287-1448km) of them, more than three times the number of miles built by Wade, although we have to give Wade the credit for planning and starting them in the first place.

Caulfeild became Deputy Governor of Inverness Castle in 1747 and built himself a house about three miles to the east of Inverness. He seems to have been quite as hospitable a character as General Wade for he had a contraption he had himself designed which was of great help to his guests when they slipped under the table, rendered helpless by over-generous libations. They would be carried out into the hall, put into a 'cradle', hauled upstairs by block and tackle and put to bed with no co-operation needed on their part.[23] The name of the house, Cradlehall, is thought to come from this useful device. Burt tells a similar story about John Forbes of Culloden (Bumper John), the brother of Duncan Forbes, Lord President of the Court of Session. His footmen pushed short poles through the dining chairs and used them to carry his guests away when they became incapable. According to one story a guest protested that he was quite sober, whereupon the footman cried, 'Very well sir, but we shall have you by and by'.[24]

Duncan Forbes himself certainly drank heavily in his youth and in later life was probably not far behind his brother. The 18th century was a great century for drinking, whether in Inverness, Edinburgh or London. Doctors actually recommended a daily intake of a whole bottle of port to maintain and encourage good health.[25]

In 1748 work was begun on the Stirling to Fort William road, 93 miles long (150km). It took five years to complete. This road went from Stirling to Tyndrum and then via Inveroran to Kingshouse and Altnafeadh, over the hills on the north side of Glencoe and down into Kinlochleven, then up again through the Mamore Hills to Fort William. It is this northern stretch of the road which is of most interest to us, passing as it does through an area which had been so closely thirled to the Great Glen in all the clan politics of many centuries, and an area which was looked upon by government as a particular haunt of thieves and broken men, and of Jacobites on the run. The MacDonalds of Keppoch in Glen Spean used to go reiving with the MacDonalds of Glencoe, in fact the two of them were off on this work in July 1689, hoping to find enough cattle to feed Viscount Dundee's army, and missed the Battle of Killiecrankie. *Colla nam Bo* (Coll of the Cows) the Keppoch chief lived a long time to tell this story but the Glencoe chief was killed with his wife in the Massacre three years later.

The road was begun at both ends at the same time and by the summer of 1748 the soldiers had made 13 miles (21km) from the Stirling end but only three (4.8km) from Fort William; probably reflecting the particularly difficult conditions at the northern end. The road was not quite finished in 1752 because of bad weather. It had rained so hard and so continuously that the army tents at Blackmount, between Inveroran and Kingshouse, rotted and had become practically useless. Nevertheless the soldiers were very discontented when they were withdrawn in the middle of September, as they lost their extra pay and felt they were in such a poor and sodden condition already that just another two weeks could not make them any worse. There cannot have been much left to do as the road was soon completed in 1753.[26]

Repair costs for this northernmost section of the road were very heavy. At Auch near Bridge of Orchy scree was constantly being washed down from Ben Dorain and at times of spate the Allt Coire Chailean tended to burst its banks and invade the road, which was on the east bank of the river. The modern road which eventually took its place is on the west bank and avoids both these hazards. Another problem was the steep ascent from Altnafeadh to the top of the pass over to Kinlochleven. A series of zigzags had to be introduced here (the Devil's

Staircase) and the results were never satisfactory. There were also difficulties in the very last section on the Lairig Mòr through the Mamores from Kinlochleven to Fort William. After struggling with expensive repairs for a long time it was finally decided to build a new road that went through Glencoe to Ballachulish. This meant taking a ferry from Ballachulish to the north bank of Loch Leven which, when the amount of traffic increased, could mean a very long wait. It was possible, in the 1960s, to calculate from one's position in the queue, whether it would not be quicker to drive right round Loch Leven. Having reached Onich by one means or the other one could then drive straight up beside Loch Linnhe to Fort William. The ferry was eventually replaced by the present bridge.

Caulfeild's third road, third as far as we are concerned, was from Fort Augustus to Bernera barracks near Glenelg. It was 43 miles long (69km) with 41 bridges and was begun in 1755, although it had been under consideration for some time. The barracks had been built at Bernera in 1722 and was large enough to hold 200 soldiers, but there was no road from there to Fort Augustus. This new road would provide a line of defence from the west coast to as far east as the barracks at Ruthven. Pennant, who visited Bernera in 1772, reported that they (the country people) 'are now quite sensible of the good effects of the military, by introducing peace and security; they fear lest the evil days should return'[27] – a delphic statement I feel, since it is not clear, to me at any rate, which evil days they meant. They may anyway just have been giving a polite or politic answer.

Caulfeild was hoping to have 600 men working on this road and thought it could be completed in one year, but only about 300 were provided (five companies). In the following year only one company was forthcoming. This suggests that the authorities were already becoming less jumpy about the possibilities of another Rising. The number of men continued to decline each year and the road may not have been completed until 1763, but we cannot be sure of this as the records do not state whether the work done related to building the road or repairing it. The repair bills were certainly very large, for instance, in 1771 there was so much rain that the floods along the line of the road washed away six bridges and badly damaged 12 others. Two years later James Boswell and Dr Johnson used the road, having come down Wade's first road from Inverness to Fort Augustus. Repair work continued up to 1784 on the Bernera road but no soldiers were used on any of the roads after 1789 and in 1790 Bernera barracks was abandoned. Telford later worked on the road but it was then re-routed through Glenmoriston, once again to avoid zigzags, this time on the hill over from Fort Augustus.

After spending the night at Fort Augustus Johnson and Boswell set out for Bernera, hoping to reach Skye via the Glenelg ferry, but they had a good look at the fort first and saw the Highland Galley. Then they began the climb up from the fort and over the hills into Glenmoriston. Quite soon they came to the series of zigzags from which there are fine views of Fort Augustus, seen alternately from the west and from the east and found it amusing that when they were going east they could see below them the baggage horse going west and vice versa. On the way over they met some soldiers working on the road, no doubt doing repairs. They stopped to talk to them and gave them some money and then went on to Aonach, which seems to have disappeared from Ordnance Survey maps but lay to the west of Achlain towards Ceanacroc. The inn there in which they were to spend the night was, as Johnson relates ' ... like other huts of loose stones, but the part in which we dined and slept was lined with turf and wattled with twigs, which kept the earth from falling'. The innkeeper's daughter was a well-educated girl who had been to school in Inverness; this must have been either the school in Church Street, which was housed in the upper storey of Dunbar's Hospital, or Raining's School, near the steps of the same name. She served tea to the two guests after dinner and Dr Johnson made her a present of a book before he left. Her father, whose name was MacQueen, gave a rather depressing account of conditions in the Highlands where, he said, rents were rising and many people who could no longer pay them were being evicted. In the evening the soldiers they had met on the road turned up at the inn and the two visitors gave them another shilling. With these gifts of money the soldiers made themselves very drunk, quarrelled and fought and had to spend the night in a barn. The army was careful to hold back much of the pay to its soldiers in the hopes of preventing drunkenness, but poor Johnson and Boswell had unwittingly defeated this sensible idea.

It was on the next day while they were sitting on a bank somewhere in Glenshiel that Johnson thought of writing an account of his journey.

They stopped at a group of houses a little further along where they were given some milk which was offered as a gift, though the giver was afterwards persuaded to ask a shilling for it, whereupon they gave her half a crown. They made a meal for themselves from the milk and the food they had brought with them and then Boswell sliced up some of the bread and distributed it to a crowd of people who had come from the houses and gathered round them; they were also given snuff and tobacco and the children were lined up and received 1d each. Everyone agreed that it was the best day they had had since MacLeod of MacLeod passed that way.

Mam Ratagan now lay before them and they found it very hard going, both up and down; Dr Johnson was persuaded to change horses to give his own a rest as he was very heavy and his mount was showing some inclination to stumble with weariness which alarmed the doctor. They got over the hill however and went to the Glenelg Inn to spend the night. 'Of the provisions', as Johnson says, 'the negative catalogue was very copious'. There was no meat, milk, bread, eggs or wine, so they settled for whisky and a fowl and used more of their own bread. They must have brought plenty of that from Fort Augustus as they had fed on it for two days and also distributed it liberally to the people of Glen Shiel, although perhaps the landlord at Aonach had been able to give them some.

They were very cheered by being sent some rum and sugar by MacLeod's factor, who lived nearby and whose servant had walked with them the last part of the way. But their hearts sank again on examining where they were to sleep. 'Out of one of the beds on which we were to repose started up, at our entrance, a man black as a Cyclops from the forge.' Johnson sent for some hay and slept on it in his riding coat but Boswell 'being more delicate, laid himself sheets with hay over and under him, and lay in linen like a gentleman'.

The next morning they reached the end of the road and, having dismissed their guides, took the ferry across to Skye where Sir Alexander MacDonald met them on the strand. Their experiences reinforce the doubts expressed by many travellers as to the standards likely to be found in inns and kingshouses along the military roads. But low though these standards were there was no lack of kindness or of hospitality along the way.[28]

But what did the Highlanders themselves think of these new roads? Burt gives us several objections made against them. The chiefs and gentlemen, he tells us, fear that they will encourage strangers whose advanced ideas might loosen the ties between clansmen and their chiefs. They also fear that easy access will compromise security. They were thinking of military security, I expect, but an ancient language and culture may need security of another kind if the pressures on it become too great. Another anxiety was that using bridges instead of wading through the rivers would make people effeminate and also less able to deal with streams which had not been bridged. Some people, agreeing apparently with this objection, refused to use the bridges and continued to wade through the water, or perhaps they were making a protest against the whole road project. Then there was the problem of having to shoe the horses because the gravel surface soon wore down their hooves and of finding a farrier to do the shoeing. And for the poorest people who could not afford to buy shoes for their own feet there was the disadvantage that the gravel was very painful to bare feet or even to feet in thin brogues.[29]

When road building was first begun it was regarded as pure madness on the part of the English and parties of Highlanders used to gather to see what on earth the soldiers were going to do next:

> The first design of removing a vast fallen piece of a rock was entertained by the country people with great derision, of which I saw one instance myself.
>
> A very old wrinkled Highland woman, upon such an occasion, standing over-against me [Burt], when the soldiers were fixing their engines, seemed to sneer at it, and said ... 'What are the fools a-doing? That stone will lie there forever for all them'. But when she saw that vast bulk begin to rise ... she set up a hideous Irish yell, took to her heels, ran up the side of a hill just by, like a young girl, and never looked behind her ... [30]

Similarly a gentleman watching the soldiers blow up a rock at the side of Loch Ness said to the officer in charge:

> When first I heard of this undertaking, I was strangely scandalised to think how shamefully you would come off; but now I am convinced there is nothing can stand before you and gunpowder.[31]

Wade himself reported that when he first travelled to Fort William in a coach and six it was 'to the great wonder of the country people who had never seen such a machine in these parts before' and he described how the Highlanders 'run from their houses close to the coach, and looking up, bow with their bonnets to the coachman, little regarding us that were within'.[32]

Although we may laugh at some of these reactions, it was certainly right to believe that easier access to these remote regions would alter the whole way of life of the natives, for good or ill and mostly for ill as it seemed to them at the time. Nor were the roads going to be of any economic value when economics then meant droving and the drovers were unhappy about them.

In Neil Munro's *The New Road* Ninian MacGregor Campbell looks forward to a change in the economic pattern when he will be able to use the roads to distribute meal, salt and herring 'and an anker now and then of brandy for the gentry ... ', and when salmon from the lochs and rivers of the Great Glen can be got to Inverness for sale.[33] He also foresees the Highlands becoming more peaceful, the soldier losing his profession and the whole fabric of life and shape of the landscape changing:

> George Wade's red sodgers, as ye ken, have been for years at the makin' o' the Big Road that is goin' to put the breeks upon the Hielanman – a bonny job for sodgers! Its killin', as ye might say, the goose that lays the golden eggs for fightin' will be by wi't in the Hielands and the trade o' war will stop. I'm tellin' you that Road is goin' to be a rut that, once it's hammered deep enough, will be the poor Gael's grave.[34]

But the deeper, more spiritual and more cultural effects of these new intrusions into the Highland landscape are also lamented by Ninian's companion Aeneas MacMaster:

> I could weep myself to think our past is there [on the old road]. Where men have walked are always left the shades of them – their spirits lingering. To your eyes and to mine is nothing on the old drove-road but grass and boulders, but if there's aught of the immortal in men's souls, there's the immortal likewise in their earthly acts. Our folk are on the old drove-road – the ghosts of them, the hunters and the tribes long-perished to the eye, *duineuasail* [gentlemen] and broken men.
> ... There is something in me, too, that little likes it.[35]

Perhaps the new roads have played a bigger part in the disintegration of Gaelic culture and language than did the Battle of Culloden and all its horrors. They have definitely played a bigger part in changes to Highland scenery.

A study of Burt's descriptions of the scenery reveals how different is his approach to it from ours. He describes the bare tops of the highest hills as having 'scabbed heads'[36] and does not see the fierce beauty of their stones and rocks in the sunlight or their soft colours under the rain. He gives us the following extraordinary lines on a group of hills:

> ... they appear still one above another, fainter and fainter, according to the aerial perspective, and the whole of a dismal gloomy brown drawing upon a dirty purple; *and most of all disagreeable when the heath is in bloom.*[37]

The italics are mine.

The new roads certainly brought new people into the Highlands, many of them coming to admire the scenery which Burt so despised. James MacPherson was one of the writers who so profoundly altered our approach to literature, ancient history and natural phenomena by his relation of the Gaelic stories he had collected. Although he must have rewritten them in his own peculiar style I am sure that they had some genuine basis and were not the total inventions that Dr Johnson declared them to be. These 'Ossianic' verses not only caused a ferment in literary circles in Britain but also, perhaps especially, in Germany where Goethe, under their influence, wrote *Die Leiden des jungen Werthers* (The Sorrows of Young Werther) which, in its turn produced 'Werther fever' throughout Europe. It is at this time that a change began and that the classical and strictly ordered literary style of the 18th century moved towards the simpler, less rational, less restricted work of the romantic poets. All these influences plus those of the works of Scott and the travels of Queen Victoria, made the Highland scenery a magnet for so many in Britain and beyond. Think, for instance, of Fingal's cave; its very name recalls MacPherson's work and the music with which Mendelssohn evokes it. Or think of the exquisite drawings of Daniell or Pennant.

So the roads, built for military purposes, did little to further conquest or military might, since the time for these had almost passed before they were finished. But they remained, some to become A or B roads, some simple footpaths, others part of the West Highland Way or the Great Glen Way, some to sink into the bog, leaving only faint traces behind them, all bringing their own drawbacks and advantages. Let us hope that the disruptions caused by these roads to the old, unique tenor of Highland life do not bring more drawbacks than advantages and that we shall not have to echo Aeneas MacMaster's words ' ... It means the end of many things ... he last stand of Scotland, and she destroyed'.[38]

XI
The Prince

Slàn do'n t-saor rinn am bàta
A thug sàbhailt' gu tir thù;
Slàn do'n iùl-fhear neo-chearbach
Thug thar fairge gun dìth dhù;
Gum b'è sud am preas toraidh
Thug an sonas do'n rìoghachd,
'S lionmhor laoch thig fo d'chaismeachd
Bheir air Sasunnaich strìochdadh.

Here's a health to the shipwright
Whose craft brought thee safely,
And one to the helmsman
Who unerringly steered thee;
Thou'rt indeed the tree fruitful
Who broughtst joy to the kingdom,
Whom many a hero will follow
To conquer the English.

Nighean Aonghais Oig (MacDonald)

ON THE SECOND of August 1745 Bishop Hugh MacDonald was returning to the west after a visit to Edinburgh. His journey took him into the Great Glen and to the River Lochy which he could cross at the ford near what we now call Gairlochy and so reach Loch Arkaig and Glen Pean beyond it. From there he could enter the country around Loch Morar and find his way to his house at Bunacaimb on the coast not far north of Arisaig. He was 46 at the time, Vicar Apostolic of the Highlands and the half-brother of Allan Ruadh MacDonald of Morar, one of the cadets of the Clanranald MacDonalds.

At the ford he was surprised to meet his uncle, Donald MacDonald of

Kinlochmoidart, fresh from a visit to Cameron of Lochiel at Achnacarry and hurrying eastwards to find the Duke of Perth. He said to the amazed Bishop: 'This night at my house you may see the Prince.' 'What Prince do you mean?' asked the Bishop. 'Who but Tearlach himself' was the answer.[1]

This was only a week since the Prince had landed on the mainland so it may have been the first occasion on which news of the arrival in Scotland of Prince Charles Edward Stuart was made known beyond the north-western seaboard.

It certainly does not seem to have been confirmed in Edinburgh and London until about the 10th August. Although it was 30 years since the failure of the 1715 Jacobite Rising and although the Highlands had been apparently quiet since then – but for the minor skirmish in Glenshiel in 1719 – the Stuarts had not been forgotten and below the calm surface of everyday life seethed the desire for the return of the native line of kings and the departure of the Hanoverians. Though many men may have become resigned to the status quo many others kept the pot boiling with talk and song about the young Stuart Prince, who seemed to be much more the man they needed to lead them than his rather quiet, retiring father King James VIII and III (or the Old Pretender, depending on your persuasion in 18th-century politics).

Alasdair mac Mhaighstir Alasdair (Alasdair son of Master Alasdair) from Dalilea at the south end of Loch Shiel (his father was episcopalian minister to a huge parish there, hence his title of Master) was one of these fiery spirits, egging his contemporaries on with his songs about the future coming of the Prince:

> O, hì-rì-rì, tha e tighinn,
> O, hì-rì-rì, 'n Rìgh tha uainn
> Gheibheamaid ar n'airm 's ar n-éideadh,
> 'S breacan-an-fhéilidh an cuaich.

> Is éibhinn liom fhìn, tha e tighinn,
> Mac an Rìgh dhlighich tha uainn,
> Slios mór rìoghail d'an tig armachd,
> Claidheamh us targaid nan dual.

> O, hi ri ri, he is coming
> O, hi ri ri, our exiled King,
> Let us take our arms and clothing,
> And the flowing tartan plaid.

Joyful I am, he is coming,
Son of our rightful exiled King,
A mighty form which becomes armour,
The broad-sword and the bossy shield.[2]

When Kinlochmoidart had assured Bishop Hugh that what he had said was no joke, the bishop wanted to know what men, money and arms the Prince had brought with him and was downcast and anxious to hear that there were very few of any of these. Instead of heading for his house at Bunacaimb he turned south to Kinlochmoidart House and on the following day met the Prince. His doubts about the wisdom of a rising without the full support of France were not what the Prince wanted to hear. He had heard them already from many of the people he had met since his arrival on the mainland on the 25th July. But he did not let himself be persuaded from his bold plan to restore his father to the throne of Britain, although he had hoped to do this with the help of France.

In 1744 Marshall de Saxe had assembled a force of 12-15,000 men at Dunkirk ready to make the crossing to Essex in merchant ships, for the French initiative at that time was directed against England and no landing in Scotland had been considered. This expedition had been dependent on whether a French fleet under Admiral de Roquefort was able to beat a British fleet under Sir John Norris. As it turned out both fleets were blown away by a great gale on the 24th February. Many of the ministers in the French government had opposed making a landing in England anyway and so the whole project was abandoned. The Prince had been ready to accompany the French fleet and its dispersal was more than he could bear. He was not prepared to return to Italy and go on living at the Palazzo Muti in Rome amidst the comings and goings of Jacobite spies, with no progress being made from one year to the next and his father's cause slowly forgotten.

With help from Irish soldiers in the French service, in the tradition of the Wild Geese, who had been leaving Ireland ever since the flight of the Earls of Tyrone and of Tyrconnell in 1607 whenever the oppression of English laws or military strength became too great, the *Elizabeth*, a captured British warship with 64 guns, was fitted out and provided with 700 soldiers from the Irish Brigade, plus a large consignment of muskets and broadswords. She left Nantes on the 22nd June 1745 accompanied by a 16-gun privateer variously called the *Doutelle*, the *Du Teillay* or the *Du Taillet*, which carried the Prince himself and his seven companions (later to be called the Seven Men of Moidart) along with a further supply of muskets and swords and 4000 louis d'or.

Once out of the English Channel they sailed to the west of Ireland to avoid encountering British navy vessels in the narrow Irish Sea; there is certainly a tradition in Co Donegal that the Prince put in somewhere along the coast there. Before this however they met HMS *Lion*, a ship of similar size to the *Elizabeth*, off the Lizard on the south coast of Cornwall. Both ships were badly damaged in the ensuing fight and the *Elizabeth* so badly that she had to put back to France. The *Doutelle* went on alone and on the 23rd July reached the island of Eriskay, which lies just off the southern tip of South Uist.

The Prince arrived on the mainland at Borrodale on the 25th July and later moved on to Kinlochmoidart House. On the 18th August he walked over the hill to Dalilea, and was rowed up Loch Shiel as far as Glenaladale where he spent the night, leaving at seven in the morning to go the rest of the way to Glenfinnan at the head of the loch. He waited there with only about 500 men, most of them MacDonalds, uncertain whether Lochiel or any of the other chiefs would join him.

Lochiel had certainly been unwilling to do so initially, unless French aid was forthcoming. At last, between three and four in the afternoon Lochiel and 800 Camerons appeared, coming down between the steep hills on either side of Glen Finnan to the head of Loch Shiel. Later on MacDonald of Keppoch arrived with 350 men making the Prince's forces up to about 1500 men.

The standard, a silken flag of red and white, was raised somewhere at the head of the loch, but probably not where the memorial tower now stands as the land there would have been too boggy. It was blessed by Bishop Hugh, although there were likely to have been chaplains of other denominations there (the army at this stage was roughly half-Protestant and half-Catholic), but they raised no objection to a Catholic priest undertaking this task. Whether they really did not mind or whether they were taken by surprise we do not know.

Meanwhile in the Great Glen news had been spread of the Prince's landing and there was consternation amongst the government soldiers up and down the line of forts built with the aim of keeping the Highlands quiet. It was generally felt that Fort William was in the greatest danger as it was more isolated than the other two. Accordingly a party of 60 soldiers was sent out from Fort Augustus on the 14th August to march south and bolster morale at Fort William. They never got there however as they were intercepted and captured by a party of Keppoch

MacDonalds. Two days afterwards two companies of the 1st Foot (later Royal Scots) – all untrained men in this case – who were also on their way to Fort William under the command of Captain John Scott were intercepted at Highbridge by Donald MacDonald of Tirnadris (Glen Spean), who had at his disposal only eleven men and a piper. Highbridge was the bridge taking Wade's Fort William to Inverness road over the River Spean. It had caused Wade some difficulties and although work on the road began in 1725 he did not build Highbridge until 1736. By whisking about in the bushes and shouting clan slogans at one another to the accompaniment of terrifying pipe music the MacDonalds so frightened the government troops that they turned and fled back in the direction of Fort Augustus. But the Keppoch MacDonalds, making a detour via Glen Gloy, intercepted them at Laggan Achadrom, between Loch Lochy and Loch Oich, where Scott was obliged to surrender. He and his men, as prisoners, were subsequently witnesses to the raising of the standard in Glenfinnan.

News of these two successes must have introduced a light, optimistic note into the campaign and cheered the Prince and his companions as they left Glenfinnan and walked along to Kinlocheil and there took the track along the north shore of the loch. This was on the 20th August, the day after the ceremony at Glenfinnan. Their intention was to get into the Great Glen and then walk up it as far as Aberchalder, a mile or two to the south of Fort Augustus, where they could turn east and link up with the Corrieyairack Pass which would take them to Garvamore and Blair Atholl. By using this road, which Wade had built to facilitate the movement of government troops, they were later able to get ahead of Sir John Cope and reach Edinburgh before him. On this 20th August however the question was how to get into the Great Glen without being observed by the garrison at Fort William. There are two theories as to the route they took. One is that they turned off at Fassfern and went up Glen Suileag which brought them down Glen Loy into the Great Glen a little north of Strone. But this would have been a very lengthy detour and heavy going too, especially when hauling the guns over – work the Highlanders detested.

Alternatively they may have stayed beside Loch Eil until Annat and then gone up the burn into Glen Laragain, thus reaching the Great Glen just south of Muirshearlich, about four miles (6.4km) from Fort William. This was very much shorter; it is also the route preferred by local tradition. The story is that three officers from the Jacobite army came to a house near Annat Farm; the woman of the house recognised one of them as Lochiel and went out to find her husband. When they came back one officer was sitting in a chair but Lochiel and the other one were still standing. Lochiel asked the man by which route they could most easily get into the Great Glen, hauling their guns with them. The man told them they should go up on the west bank of the Annat Burn and that he would go with them to make sure they avoided boggy ground. Lochiel thanked him and then, turning to the officer seated in the chair, said: 'This is your Prince'. The Prince shook the man's hand and, going outside, signalled to the army to advance and turn up the Annat Burn, as instructed. Since that time the man and his wife only allowed their closest friends to sit in the Prince's chair and kept a length of string tied between the arms to prevent anyone else from doing so.[3]

It is thought that the Prince's army, once in the Great Glen and on the west bank of the River Lochy, forded the river at Moy on the 26th August, crossed the Spean gorge at Highbridge and then continued on Wade's road and bivouacked at Laggan while the Prince and his party went on to Invergarry Castle beside Loch Oich. Blaikie's Itinerary says that on the way the Prince stopped briefly at an old inn 'now [1897] sometimes used for changing post horses'.[4] This must have been the kingshouse at Letterfinlay. On the following day the entire army went on to Aberchalder where they bivouacked. The next morning, the 28th August, starting at 3am, they turned right into Glen Buck and then went along beside the Allt Lagan a' Bhainne, joining the Corrieyairack at the bridge where Wade had given his soldiers an ox roast and which they had named Snugborough. There had been no chance of their being observed from Fort Augustus. When they reached the eastern end of the Corrieyairack they realised that Sir John Cope, who was marching north along the line, more or less, of the modern A9, had given up any idea of confronting them and was heading for Inverness, so they went on to Blair and then, via Perth and Stirling, to Edinburgh.

The Great Glen was not to see them again for a long time for, having taken Edinburgh and won the Battle of Prestonpans, they began their descent into England and did not get back into the Highlands until February 1746.

Between their departure from Edinburgh and their return to the Highlands the Prince's army had gone into England and advanced as far as Derby without encountering much resistance. Government troops were either in England, but in the wrong place, or on the continent. London was in a turmoil, believing that hordes of barbarians were likely to fall upon them any day. King George was said to be packing his bags. On the other hand English and Welsh Jacobites had made a negligible response to the call to join the Prince. They were steadfast in the toasts they drank to the King over the Water but, as a supporter of the Prince declared, had they waved their swords as enthusiastically as they waved their wineglasses things might have gone a lot better. Some think that they were fearful that the Scots might withdraw to Scotland and leave them in the lurch. At Derby on the 5th December the clan chiefs were given false information about the size and movements of the enemy armies by a government spy. This encouraged them to advise the Prince to go back to Scotland, for they felt they were far too few in number to withstand government forces which were by then showing clear signs of getting to grips with the situation. A retreat was greatly against the Prince's wishes; he still thought they had a good chance of success and believed firmly in the strength and courage of his Highlanders. And who can say he was wrong? Both strategies have their supporters today. The life went out of the clansmen and of the Prince as the retreat began. The Prince, who had marched at the head of his army and sometimes gone too fast even for them, was more likely now to be found on horseback or in a carriage.

A Jacobite victory at Falkirk on the 17th January cheered everyone up, but their spirits were only to be dashed again when Lord George Murray and the clan chiefs informed the Prince that his army had shrunk to a third due to desertions and that instead of taking advantage of their victory they should again retreat, this time to the far north of Scotland. This assessment of army strength was subsequently found to be misleading as the Highlanders had merely been following their age-old practice of going home from time to time, whenever there was a pause in hostilities, to see how their people were getting on. They would appear again, and did. The chiefs must have known this and one cannot help thinking that they were merely using the temporary absence of some Highlanders as an extra argument to persuade the Prince to do what they had suggested. He had little choice in the matter as none of the army leaders seemed to support him. Later on when he found out this 'mistake' he was very angry. If he ever really did lose his trust in the Scots, as one so often hears, it must have been at least partly because of manoeuvres of this kind.

His army entered Inverness in February. He himself spent the first week of March in the town, lodging with the Dowager Lady MacIntosh in a house in Church Street (it was pulled down in 1843). After this he spent some time in Elgin where he became very ill, but he had recovered by the 1st April and returned to Inverness.

The obvious first task was to gain control of Fort George. At that time it stood on the site of Inverness Castle where there had been a castle since at least the eleventh century and where there is a reconstructed one today. Its governor was Major George Grant and he had at his disposal two independent companies supplied by the Laird of Grant and the Master of Ross and about 80 members of Guise's 6th. The siege was begun on the 20th February with Colonel John O'Sullivan, one of Charles's devoted Irish adherents, and the Marquis d'Eguilles, representing Louis XV, in charge. The foundations of the castle, which had been seen to be unstable, were mined by the Jacobites who then proceeded to fire at the walls. The defenders were unable to respond adequately to this fire as their cannon could not be lowered enough to take proper aim at the besiegers. On the following day, the 21st, Major Grant surrendered to avoid being blown up.

After this very easy victory it must have seemed only sensible to see whether they could have the same good fortune with Fort Augustus, so they marched down the Great Glen and began the siege there on the 3rd March. The Governor was Major Hugh Wentworth, the man who had sent out two parties of men to Fort William, only to hear that they had been intercepted and taken prisoner by the Keppoch MacDonalds. Wentworth had three companies of Guise's 6th; two of these were in the new (Wade) fort and the third in the old barracks a little distance away. Besieging them were the Irish Picquets, the Royal Eccosais and 1500 Camerons and MacDonalds, all under the command of Lieutenant Colonel Walter Stapleton of the Irish Picquets. Colonel James Grant, Master of Ordnance to the Prince, was in charge of the guns as at Fort George. They began to fire at the new fort from the old one, having first evicted the occupants, and were soon successful; a shell landed in the powder magazine and Wentworth surrendered on the 5th March.

This left only Fort William at the southern end of the glen. It is sometimes said that the Prince was very uneasy about having part of his army such a long way from the main body and this is very understandable, but I feel that initially at least he must have been in agreement with this third siege, for if it succeeded it would mean the destruction of the whole line of defence which Wade had created as the basis for his Highland road system and the security of the Highlands. The chiefs and their clansmen were naturally in support of a siege as the Fort had been an affront and a danger to the whole of Lochaber since it was first constructed. Lochiel will have been particularly sensitive on this point, remembering the difficulties his grandfather Sir Ewen Dubh had had with it in Cromwell's time.

The garrison at Fort William was commanded by Captain Caroline Frederick Scott, who showed himself after Culloden to be one of the most brutal of Cumberland's officers. His very unusual name came from his godmother, Princess Caroline of Ansbach, who married George II. Scott had a garrison of 400. On the Jacobite side were the same people as had reduced Fort Augustus, but unfortunately Colonel James Grant was injured by a cannonball at an early stage in the proceedings and Stapleton had to send to Inverness for Mirabelle de Gordon – a Scots Frenchman – who was generally thought to leave much to be desired as a director of sieges; he had already failed at the siege of Stirling. Sadly his skills had not improved by the time he reached Fort William and the Jacobites were also hampered by difficulties in obtaining supplies, particularly heavy guns, as part of Wade's road had been swept away at Letterfinlay by continuous rain. The garrison at Fort William, in contrast, could be supplied by sea and although the Jacobites had placed a guard at the Corran Narrows to prevent any supplies getting through, boatloads of troops had been sent down Loch Linnhe from the Fort before the siege began; they disposed of many of the Jacobite troops there.

With all these drawbacks, along with many disagreements amongst the besiegers, progress was very slow, if evident at all, and at the beginning of April the Prince was obliged to recall them all to Inverness as he had feared would be necessary, for Cumberland's forces were known to be advancing on the town from the east.

The Prince and his staff moved to Culloden House to the east of Inverness on the 14th of April. Its owner, Duncan Forbes, the Lord President of the Court of Session and the man whose brother offered such generous bumpers to all his guests, had gone off to the north-west with Lord Loudon to avoid the Prince!s army. Culloden House became the Prince's headquarters for the brief period before the battle.

This battle began at about one o'clock in the afternoon of the 16th April. It was very quickly over, with terrible casualties for the Jacobite army. There are many different opinions as to why Culloden Moor was chosen for this confrontation between the Prince and the Duke of Cumberland; the ground was boggy and flat and quite unsuitable terrain on which to carry through that so successful tactic of Highland armies – the Highland charge. This was not the only drawback; organisation of the food supplies had broken down. When the Prince's secretary, John Murray of Broughton, fell ill in Elgin at the same time as the Prince he had been replaced by John Hay of Restalrig, who appears to have had no idea how to victual an army. When the battle began many Highlanders were still in Inverness, trying to find food, while many of those on the battlefield were in a semi-starving condition. The weather too was against the Prince and easterly winds brought in showers of rain and sleet. The moor is seldom anything but a brisk place and when the wind blows from the snowy Cairngorms or sweeps over the Moray Firth from the wilds of Sutherland, it chills the blood even in the heat of war. Unlike the Prince's army Cumberland's troops were well fed, well rested and had their backs to the wind.

But this disaster has been discussed and described and lamented over too often and too extensively to need any more mention here. It did not in any case, strictly speaking, take place within the Great Glen, but its consequences affected the whole of the Highlands.

As the Jacobite army crumbled before the assaults of the weather and the larger and better-equipped government troops the Prince tried to rally some of those escaping from the battle. His horse had been shot under him and his groom killed beside him as he brought up a fresh horse. The devoted O'Sullivan at last persuaded him that there was no hope left and he was led reluctantly from the field, escorted by a detachment of Fitzjames's Horse. They went with him as far as the ford at Faillie and were then dismissed, leaving him to go on with Lord Elcho, Sir Thomas Sheridan, O'Sullivan and Felix O'Neill (an Irishman in the French service). The Prince's aide-de-camp, Alexander MacLeod Yngr of Muiravonside, was also with him, bringing his servant Ned Burke from North Uist who was to act as guide. Crossing the River Nairn by the Faillie ford they went down Strathnairn and into Stratherrick to Gorthleck where Thomas Fraser, Lord Lovat's factor, lived. It is possible that Fitzjames's Horse stayed with the Prince as far as Gorthleck. Stratherrick was a favourite part of Simon Lovat's lands and he often visited it, staying at his factor's house. It stands on a ridge overlooking what is now Loch Mhor, which was formed in 1895 from lochs Farraline to the north and Garth to the south to provide water for an aluminium works at Foyers.

Lovat was there to greet the Prince. He had for years wavered between Jacobitism and loyalty to the House of Hanover; he was probably a Jacobite at heart but financial and territorial ambitions often gained the upper hand. He needed above all things to be on the 'right' side and had so far been fairly successful, but now, at the end of his life, he made the mistake of backing the wrong horse. Even that backing was half-hearted and circumspect. He mustered a body of clansmen and ordered his son, the Master of Lovat, to lead them in support of the Prince, but at the same time was careful himself to avoid coming face to face with the son of the king they were to fight for. He hoped the Prince would win this battle but he also hoped that by keeping away from the Jacobite army and remaining quietly on his estates he might give the impression of disapproving of the Rising and so be safe whatever the outcome. This unexpected meeting with the Prince threw the wrong light on his policies and cannot have been welcome, but native Highland courtesy and political expediency did not allow this to show when the Prince arrived. They took several glasses of wine together and according to O'Sullivan, 'he [the Prince] supt at Ld. Lovets the night of the battle',[5] though some believe his stay there was shorter. The visitors certainly needed to put as much distance between themselves and the battlefield as they could and as quickly as they could. They continued on General Wade's road, down the long slope to Loch Tarff and down the final long twists and turns to Fort Augustus which they reached in the early morning of the 17th while it was still dark. The fort had been empty since it had surrendered to Jacobite forces six weeks before. They rode on to Invergarry Castle on the shore of Loch Oich; here also they found no-one but were lucky to discover two salmon in a stake-net which when boiled and eaten with oatcakes, made a meal for them all. After they left Loch Oich side they turned towards Kilfinnan and rode down beside Loch Lochy to Lochiel's house at Achnacarry. The Achnacarry people had heard nothing of the battle and Lochiel was still on his way to them, having been carried off the field of battle with both his ankles broken by grapeshot. The Prince continued his journey beside Loch Arkaig to Glen Pean and the west. He now had only three companions – O'Sullivan, Father Allan MacDonald, who had served as Chaplain in the Clanranald regiment, and Ned Burke.

Meanwhile the Duke of Cumberland had embarked on his policy of 'deliberate frightfulness designed to stamp out any remaining vestige of resistance', as Sir Fitzroy Maclean so accurately expressed it.[6] Cumberland himself thought of it as 'pacification'.

This had begun on the battlefield where the wounded received no mercy and many were despatched with bayonet or rifle butt. The 'excuse' for this was that the Jacobite orders for the battle had said no quarter should be given to Cumberland's army. This was a lie, there had been no such orders given. nor would the Prince have permitted it.[7] Those wounded who were lucky (or unlucky) enough to have survived were left for days on the moor without food or drink or medical attention, apart from the care given them by three local women.

Cumberland's cavalry pounded after the clansmen retreating from the moor and killed or wounded as many of them as they could, following them all the way to Inverness. Many people who had come out from the town to see the battle or were on that road in the course of their normal occupations found themselves caught up in this slaughter; the victims included women and children.

Wounded officers of the Prince's army who had sought shelter in or around Culloden House were put up against a wall and shot. In Inverness the gaols were crammed with prisoners and, when they overflowed, houses and cellars in the town and even the holds of vessels lying in the Beauly and Moray firths were commandeered. Here again no medical aid was offered to the wounded, nor was food or drink given to them. John Fraser, who was Provost of Inverness and John Hossack, who had been Provost before him, went to General Hawley (known as Hangman Hawley and still high in Cumberland's regard in spite of his abysmal defeat at the Battle of Falkirk) to plead for better conditions for the prisoners. When Hossack was so unwise as to speak of mercy:

> Hawley shouted 'Damn the puppie. Does he pretend to dictate to us? Carry him away.' And another cryed 'Kick out', which Sir Robert Adair did on the top of the stairs with such a force that he did not touch them till he was at the end of the first flat.[8]

Lord President Duncan Forbes who had visited Cumberland on a similar errand was described by the duke as 'that old woman who spoke to me of humanity'.

A letter to Bishop Forbes from an eyewitness shows the true horror of the situation. The writer claimed to be an officer in the government army who had come to think with shame of the part he had played, but he was actually John Farquharson of Allargue, a captain in the Jacobite army (the Farquharson regiment). He wrote 'in disguise' as he was an escaped prisoner and was fearful of revealing his whereabouts.

> When we had filld all the goalls, kirks, and ships at Inverness with these rebell prisoners, wounded and naked as they were, we ordered that non shoud have any access to them either with meat or drink for two days. By means no doubt we thought at least the wounded woud starve either for want of

food or cloaths, the weather being then very cold. The two days being passed, there was a corum of officers pitched upon to goe and visit them in order to take down their names and numbers ... Amongst the number I was myself but, oh Heavens! what a scene open to my eyes and nose all at once; the wounded feltring [festering?] in their gore and blood; some dead bodies covered quite over with pish and dirt, the living standing to the middle in it, their groans woud have pirsd a heart of stone ... That night it was determined in the privy counsell that each prisoner should have half a pound oat meall per day (but Haly [Hawley] thought it too much) and accordingly they sent some of their commissarys to distribute the meall. I could not help laughing in the time of the distribution when the poor things had nothing left them to hold their meall but the foreskirt of their shirts, rather exposing their nakedness to the world than want their meall. They made very odd figures every on with his half pound meal tied up in his shirt lap, and all below naked ....We allways took care not to bury their dead untill such time, as we had at least a dozen of them. Only imagine to yourself what for an agreeable smell was there – their own excraments with the stink of the dead bodyis ... 9

These poor prisoners, we subsequently learn, were held until the 29th May and those who survived were then crowded onto ships and carried off to London, under conditions if anything worse than in their Inverness gaols.

In the starkest contrast to all this is a letter written by Prince Charles Edward to his father after the battle of Prestonpans:

... I am now charged with the care both of my friends and enemies. Those, who should bury the dead, are run away as if it was no business of theirs ... I cannot bear the thoughts of suffering Englishmen to rot above ground.

I am in great difficulty how I shall dispose of my wounded prisoners. If I make an hospital of the church it will be looked upon as a great profanation ... Come what will I am

resolved I will not suffer the poor wounded men to lie in the
streets, and if I can do no better I will make an hospital of the
palace, and leave it to them.[10]

Cumberland, having stayed in Inverness for about one month after the battle,
began to move troops down to Fort Augustus on the 16th May and joined them
there himself at the end of that month. The fort had been badly damaged during
the siege, though it could still provide some accommodation for officers. It was,
however, not considered good enough for Cumberland and the soldiers are
believed to have built a 'bower' for him out of the trunks and branches of trees.
The association of this coarse and brutal figure with so romantic a structure as a
bower, would be laughable were the events surrounding it less tragic.

Parties of men were sent out from the fort into the surrounding glens where
they took prisoners, shot people at work in the fields, burnt houses, raped women,
rounded up cattle and drove them away, depriving the inhabitants, many of whom
had taken no part in the Rising, of any means of supporting life. The glens worst
affected, being the nearest to Fort Augustus, were Glenmoriston and Glen Garry,
but the parties of soldiers ranged up into Glen Urquhart and down into Lochaber,
burning and looting as they went. Huge sales of cattle were organised and people
came from the south of Scotland and from far beyond the border to buy them.

Glenmoriston and to a lesser extent Glen Urquhart were particularly badly
afflicted as a result of the actions of Ludovick Grant of Grant. He was the eldest
son of Sir James Grant, the chief of the clan. When the Rising began Sir James
was 66 and feeling that he needed a quiet life. He went off to London, leaving
the management of the clan to Ludovick. He advised him to take no action either
for or against the government unless his own territory was attacked. The Grants
were a divided clan in that the chief, with his main territories in Strathspey, had
always supported the Hanoverians while the cadets of the clan in Glenmoriston
and Glen Urquhart had always been Jacobites, fighting in the first Rising of 1689
in Bonnie Dundee's army and coming out again in the '15 and the '45. In 1746
Ludovick was regarded with a certain amount of suspicion by Cumberland
because he had not supported government troops in his area and had been reluctant to supply an Independent Company when asked to do so; he did however
eventually produce a company to defend Fort George. In the hope of ingratiating
himself with the conquerors he went to Glen Urquhart and Glenmoriston and
urged those who had taken part in the Rising to surrender, promising that he

would speak for them to Cumberland and secure pardons for them. Sixty-eight Glenmoriston men and 16 Glen Urquhart men surrendered. Several of their wives tried to prevent them leaving. In one case Ewen MacDonald of Levishie (in Glenmoriston) was followed by his wife, carrying their small child and pleading with her husband to remain until, just beyond Achnaconeran, she threw the child in a bush and, turning back home, cried out that it would remain there and die unless he picked it up and brought it home. In this way he was saved from the fate of the other men. When old Grant of Sheuglie in Glen Urquhart mounted his horse to accompany Ludovick the horse turned three times – *tuaitheal*, that is, anti-clockwise, a very bad omen – but he still went on and never came back again, dying in London where he was held prisoner.

Ludovick took them all to Inverness but once there just handed them over 'that His Royal Highness might dispose of them as he should think fit'.[11] He said not a word in their favour and most of them were transported to the West Indies. By 1749 only 18 were still alive there and only eight of these ever got home again. As the entries in Prince Charles Edward's Muster Roll for the Glengarry regiment show, the Grants, fighting under the banner of the Glengarry MacDonalds, suffered far more than did the MacDonalds (or MacDonells) themselves.[12]

There were at least 12 Catholic priests as chaplains with the Prince's army, four being associated with the clans of the Great Glen. One of them was Aeneas MacGillies, a priest attached to Glengarry's regiment, who managed to escape. The other three were all serving with Lochiel's Camerons. One was his brother, Alexander Cameron, a Jesuit priest and the only Catholic in Lochiel's family, who was captured and eventually imprisoned in Inverness but was later transferred to the hulks in the Thames (abandoned and rotting navy ships), where he died under the particularly awful conditions there.[13] (These hulks or similar vessels were still in use 50 years later to hold French prisoners during the Napoleonic period). The other two were the episcopalian minister Duncan Cameron of Fortingall who appears to have escaped and John Cameron (Church of Scotland) of Fort William who also escaped and turned up later on in the Prince's company. (John Cameron was one of the few Ppesbyterians in the Prince's army which was composed mainly of catholics and episcopalians.) The Prince was at this time beside Loch Arkaig, somewhere near Achnasaul. Cameron of Clunes asked him to meet him in a wood two miles away. To this meeting Lochiel, who could not come himself sent his brother Dr Archie Cameron, who brought John Cameron with him. The Rev John later gave a description of the

Prince as he then saw him, He was:

> 'bare-footed, had an old black kilt on, philabeg and waistcoat,
> a dirty shirt and a long red beard, a gun in his hand, a pistol
> and dirk by his side. He was very cheerful and in good health,
> and in my opinion fatter than when he was in Inverness'.[14]

Bishop Hugh MacDonald, whom we met crossing the River Lochy at the beginning of this chapter, probably left the Prince's army not long after blessing the standard, as he needed to fulfill his duties as Vicar Apostolic to the Highlands. On the 20th September 1746 Bishop Hugh left Loch nan Uamh on *le Prince de Conti*, bound for France along with the *L'Heureux* on which the Prince himself escaped. He was taken in by the Scots College in Paris but returned to Scotland in 1749. In 1756 he was tried and condemned to perpetual banishment but he nevertheless remained in Scotland, constantly on the move to avoid his presence being discovered. In 1761 he moved into the Great Glen, to Aberchalder, between Loch Oich and Loch Ness, and lived there in a small house near General Wade's road for the rest of his life, dying nearby in 1773 in a house a little to the north of Aberchalder belonging to Allan MacDonell of Cullochy. He was buried in the old burial ground at Kilfinnan at the northern end of Loch Lochy and on its west bank. In 1803 Telford began to build the Caledonian Canal. During the construction of Laggan Locks near Kilfinnan, the level of the water in the loch was raised and engulfed Hugh's grave, so his exact burial place is now uncertain, but a Celtic cross was put up there in his memory in 1900.[15]

Of the chief gentlemen of the Great Glen clans Lochiel himself, after many wanderings, escaped to France on the same ship as the Prince. His brother, Dr Archie, also escaped but returned many times, hoping to create good conditions for another Rising. Eventually he was captured and executed (hanged, drawn and quartered) in 1753, without a trial but on the basis of an earlier attainder. Lochiel's Catholic brother Alexander died on a prison ship as we have already seen, while his uncle, Ludovic of Torcastle, escaped.

He was with Lochiel when the latter was in hiding near Loch Shiel. They were advised by Stewart of Ardshiel to cross Loch Linnhe to Appin as that country was felt to be safe at the time. This they did, their party including Dr Archie, Murray of Broughton the Prince's secretary and the Rev John Cameron. When the Appin country became dangerous again the party split up and Lochiel headed for

Ben Alder and the shelter provided by Cluny MacPherson in his famous 'Cage'.

The men of the Glengarry regiment had been raised by Donald MacDonald of Lochgarry, the chief being elderly and his eldest son Alasdair Ruadh being in prison. Lochgarry managed to escape and of his junior officers Alexander Grant of Corriemony in Glen Urquhart was wounded at Culloden but does not appear to have been captured; old Sheuglie, as we have seen, was one of Ludovick Grant's victims. Alexander Grant of Inchbrine (Alasdair a' Chlaidheimh – Alexander of the sword) – was thought to have died at Culloden but, according to a family tree in my possession, escaped and may have gone to America afterwards; his brother James was mortally wounded at Culloden and was met by his cousin (Kate Baillie) as he was being carried away from the field. She took him to her mother's house at Dunain (according to the same family tree, but MacKay says Cradlehall), where he died two days later.[16]

Of the Keppoch MacDonalds Alexander the Chief was killed at Culloden in that famous and much discussed moment when the command to advance sent by the Prince had failed to arrive because the messenger had been killed before he could deliver it. The chief, incapable of remaining inactive amongst all the clamour of battle, rushed forward alone, giving the impression that his men would not follow him, and was shot down at once. This is one generally accepted version, but the whole episode remains unclear. His brother, Donald, was killed at the same time while another brother, Archibald, had met his death at the Battle of Prestonpans the previous year. A nephew, Donald, had been captured at Carlisle and was executed. in August 1746, while Major Donald MacDonald of Tirnadris, a cousin, who had fooled the redcoats with his eleven men at Highbridge, was captured at Falkirk, having mistaken some of the enemy for his friends; he was executed in October 1746. Keppoch's wife with her newborn son managed to get away before their house was set on fire and hide in the mountains, while the children of Tirnadris, whose house was also burned, took refuge on the slopes of Stob Ban behind Ben Nevis and close to the ancient and hidden track of the Lairig Leacach. They were later reunited with their stepmother at a house near Loch Treig.

Many of the Frasers in the Jacobite army came from the Fraser lands to the west of Inverness, from Beauly and Kilmorack for example, but many also were from Stratherrick on the east bank of Loch Ness. Their chief, Lord Lovat, was captured on an island in Loch Morar and taken to London, where he was beheaded in 1747.

During this period of murder and destruction, when the very means of liveli-hood was being snatched from those who had missed death from sword or bul-let, the Prince himself was engaged on his intricate journeys through the western highlands and islands. He had been brought to the conclusion that further attempts to continue the Rising were bound to fail, one very good reason being presumably that there was no money to support another army. A French ship bringing money and supplies had been lost to the Royal Navy on the north coast in February and another contribution from France amounting to 36,000 *louis d'or* eventually reached Loch Arkaig where it was either buried or disappeared and subsequently became a source of much recrimination and resentment. While the chiefs concentrated on arranging rendezvous here and there in the Highlands (one in Lochaber where only 300 Camerons and 300 of Clan Donald assembled) in the hope of continuing the Rising or at least protecting the population from the brutalities of the government army, Prince Charles was bent on finding one of the French ships sent out to rescue him, so that he might come back again with French troops, a plan which at that stage he seems to have thought quite achiev-able.

After a dozen narrow escapes, after days in the rain, days spent nose-down in the heather (and the midges) or crossing the Minch in a storm, after weeks of searching cold and wet or burning sun, he at last found himself back near the Great Glen and at the top of Glen Moriston. Here the forethought and courage of Roderick Mackenzie, a merchant from Inverness and an officer in the Jacobite army, had earlier helped him avoid capture. Roderick, who was the same height as the Prince and bore some resemblance to him, was surprised by a group of red-coats and defended himself as well as he could, but as they dealt him the final and fatal blow he had the presence of mind to call out: 'Villains, you have slain your Prince'. The excitement of his attackers on realising that they might be with-in inches of being able to claim the £30,000 which Cumberland had offered to anyone apprehending the Prince must have been immense. They removed his head and took it or sent it to Fort Augustus. It happened that one of the prison-ers at the fort at that time was MacDonald of Kingsburgh, the future father-in-law of Flora MacDonald. He was asked whether he would know the Prince's head if he saw it and he replied that he would indeed were it between his shoulders, but otherwise he would know nothing at all about it. This rather oracular answer was received with some misgivings by the authorities who packed up the head and sent it to London as a further attempt at identification. By the time it reached there however it was too far decomposed to be recognised as anyone. The great advantage all this gave to the Prince was that the search for him, which was getting far too close to be comfortable, was slackened for a few days and he thus had time to slip out of his dangerous position in the hills and get into safer surroundings. Roderick Mackenzie now has a cairn to his memory on the south side of the glen a little to the east of Ceannacroc; just opposite it on the north side is his grave, immediately adjacent to and just below the level of the present road.

It was here on a hillside overlooking Loch Cluanie that the Prince first met that band of 'robbers' who later became known as the Seven Men of Glenmoriston. They were Patrick Grant and John MacDonald from Tom Crasky, Alexander MacDonald from Aonach, Alexander, Donald and Hugh Chisholm from Bhlaraidh and Grigor MacGregor, a native of Strathspey. Hugh Macmillan joined them later, making them eight in all. They had banded together, determined to continue resistance to the government army, and were living off the land, attacking redcoats whenever they came upon them. When they first met them in early August in the Coire Dho the Prince and his companions had just spent a miserable night in a cave which gave little protection against the weather and which was too small to permit them to lie down. The Seven Men took them to another cave further up the hill. It had a floor of smooth gravel and a little stream ran through it beneath a sturdy roof of rock. There they were safe and well cared for and their guardians brought them better food than they had enjoyed for a long time. They stayed for three days and then went to another cave two miles away where they remained for four days before making their way northwards to Strathglass. The so-called 'robbers' who had helped them in this extremity could easily have handed the Prince over in exchange for the £30,000 reward but they were men of honour. They had sworn to each other:

> That their backs should be to God and their faces to the
> Devil, that all the curses the Scriptures did pronounce might
> come upon them and all their posterity if they did not stand
> firm to help the Prince in his greatest dangers.[17]

They kept a very tight eye on the Prince's behaviour, for his own safety, and told him when he might eat and when it was safe for him to move on. As Charles said: 'Kings and Princes must be ruled by their privy council but I believe there is not in all the world a more absolute privy council than what I have at present'.[18]

By the 15th August they were back by Loch Arkaig which they had reached after miserable nights without proper shelter in Glenmoriston and Glengarry. Beside the loch they met Dr Archie Cameron and the Rev John Cameron from Fort William, whose description of the Prince has already been quoted. They went east as far as Achnacarry and observed the burnt ruins of Lochiel's house which had been built by his grandfather, the great Sir Ewen Dubh; it was said to be built 'all of Fir-planks, the handsomest of that kind in Britain'.[19] At Achnacarry the Seven Men, except for Patrick Grant, were dismissed. Patrick stayed until the River Lochy was reached when the Prince said goodbye to him and gave him 24 guineas to be divided amongst the seven (really eight) men.

The Prince and MacDonald of Glenaladale, who had been with him during some of the most dangerous parts of his wanderings, then crossed the Lochy and set out for Badenoch where he was to join Lochiel and where they spent about a week together in Cluny MacPherson's 'Cage'. On the 13th September they heard that there were French ships in Loch nan Uamh and they at once started the long trek to the coast. By the 15th they were in Glen Roy and on the night of the 16th crossed back over the Lochy. This was their last sight of the Great Glen and it is cheering to recall that their crossing of the river was attended by some merriment:

> As they were approaching Lochiel's seat, Achnicarry, they came to the river Lochy at night, being fine moonshine. The difficulty was how to get over. Upon this Cluns Cameron met them on the water side, at whom Lochiel asked how they would get over the river. He said, 'Very well, for I have an old boat carried from Lockharkaig that the enemy left unburnt of all the boats you had, Lochiel'. Lochiel asked to see the boat. Upon seeing it he said 'I am afraid we will not be safe with it.' Quoth Cluns 'I will cross first and show you the way'. The matter was agreed upon. Cluns upon reflection said, 'I have six bottles of brandy, and I believe all of you will be the better of a dram'. This brandy was brought from Fort Augustus, where the enemy lay in garrison, about nine miles from that part of Lochy where they were about to cross. Lochiel went to the prince and said, 'Will your Royal Highness take a dram?' 'O,' said the Prince, 'can you have a dram here?' 'Yes,' replied Lochiel, 'and that from Fort Augustus too.' Which pleased

the prince much that he should have provisions from his enemies, etc. He said, 'Come, let us have it.' Upon this three of
the bottles were drunk. Then they passed the river Lochy by
three crossings, Cluns Cameron in the first with so many,
then the prince in the second with so many, and in the last
Lochiel with so many. In the third and last ferrying the crazy
boat laked so much that there would be four or five pints of
water in the bottom of the boat, and in hurrying over the
three remaining bottles of brandy were all broke. When the
prince called for a dram it was told that the bottles were
broke, and that the common fellows had drunk all that was
in the bottom of the boat as being good punch, which had
made the fellows so merry that they made great diversion to
the company as they marched along.[20]

On the 19th September the Prince, with Lochiel and many other Highland gentlemen seeking refuge in France, went aboard *L'Heureux* which set sail very early
the next morning. They left behind them a country destroyed, its people dead, or
scarce able to find the means to live. The Great Glen was filled with burnt or
ruined houses, with silence where once the herds of cattle had lowed; its side
glens were ravaged and depopulated, its lochs and rivers with hardly a boat upon
them. Only the summits of the great hills seemed untouched, looking down on
a transfigured landscape from their refuge in the sky.[21]

XII
The Canal

The Caledonian Canal is a very wonderful piece of engineering, but travelling by it is very tedious.

Queen Victoria

THOMAS TELFORD, THE famous Scots engineer, worked his way up the Great Glen from Fort William to Inverness in the summer and autumn of 1801. This was nearly 13 centuries after the visit of Calum Cille to Brude, the King of the Picts, which covered the same ground. But Telford was not going to meet a king, or to talk about founding a monastery or to discuss peace between the Picts and the Scots; he was going to make a survey of conditions with a view, amongst other things, to building a canal from Loch Linnhe to the North Sea.

Telford. Some called him the 'Colossus of Roads', a name given him by the poet Southey, while others knew him as *Pontifex Maximus*. Thus were his contributions to the roads and bridges of Britain recognised, but unfortunately, from our present point of view, he had no name to honour his work on canals.

He was a bright, energetic man of reasonably ample proportions, with thick, dark, curly hair and dark eyes. Though he got through a prodigious amount of work in his life this did not prevent him from making friends wherever he went. In 1819 Southey, the Poet Laureate, accompanied him on one of his tours of inspection and did not fail to notice how warm was the welcome he always received and how many were the people he was on Christian-name terms with. He was an amusing conversationalist, full of jokes and funny stories. His headquarters in London for a long time were at the Salopian Coffee House at Charing Cross, where he lived and where some of his assistants and pupils also lived and he could always obtain extra accommodation there whenever he needed it. It must have been a jolly place with Telford at the head of the dinner table. When he finally left it late in life to move into a house of his own – it was opposite the Houses of Parliament – the landlord of the coffee house, who had just bought that establishment, protested at his leaving, saying that he had just paid £750 for him.[1]

The poet Thomas Campbell was one of his guests at the coffee house. It may perhaps seem strange that an engineer, busy with some of the most practical things in life, should seek the friendship of poets, but Telford was devoted to literature in general and poetry in particular; although he had had little formal education he had read widely and never liked to be without a book to his hand. He wrote poetry himself but we have to admit that it was of a rather pedestrian kind.[2]

The possibility of a canal in the Great Glen had been foreseen by the Brahan Seer, *Coinneach Odhar Fiosaiche* (Sallow Kenneth, soothsayer). He was born at Baile na Cille in Uig in the island of Lewis in the late 16th or early 17th century. His mother is said to have given him a small, round, blue stone which she found in a loch by following the instructions given her by the ghost of a Norwegian princess, who had been drowned while bathing near Baile na Cille. The princess told her that the stone would enable her son, Kenneth, to foretell events, which he certainly did with great enthusiasm. One of his prophecies runs: ' ... strange as it may seem to you this day, the time will come, and it is not far off, when full-rigged ships will be seen sailing eastward and westward by the back of Tomnahurich at Inverness'.[3] Tomnahurich (the hillock of the yew trees) is a conical hill a little to the north-west of the canal bridge at Inverness on the A82 and forming part of the burial ground there. It is an esker, a feature produced by glacial deposits.

The Brahan Seer's prediction has come true as did many of his prophecies, although it may not have materialised quite as he had expected. He came to a sticky end himself for, having infuriated the wife of the Earl of Seaforth by saying that 'he [Coinneach] saw more in the company of the children of footmen and grooms than of the children of gentlemen', which the countess and her guests seem to have understood to have cast some doubt on the paternity of the latter group, he was seized and declared a witch and put to death by being thrust into a burning tar barrel. It is believed that the earl himself was away from home at the time and arrived to see the smoke rising from Chanonry Point, where the unfortunate Seer was being immolated; he rushed madly to the scene to stop the proceedings but arrived too late.[4] But there are so many stories about the Brahan Seer (the cottage in which he lived was at Brahan, not far from Conon Bridge) that I cannot guarantee that this one is true. You must select your favourite as you come across it.

Telford was not the first to consider building a canal through the Great Glen. James Watt wrote about it in his *Survey and Estimate of the Expence of making a Navigable Canal with ten feet of water from Fort William to Inverness*, which appeared in James Anderson's disquisition on the state of the west coast and western islands of Scotland.[5] Both Anderson and Watt felt that there would be little difficulty; the glen was wide enough to provide space for the canal as well as the rivers; the three lochs, which never froze, could be used to provide a good part of the waterway, leaving only a short distance (22 miles, 35.4km) to be cut. One problem that Watt identified was that the wind often blows from north or south for a long time without changing tack and seldom blows across the glen; tall ships might therefore have difficulties making headway against a strong wind.[6] It was thought however that a much deeper canal which could take big ships going from Holland and the Baltic to the west of Britain and Ireland would be needed and could be commercially viable; it would be especially valuable in time of war, but would only thrive if some large towns and industrial complexes could be established nearby.[7] There was however little commercial activity at either end of the glen or in the glen itself. At Inverness salmon caught in the River Ness were exported and there was a factory making sailcloth and twine, while at Fort William the town of Maryburgh which had grown up around it was only small, its sole occupations being the victualling of the garrison and the sale of salmon from the river. 'It will be enough', Anderson thought, 'if we can put things into such a train to render this great work at some future period a necessary undertaking'.[8]

Meanwhile the British Fisheries Society had been formed in 1786, its aim being to improve conditions in the Highlands which had been so harshly treated after the '45. It is satisfying to note that the terrible nature of the reprisals inflicted on the Highlanders was being recognised at last. It was thought that the establishment of coastal towns to encourage and facilitate the catching and sale of fish would be some contribution to the Highland economy. But although fishing ports had been built at Ullapool and Tobermory the distribution of the fish caught was made difficult by the lack of good roads. It was to deal with this problem that Thomas Telford was asked in 1801 to make a survey of Highland communications in general.

Telford was a Scot, a Borderer, born on the 9th August 1757 in a cottage at Glendinning in Eskdale. His father John, who was a shepherd, died, aged 33, before Thomas was a year old. This left his mother in particularly hard circumstances, especially as their cottage was a tied one and they had to move into one room of a two-roomed cottage. But their neighbours were very good to them and Thomas's uncle Jackson paid for Thomas to go to the parish school in Westerkirk. Here he worked hard and spent school holidays helping with farm work or herding cattle and sheep. He was eventually apprenticed to Andrew Thomson, a master mason in Langholm. This employment enabled him to gain plenty of varied experience as Thomson worked for the Duke of Buccleuch who was improving his land at the time, together with its roads and bridges. By 1782 Telford was in London where he was introduced to Robert Adam and worked on many commissions in England and Scotland until in 1793 he became agent, engineer and architect to the Ellesmere Canal Company. This was the first canal he built; it included the famous aqueduct at Pont Cysyllte in the Vale of Llangollen, where earth-bound spectators could look upwards and see ships and their passengers passing as it were across the sky above the trees and rocks. It was a long passage, for the Vale of Llangollen at this point is 2500 feet (762m) wide.

By the time Telford produced his survey in 1801 Wade's roads were in a neglected state and had in any case been built for military purposes; they were not suitable for commercial use, often included unduly steep gradients (the Fort Augustus to Laggan road over the Corrieyairack, for instance) and were generally poorly surveyed (in Telford's opinion).

Telford had become engineer to the British Fisheries Society and it was they who had asked him to make the survey of Highland communications. He was so enthusiastic about it that he did not wait to receive detailed instructions and when they did arrive had already completed most of the journeys he needed to make. He worked so fast on the project not only because of his great interest in it but also because he wanted to finish the survey before the winter, when conditions would be too bad to make many of his journeys possible.[9] His report was so well received that he was asked to make further surveys, and presented a second report in 1803 which suggested a scheme for the building of roads, bridges and canals in the Highlands. It was as a result of this suggested scheme that he was given the job of building the Caledonian Canal.

When he began work on this canal he was still superintending the construction of the Ellesmere Canal in Shropshire; Pont Cysyllte aqueduct was not finished until 1805. What with the Caledonian Canal and the roads and bridges he was building in the Highlands, requiring at least one extensive tour of inspection every year, plus a number of other smaller engineering works throughout

England and the south of Scotland, not to mention surveying and superintending the building of the Gotha Canal, a ship canal from the North Sea to the Baltic, which he began in 1808, he must have been constantly on the go. 'I am toss'd about like a tennis ball' he wrote to one correspondent, but felt it rather suited his disposition.[10]

Telford brought to his assessment of the Highland situation the attitude of a countryman and of a Scot. He could see that the state of misery in which he found the Highlanders was occasioned by the disruption of their particular agricultural methods which, inefficient though they may have been, had been quite capable of supporting the population, except at times of very poor harvests or very harsh winters. The Clearances, which began in the late 18th century and continued well into the 19th, were the result of the introduction of sheep to replace cattle and arable crops, and affected most areas of the Highlands, although the Great Glen was not so severely affected as the islands and the western seaboard. People were evicted from their land and their houses were destroyed. Sometimes they were moved to other areas but the land was usually poorer and could hardly support them even at the lowest level of existence. Some crowded into the new factories set up in Glasgow, some struggled on trying to wrest a living from unrewarding soil, some emigrated, either by choice or by compulsion.

The year 1792 came to be known as *Bliadhna nan Caorach* (the Year of the Sheep). These innocent, woolly creatures arrived from the south accompanied by their Lowland or English shepherds and by the 1790s had got as far north as the Great Glen. Their arrival coincided with the decline of the clan system. Previously the chiefs were regarded as the fathers of their people, caring for them in times of poor harvests, acting as a sort of social service, leading them out in war to protect their territories or to protect their political affiliations. In the last half of the 18th century this system was broken up, partly by the terrible reprisals taken after the '45 Rising and partly by general political and social changes. The chiefs lost much of their power and they no longer counted their wealth in the number of fighting men they could call on. They abandoned their patriarchal duties, or had them snatched away from them and became much the same as ordinary landowners. They looked for profits from their estates and welcomed the arrival of the sheep which demanded relatively little in the way of husbandry. The Lowland shepherds, who could pay higher rents than the clansmen they replaced, were welcomed by the landowners, who regarded themselves as improvers of the land rather than destroyers of a more primitive but more satisfying way of life. The building of roads, bridges and a canal was looked upon as a possible way of providing work and thus preventing emigration or wholesale movement of workers to the industrial belt.

On the basis of his survey of communications in the Highlands Telford was asked to undertake the building of a canal through the Great Glen linking the west coast and the western islands to the North Sea and avoiding the dangerous passage through the stormy Pentland Firth where there had been massive losses of shipping. French privateers lurking in and around the English Channel would also be less of a problem as the alternative route down the east coast of England could be avoided. When Telford agreed to undertake this work he appointed William Jessop as consulting engineer for the whole canal; he had worked on the Pont Cysyllte aqueduct. The resident engineers were Matthew Davidson in the north-east and John Telford, who was no relation, in the south-west; he too had worked at Pont Cysyllte. They were each to have £200 a year with a house and a horse.[11]

Work began in 1803. The canal was to be 50 feet wide (15.2m) at the bottom and 15 feet deep (4.6m). The earth that was dug out was used to build banks on both sides to a height sufficient to hold 20 feet (6.1m) of water. It was decided that they would start at both ends at the same time, that is, they would cut from Clachnaharry to the north end of Loch Ness and from Corpach to Gairlochy. They would then concentrate on the middle section. This would mean that the completed stretches of canal could be used to transport materials to the middle section.

Workshops and huts for the workers were built to the east of Clachnaharry and a 50-ton sloop, the *Caledonia*, was built at Kessock to carry stone from Redcastle on the north bank of the Beauly Firth to Clachnaharry. Fir and birch wood came from land around Muirtown. In Inverness the row of six three-storeyed houses of superior design in Telford Street was built for the canal contractors, and Joseph Mitchell, Telford's superintendent of roads also spent some time there.

Along the whole length of the canal there was to be a towpath on the south-east side so that ships could be towed by horses where necessary, but this path was not needed along the sides of the lochs.

The northern section was to start with a sea lock at Clachnaharry followed by four more locks at Muirtown. A further lock was built at Dochgarroch; this was a regulating or guard lock to prevent the loch overflowing into the canal during unduly wet weather. Loch Dochfour then took over until the entrance to Loch Ness was reached. The River Ness had to be moved out of its bed between Dunain and Dochgarroch to provide easier passage for the canal.

At the west end the canal began with a sea lock and continued with a flight of eight locks, now known as Neptune's Staircase, at Banavie. A lot of work was needed between Banavie and Gairlochy to cope with the streams feeding the River Lochy from the west; small aqueducts were built at Lower and Upper Banavie with two arches and one arch respectively. Further along the Allt Sheangain in Gleann Laragain needed three arches to take the canal over it. At Muirshearlich only one arch was needed but Strone required the longest aqueduct with a 25-ft (7.6-m) arch for the river and two arches each 10-ft (3-m) wide for carts and farm animals. At Moy it was found inadvisable to build an aqueduct over the Allt Coire Chraoibhe because of difficulties with land levels and instead the burn was allowed to enter the canal and then leave it again on the other side; any earth and gravel brought down into the canal was dealt with by a series of waterfalls and pools. Finally, at Gairlochy, the engineers were faced with the problem of getting both the River Lochy and the canal through a relatively narrow space. It was decided to divert the Lochy river by cutting a new channel for it a little to the east and allowing it to join the River Spean at Mucomir Farm; the canal then flowed for a short distance in the river's bed. One lock, a regulating lock, was then built at Gairlochy. Telford used to stay at the lock keeper's house here and the middle room upstairs is still known as Telford's room.

A glance at the map shows the canal and the River Lochy elbowing their way from Banavie to Gairlochy, sometimes almost bumping into one another and leaving thin slips of land between, at times isolating farms and houses from the land to which they had before always been anchored. Tor Castle, the old stronghold of the Cameron chiefs, was cut off in this fashion, but the underpass for the Allt Sheangain can be used to reach it and also the beautiful tree-lined and mossy stretch known as Banquo's Walk. Shakespeare's Banquo is billed as a general in Macbeth's army but whether he ever really existed we do not know; he is traditionally believed to have been Thane of Lochaber, which explains why he puts in an appearance in this context.

Telford's workmen built a road to the west of the canal which involved the construction of 56 one-arched bridges within a distance of ten miles (16km) between Banavie and Gairlochy. The specification for the gravel to be used on the road required that all stones more than the size of a hen's egg must be removed. This rule was observed very carefully and all road inspectors carried a ring gauge with them so that they could check any suspicious-looking stones. I do not remember hearing that General Wade was so particular about his gravel.

When the northern and southern stretches of the canal were finished they turned their attention to the middle sections, that is, from Laggan at the head of Loch Lochy to the southern end of Loch Oich and from Aberchalder at the northern end of Loch Oich to Fort Augustus. Two locks were built at Laggan, which took a long time as the difficulties experienced in digging and dredging here were phenomenal. When they were at last completed and the old channel of the River Lochy at Gairlochy dammed to the necessary height, the level of the loch was raised by 12 feet (3.7m). This was what caused the drowning of Bishop Hugh MacDonald's grave at Kilfinnan.

Telford had had no difficulties up to this point in agreeing a price for the land they needed with the landowner, Donald Cameron of Lochiel, the 22nd Chief, but Alasdair Ranaldson MacDonell of Glengarry, into whose territory the canal contractors were now moving, was a difficult and complex character. He had been enthusiastic at the outset about the canal project but probably had not realised the impact it was likely to have on his lands. He feared that the ships passing through Loch Oich would interfere with the fisheries there and he was also very unwilling to have ships full of inquisitive passengers sailing past his drawing-room windows; the new Glengarry House was, like the old castle, on the west bank of Loch Oich, which explains his demand that shipping should be confined to the eastern side of the loch. He also disputed the price offered for the land to be used for the canal. This dispute was taken to the courts where he was offered £10,000, but he still did not consider this enough and arguments continued for years, much to the aggravation of the canal builders. There were also claims and counterclaims made over the construction of bridges, where they should be sited or whether they should be constructed at all.

All these matters took years to settle. At one point Glengarry became so exasperated over not getting his own way that in 1816 he appeared early one morning with his brother, Colonel James MacDonell, Captain Morgan, adjutant of the local militia and 30 armed men and seized one of the contractors' boats; he threatened the men working on the canal until they stopped work and caused considerable delays.[12] He was not used to having his wishes disregarded. He behaved in many ways more like a 17th-century chief and always appeared in full

Highland dress and with his 'tail'. The 'tail' might be composed of gentlemen such as bard, *seanachaidh* (historian), piper, *teachdaire* (herald), *fear sporain* (treasurer), and of attendants such as *gille cupa* (cup bearer), *gille cas fliuch* (wet foot servant – the man who carried the chief over streams). He delighted Sir Walter Scott, being more like a character in a romance than a real person and Scott is thought to have based Fergus MacIvor in *Waverley* upon him. There are however quite a few other people on whom MacIvor is believed to have been based. Scott thought him 'a jewel', but then he was not dependent on him as were the many clansmen who were cleared from the Glengarry estate to make room for sheep. At the same time however he was kindly, generous and hospitable and was genuinely missed by many people at his early death in 1828, caused by going to help his daughter during an accident on Loch Linnhe.

Loch Oich had its own problems, quite apart from those caused by Alasdair Ranaldson. It is a small loch, four miles (6.4km) long by one-fifth of a mile wide (322m), very quiet and intimate and with beautiful trees on both banks, but it is shallow, particularly down the middle, where more than half of it is less than 50-ft (15.2m) deep and only 20 feet (6.1m) at the mouth of the River Garry.[13] It draws most of its water from this river, which in turn is fed by Loch Garry and Loch Quoich, and brings down gravel and sand, which account for the shallowness of the loch at the river mouth. Dredging was needed on a large scale.

The River Oich between Cullochy and Fort Augustus had to be diverted into a new channel so that its bed could be used for the canal; this was done to avoid the river flooding the canal. The two waterways lie close together most of the way and at Fort Augustus are only a few yards apart where they enter Loch Ness.

The construction of the canal coincided with that painful period of Highland history known as the Clearances, to which we have already referred; it resulted in many people all over the Highlands being destitute and without work. Work on the canal now became available, but although Highlanders knew very well how to build their own houses Telford's work required engineering knowledge of a very advanced kind of which they had no experience. The work available to them was therefore of a sort which they would be inclined to describe as unsuitable for a Highland gentleman, that is, digging, carting soil and sawing wood. Even in time of war they always avoided work of this nature if they could – digging defences for instance, or hauling cannon over hills. Telford brought in trained men to teach them how to do the more complicated kinds of work and they learnt quickly. He also brought masons from Wales – not necessarily Welshmen but men who had worked on the Pont Cysyllte section of the Ellesmere Canal. These 'foreigners' often found the vastness of the Great Glen disturbing and the presence of such high mountains frightening rather than inspiring, for mountains at that time were still regarded as 'horrid', though this was soon to change under the influence of Sir Walter Scott and Queen Victoria. It seems to me howeever unlikely that they found it quiet and lonely as some people seem to believe, for there were so many of them working together and living and eating together.

One of Telford's inspectors, Joseph Mitchell, in his book entitled *Reminiscences of My Life in the Highlands*, describes the time he spent living with 30 masons in the lock-keeper's house at Cullochy which must have been a squeeze. They slept in what Mitchell calls 'temporary beds, one above the other, like the berths on a ship'. They took it in turns to cook, breakfast being porridge and milk and oaten bannocks; this was at nine o'clock, three hours after work began. It is to be hoped that they had a little something first thing in the morning to last them until nine. They then had to wait until two o'clock for their next meal, which was the same as breakfast. Their main meal was at eight in the evening when they usually ate potatoes and herring. The diet did not seem to alter during the week but on Sundays they had tea, oaten bannocks and butter for breakfast.[14] There seems to have been very little alcohol consumed, but then there were no public houses anywhere near. A brewery had been built at Corpach which, it was hoped, might encourage the Highlanders to drink less whisky, but Corpach was up to 30 miles (48.3km) away for anyone working on the middle section of the canal. General Wade, it will be remembered, had allowed his soldiers to brew their own beer, but no such arrangement was made for the canal workers; they had to catch up with drink at Fort Augustus when they collected their wages.

There were frequent disruptions to the work. Sometimes this was because building materials had not arrived, but at other times there were disputes about wages, althousrh the major delays were likely to occur at harvest time when the Highlanders would go back to their homes, if they were lucky enough still to have any, to make sure all was well there and to help with the harvest. This was a long-established tradition in the Highlands and had always caused problems to the commanders of Highland armies, who might suddenly find their forces reduced by a half or more at a tricky moment. Harvest absences were expected and most of the men returned within a reasonable time, although a few were late or never returned.

After the canal was finished there were claims that it had been built by Irishmen, who were regarded by some as superior to the Highlanders, but wage records reveal very few Irish names. The labourers came from Inverness-shire, Argyll and the islands. There were masons from Moray and blacksmiths and carpenters from Inverness.[15] Matthew Davidson, the resident superintendent at Clachnaharry, was said to be addicted to literature, bathing in cold water and cursing Scotsmen, although he was a Scot himself; with the relatively local workers at his disposal he would have had plenty of opportunity for cursing.[16]

The canal was completed in 1822, nineteen years after work on it had begun. Telford had hoped to complete it in seven years but the difficulties encountered when digging through solid rock, as at Corpach, or through very loose, porous soil, as at Clachnaharry, the problems at Laggan, the need to resort to puddling[17] at many points to avoid leaks, not to mention Glengarry's constant objections, made the original timescale impossible.

The ceremonial opening took place in the autumn. A large party of gentlemen, headed by the commissioners of the canal, set sail from Inverness in the SS *Stirling* on the 23rd October 1822 and reached Fort Augustus that evening. They left Fort Augustus at six o'clock the next morning, making such an early start to avoid Glengarry, as they were afraid he would stop them from entering Loch Oich; he was still quarrelling fiercely, but they failed to take into account the quicksilver nature of his character, for when he did turn up beside Loch Oich, having missed them at Fort Augustus on account of their early start, he was in the very best of humour and as enthusiastic about the whole undertaking as he had been at the very beginning.

There was a band on board the SS *Stirling* and as she passed Glengarry House the bandsmen struck up *My name it is Ronald Macdonald, A chieftain of high degree*. The ladies of Glengarry's household stood in front of the house and waved their handkerchiefs and a salute was fired from the ship and answered from the old castle. All of this must have been most inspiring and elevating to Glengarry himself – just the sort of thing to enhance his reputation as a chief of the old style. One might imagine it would have been enough to make him forget all the arguments over money, if not those over fisheries, interference with privacy, the siting of bridges, etc., but the money problems went on for years after the great opening day and his son inherited them along with the chiefship.

After a successful passage through Loch Oich and Loch Lochy and through the many locks, they reached the end of their journey in the early evening, having travelled from the Moray Firth to the junction of Loch Linnhe and Loch Eil, and at half-past seven sat down, 67 of them, to dinner. There was a vast number of toasts to be drunk, but at midnight, when most of these were over, some gentlemen including Glengarry retired, although the Inverness Courier reported that those who remained prolonged the session 'with genuine Highland spirit'.[18]

In the years that followed faults and weaknesses in the construction of the canal became evident, many the result of hurried work in response to the general impatience of the government and the public. These faults were greatly exacerbated by the bad weather of 1834. Very heavy rain in November raised the level of the water in all the lochs so much that acres of farmland were flooded and the canal banks broken at many points. By 1840 the state of the canal was such that it had to be closed and it remained closed until 1847; it underwent a complete overhaul during those seven years.

When the canal was first opened George IV was on the throne but by the time it closed for repairs George and his brother, William IV, had died and Victoria had been Queen for three years. Long after it had re-opened she records in her diary entry for the 16th September 1873 that she and Princess Beatrice travelled to Inverness in the SS *Gondolier*, the best remembered of all canal craft. They had been staying at Inverlochy Castle (the new house, now an hotel, a mile or two to the north of the old castle) and joined the *Gondolier* at Banavie, disembarking at Dochgarroch, where a landau was waiting to take them to Inverness station; there they took the train to Ballater and went on to Balmoral in an open landau. On the way up the canal they had stopped in one of the locks at Fort Augustus and had luncheon there, going below decks to do so. This meant that they were below the level of the many people gathered at the lock side, who gazed down at them as they were eating, an attention which the queen did not much appreciate.[19] She remembered that 26 years earlier Albert had gone up to Inverness to attend a ball, leaving her at Ardverikie, the house by Loch Laggan which at one time they thought of buying, but Albert found it too cold and damp and too remote and the sport poor. They eventually bought Balmoral instead, which had none of these drawbacks. After the ball in Inverness Albert had spent the night at Dochfour, which was then a new house and 'very elegant'. He must have returned by way of the canal, for he saw the Falls of Foyers on the following morning and had reached Fort William before half-past six that evening. The queen joined him there.[20] At the time of Albert's visit, the 16th to 17th September 1847, the canal had just re-opened after its major overhaul.

But this fine canal, demonstrating all the genius and talent of its builders, has never been a commercial success. The reservations of Anderson and of Watt had been forgotten and it had been built without an appropriate expansion of trade and industry at either the north or south end. (We must all be thankful for that!) It was also overtaken by the age of steam and of railways and by the growth in size of commercial shipping which could no longer fit between its banks. But during the First World War a barrage was placed between Orkney and Norway to combat German U-boats and the parts for 70,000 mines, which arrived on the west coast from the USA, were shipped through the canal to Clachnaharry and assembled nearby at Muirtown and Dalmore; this would have taken so much longer without the canal.

Today, although some fishing vessels still use it, it exists mostly by transporting an increasing number of tourists who, caught up in the joys of managing their own craft or of watching the changing scenes of mountain and forest slip by them, do not find the slow pace of their boat a drawback or the long process of filling and emptying the locks tedious. The cool water laps at the sides, the green banks and fields beyond the canal water fill in turn with daffodils, primroses, bluebells and great bushes of whin, that scent the air with honey and coconut, the heather opens its tiny flowers in August and in the autumn the silver trunks of the birches shine through their burden of golden leaves.

Who can regret the hours spent among them?

EPILOGUE

THROUGH ALL THE events within the pages of this book – the Celtic saints, the battles and struggles for power, the attempts to overthrow an alien dynasty, the development of new ideas and their conversion into solid form – there runs a thread of music and the words which arise from it or which themselves produce it.

The Keppoch MacDonalds from Glen Spean were a particularly rich source of poetry. One of the greatest Gaelic poets, Iain Lom, who was born in about 1624, was descended from the 4th Keppoch chief, Iain Aluinn, and could truly be called the historian's poet since so many facts relating to the history of his times might be forgotten or remain obscure but for him. He brought us an account of the second Battle of Inverlochy in his song *Là Inbhir Lochaidh*[1] and in two other songs described the build-up to the Battle of Killiecrankie – *Oran air Feachd ri Seumas* – and the battle itself – *Cath Raon Ruairidh.*[2] He recorded the Keppoch murder[3] and stayed with us long enough to write a song against the Union – *Oran an Aghaidh an Aonaidh*[4] – that is, the Union between the Scottish and English Parliaments in 1707. He had an excellent sense of humour. The Marquis of Argyll is said to have offered a reward to anyone who would bring him his head and was astounded when one day Iain himself turned up at Inveraray Castle to claim the reward. Argyll was so amused that he kept Iain there as his honoured guest for a week! Iain died in about 1710 and was buried somewhere in the grave-yard at Cille Choireil in Glen Spean. A great stone now stands there near the church door in his memory, but no-one is sure exactly where his grave lies.

Near his stone is a memorial to a 16th century poet, Domhnall mac Fhionnlaigh who, though he came from Glencoe, was closely associated with the Keppoch MacDonalds. His *Song of the Owl* is centred on Loch Treig which stretches from Fersit, near Glen Spean, in the north, down nearly to Corrour in the Moor of Rannoch. Countless local place-names are mentioned in this poem and there is a knitting together of history and topography and natural phenomena. Domhnall speaks of his contemporary, Alasdair Carrach, the 1st Keppoch chief, who fought in the first battle of Inverlochy:[5]

Chunnaic mi Alasdair Carrach,
Duine b'allail' bha an Alb 'e;
'S tric a bha mi seal ga eisteachd
'S e ri reìteach an tuim-shealga.

I saw Alasdair Carrach,
the most eminent man in Scotland;
often I spent a while listening
as he shared out the hunt's booty.[6]

Some of the verses seem to herald Duncan Ban MacIntyre's *Moladh Beinn Dòbhrain*, for instance the description of the hind:

Chan eil do chèil' aic' ach an damh,
'S e s' muime dhi am feur 's an creamh;
Mathair an laoich bhall-bhric mhir,
Bean an fhir mhall-rosgaich ghlain.

No mate has she but the stag,
her sustenance is the garlic and grass;
mother of the dappled agile fawn,
wife of the noble one of stately gaze.[7]

Sileas na Ceapaich, a sister of the 16th Keppoch Chief, *Colla nam Bo*, wrote much of her poetry after she had married and moved out of the Great Glen, but she left a lament that relates to the place of her birth; it is for Alasdair Dubh of Glengarry. He was the 11th chief of the Glengarry MacDonalds and became famous for his exploits in the battles of Killiecrankie and Sheriffmuir. She wrote of him:

Bu tu 'n t-iubhar thar gach coillidh,
Bu tu 'n darach daingean làidir,
Bu tu 'n cuileann 's bu tu 'n draigheann,
Bu tu 'n t'abhall molach blàthmhor;
Cha robh do dhàimh ris a' chrithean
Na do dhligheadh ris an fheàrna,

Cha robh bheag ionnad de 'n leamhan;
Bu tu leannan nam ban àlainn.

You were the yew above every forest,
you were the strong steadfast oak,
you were the holly and the blackthorn,
you were the apple-tree, rough-barked and many-flowered.
You had no kinship with the aspen,
owed no bonds to the alder,
there was none of the lime-tree in you;
you were the darling of beautiful women.[8]

Another lament by Sìleas is for Lachlann Dall, a blind harper who travelled all over the Highlands bringing music and the latest news to the families he visited. Sìleas, who must have known him at both her childhood and her married homes, laments how much she will miss him and his songs now he is dead:

Slàn a chaoidh le ceòl na clàrsaich
Ona ghlac am bàs thu, Lachlainn;
Cha bhidh mi tuille 'gat iargain,
nì mò dh'iarras mi chaoich t'fhaicinn;
...
Iaram air Dia bhith riut iochdmhor
'S do leigeil am miosg nan Aingeal;
O bha do thlachd 's a' cheòl 's an t-saoghal,
Ceòl am miosg nan naomh dha t'anam.

Farewell forever to the music of the harp,
since death has taken you, Lachlann;
no more shall I bewail your absence,
nor ever seek to see you ...

I beseech God to be merciful to you
and to admit you among the angels;
since your delight on earth was in music,
may your soul have music among the saints.[9]

There are other poems, some from the pen of that prolific writer Gun Urra (anon) which appear from their content to have originated in the Great Glen, for instance the poem entitled *Achadh nan Comhaichean* (the Field of the Covenant) which lies in Brae Lochaber, again in Keppoch territory. The words are spoken by a young girl who believes herself in love with a man of much higher rank, in fact with Prince Charles Edward himself:

> A Theàrlaich òig a laoigh mo chéille,
> Chunna mi 'n tòir mhòr an déidh ort,
> Iadsan gu subhach is mise gu deurach –
> Taobh Ghlinn Laoigh a rinn sinn éirigh.
>
> A Theàrlaich òig, a mhic Righ Seumas,
> S mise bha brònach gad fhògradh aid béistibh –

> O young Charles, calf of my senses,
> I've seen the massive pursuit at your heels,
> They are so cheerful and I am so tearful
> The side of Glen Loy is where we arose.
>
> O young Charles, O son of King James,
> I was so sad that you were banished by beasts – [10]

and she follows this up with a verse lamenting Culloden and its cruel aftermath:

> Mharbh iad m'athair, mharbh iad mo bhràithrean,
> Mhill iad mo chinneadh is chreach iad mo chàirdean,
> Loisg iad mo dhùthaich is rùisg iad mo mhàthair –
> 'S cha chluinnte mo mhulad nam buinnigeadh Teàrlach.

> They've killed my father, they've killed my brothers,
> they've savaged my kindred and plundered my kinsfolk,
> they've burned my country and raped my mother –
> and if Charles won no one would hear me grieving.[11]

There were no pipers in the Great Glen who could rival the MacCrimmons –

hereditary pipers to MacLeod of Dunvegan in Skye – or the Rankins – pipers in turn to the MacLeods of Raasay and of Coll – but that does not mean that the pipes were silent there; far from it, for we have only to think of the players of Black Donald's pibroch, that great pibroch tune that laments the defeat of the Camerons who fought against Alasdair Carrach at the first Battle of Inverlochy.[12] The pipes came to be regarded as a weapon of war, inciting the clansmen to battle and leading them bravely into the fray however slim their chances there; as such they were proscribed after Culloden but survived triumphantly by being adopted into the music of the British army.

It is believed that before they were used in battle their place was filled by the clarsach, the little Highland harp, although it has always seemed to me far too gentle an instrument, even in its most impassioned moments, for such a function. The clarsach began to decline in general use in the early 18th century, one of its last players, before its modern revival, being Alexander Grant of Sheuglie in Glen Urquhart. He was born in 1675 so he was 71 at the end of the last Jacobite Rising, when he had the misfortune to fall victim to the machinations of Ludovick Grant of Grant, as described in an earlier chapter. He is thought to have played the fiddle and pipes as well as the clarsach and also wrote a number of poems, the Gaelic of which has been lost. But he still had time to marry twice and produce 14 sons and six daughters. The tune of one of his poems, *Mairi Nighean Dheorsa* (Mary, George's Daughter), which represents a dispute between harp, pipes and fiddle, appears in Captain Fraser's collection, where it is given the English title of *Grant of Sheuglie's contest between his Violin, Pipe and Harp.*

Captain Simon Fraser lived on the east side of Loch Ness in the late 18th/early 19th century. He was a renowned fiddle player and collector of tunes. In 1816 he published his collection together with collections made by his father and grrandfather, under the title of *The Airs and Melodies Peculiar to the Highlands of Scotland and the Isles.* But he only published the music; even at that late date, 70 years after the last Jacobite Rising and after the deaths of both Prince Charles Edward and his brother, Cardinal York, he was afraid to give the words of the songs because of the Jacobite sympathies most of them express.

Now we can express these same sympathies, if we wish, without fear of reprisals; the views and prejudices of those days now seem of little importance or have been forgotten altogether. The days when Christianity first came to the Great Glen, when the kindred of Loarn fought against the kindred of Gabhran, when the Lords of the Isles still tried to hold their ground against the Kings of

Scots, when there was civil war between King and Covenant, when soldiers toiled at the making of a road, a highway for a new dynasty of kings, and when a new waterway was cut linking the three lochs in the glen – though much of all these activities has been remembered in these pages, yet how much more has been forgotten and can perhaps never be retrieved.

But the sweet, light notes of the little handbell so beloved of the Celtic saints, the silvery runs on the strings of the clarsach, the wild piercing notes of the great Highland bagpipe, the shivering song of bow against fiddle string, the flights of the human voice turning music into words and words into music – these sounds will echo in the Great Glen and in all the Highland glens until the rocks melt in the sun and the sun destroys the music of running water and all the music of nature and of man.

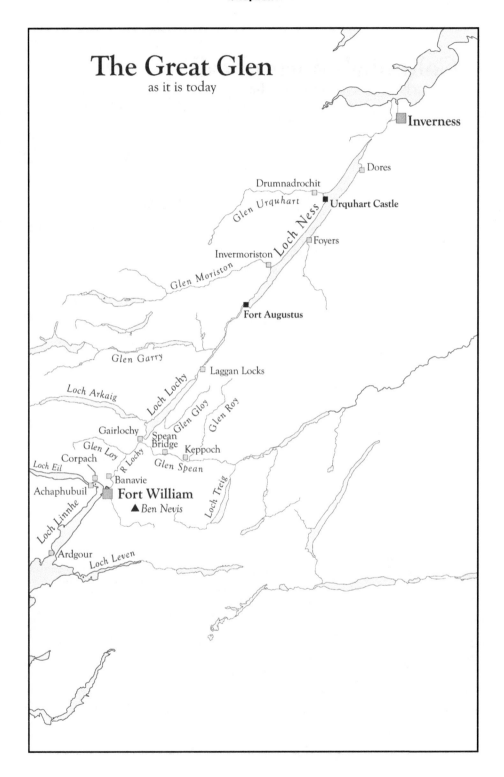

Chapter I

The Great Glen
as it is today

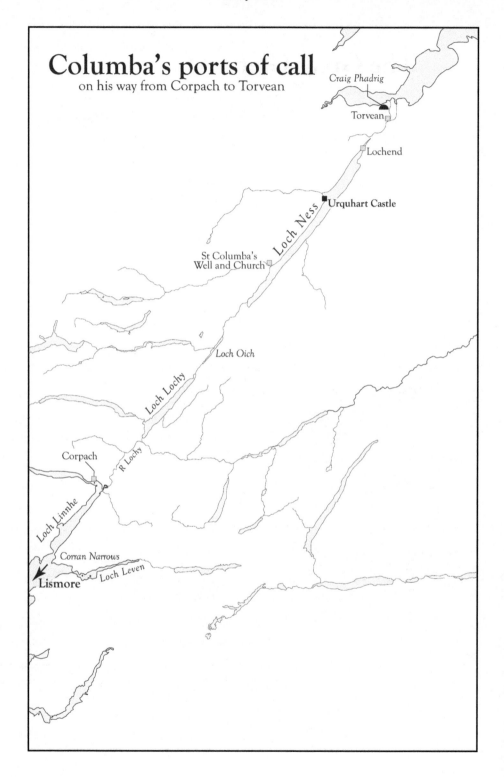

Columba's ports of call
on his way from Corpach to Torvean

Craig Phadrig

Torvean

Lochend

Loch Ness

Urquhart Castle

St Columba's
Well and Church

Loch Oich

Loch Lochy

R Lochy

Corpach

Loch Linnhe

Corran Narrows

Loch Leven

Lismore

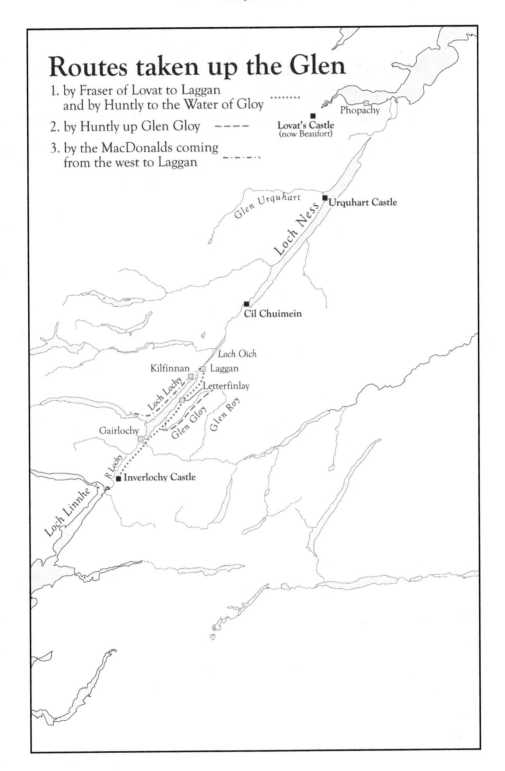

Routes taken up the Glen

1. by Fraser of Lovat to Laggan
   and by Huntly to the Water of Gloy ·········

2. by Huntly up Glen Gloy – – – –

3. by the MacDonalds coming
   from the west to Laggan – · – · –

Phopachy

Lovat's Castle
(now Beaufort)

Glen Urquhart

Loch Ness

Urquhart Castle

Cil Chuimein

Loch Oich

Kilfinnan   Laggan

Letterfinlay

Loch Lochy

Glen Gloy   Glen Roy

Gairlochy

R. Lochy

Inverlochy Castle

Loch Linnhe

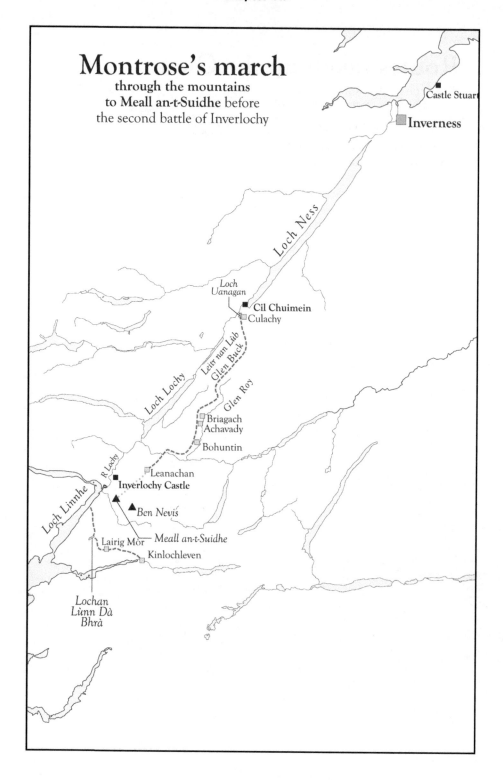

Montrose's march
through the mountains
to Meall an-t-Suidhe before
the second battle of Inverlochy

Castle Stuart

■Inverness

Loch Ness

Loch
Uanagan
■ Cil Chuimein
Culachy

Leitir nan Lùb
Glen Buck

Loch Lochy

Glen Roy

Briagach
Achavady

Bohuntin

R. Lochy

Leanachan
■ Inverlochy Castle

▲ Ben Nevís

Loch Linnhe

Lairig Mòr — Meall an-t-Suidhe
Kinlochleven

Lochan
Lùnn Dà
Bhrà

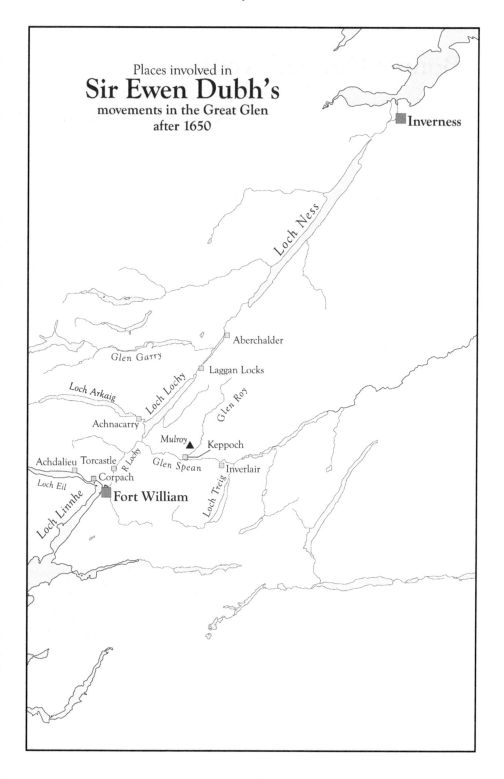

Places involved in
Sir Ewen Dubh's
movements in the Great Glen
after 1650

Inverness

Loch Ness

Aberchalder

Glen Garry

Laggan Locks

Loch Lochy

Loch Arkaig

Glen Roy

Achnacarry

Mulroy ▲ Keppoch

Achdalieu Torcastle

Glen Spean   Inverlair

R Lochy

Loch Eil Corpach

Loch Treig

Loch Linnhe

Fort William

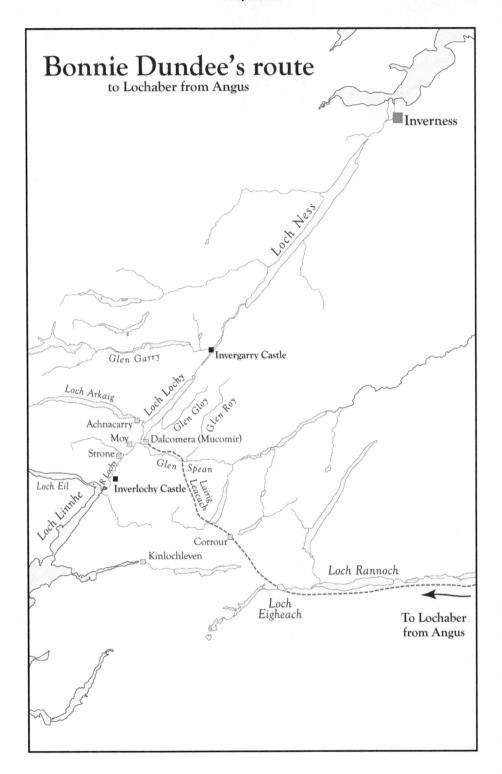

Bonnie Dundee's route
to Lochaber from Angus

Inverness

Loch Ness

Glen Garry

Invergarry Castle

Loch Arkaig

Loch Lochy

Glen Gloy

Glen Roy

Achnacarry

Moy

Dalcomera (Mucomir)

Strone

R. Lochy

Glen Spean

Loch Eil

Inverlochy Castle

Lairig Leacach

Loch Linnhe

Corrour

Kinlochleven

Loch Rannoch

Loch Eigheach

To Lochaber
from Angus

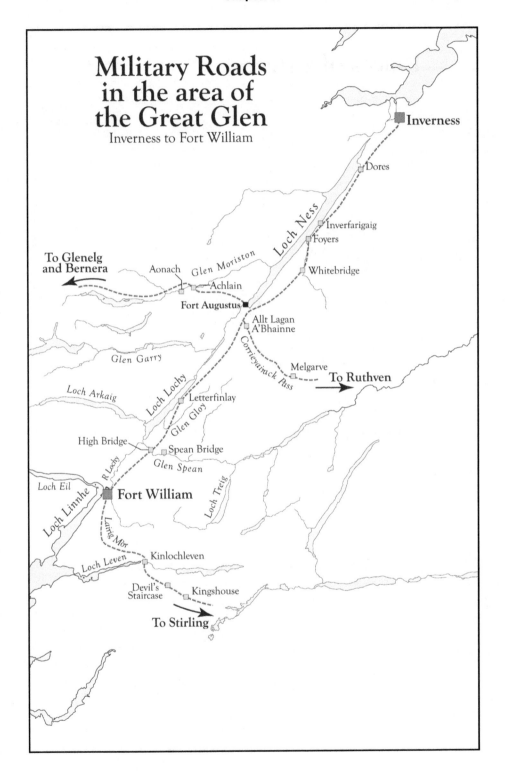

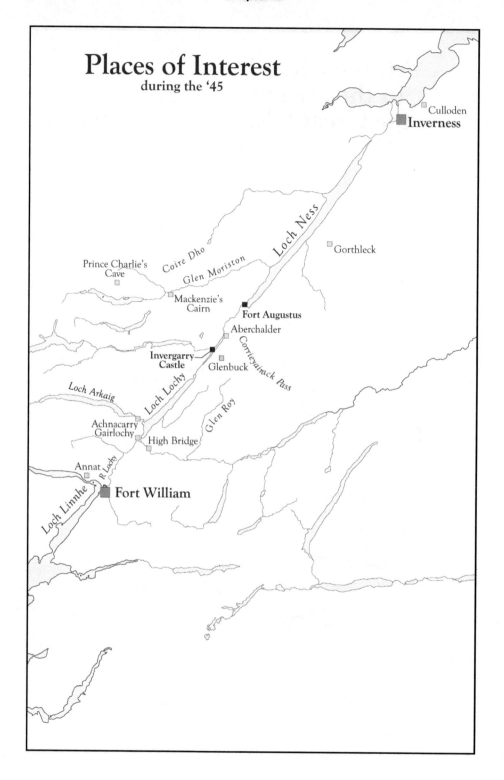

Places of Interest
during the '45

Culloden
Inverness

Loch Ness

Gorthleck

Prince Charlie's Cave

Coire Dho

Glen Moriston

Mackenzie's Cairn

Fort Augustus

Aberchalder

Invergarry Castle

Glenbuck

Corrieyairack Pass

Loch Arkaig

Loch Lochy

Glen Roy

Achnacarry
Gairlochy

High Bridge

Annat

R. Lochy

Fort William

Loch Linnhe

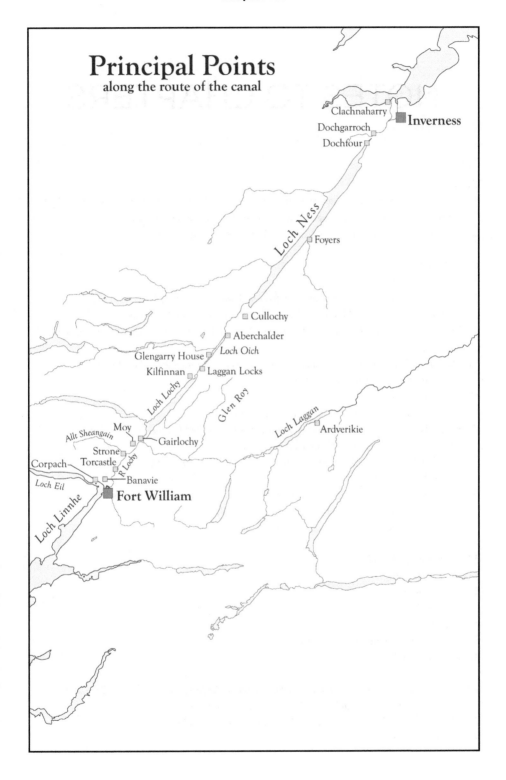

Principal Points
along the route of the canal

Clachnaharry
Dochgarroch
Dochfour

Inverness

Loch Ness

Foyers

Cullochy

Aberchalder

Glengarry House

Loch Oich

Kilfinnan

Laggan Locks

Loch Lochy

Glen Roy

Loch Laggan

Ardverikie

Allt Sheangain

Moy

Gairlochy

Strone

Torcastle

Corpach

R Lochy

Loch Eil

Banavie

Fort William

Loch Linnhe

NOTES TO CHAPTERS

CHAPTER I

1 kingshouse. Any inn that developed from a camp of soldiers/road-builders during the 18th-century road construction programme of Generals Wade and Caulfeild.

2 WC Sellar and RJYeatman: *1066 and All That*, London, 1934, p5.

CHAPTER II

1 Duke of Argyll: *Iona*, 1884.

2 Adamnan: *Vita Columbae*, ed. William Reeves, Lampeter, 1988, p17.

3 *Carmina Gadelica*, ed., Alexander Carmichael, Edinburgh, 1928, I. pp162-3.

4 Manus O'Donnell: *The Life of Colum Cille (Beatha Cholaim Chille)*, ed. Brian Lacey, Dublin, 1998, p18.

5a Duncan M MacLennan: *The Cathach of Colum-cille* in *Transactions of the Gaelic Society of Inverness*, XXXV, Inverness, 1929, p24.

5b Adamnan, p35.

6 John A Duke: *The Columban Church*, Edinburgh, 1950.

7 breastplate = *lorica* = leather cuirass. A song/poem so called because it was believed that singing it would keep one from harm.

8 Translated from the Irish by Mrs Cecil Alexander, wife of the Bishop of Derry and Raphoe: *Poems*, London, 1896.

9 Translated from the Irish of a manuscript in the Burgundian Library, Brussels and quoted in Peter Berresford Ellis: *Celtic Inheritance*, London, 1992, p107.

10 *St Patrick's World*, ed., Liam de Paor, Dublin, 1996, p133.

11 O'Donnell, pp68-9.

12 Adamnan, pp128-131.

13 O'Donnell, p97.

14 Adamnan, p83.

15 ibid., p25.

16 ibid., p34.

17 Duncan M MacLennan, XXXV, p7.

18 O'Donnell, p9.

19 ibid., p100.

20 *Treasures of the National Museum of Ireland. Irish Antiquities*, ed: Patrick F Wallace and Raghnall F Ó Flionn. Dublin, 2002, p269 (7:21) and p288.

21 Thomas Cahill: *How the Irish Saved Civilization*, London, 1995, p171.

22 Adamnan, p35.

23 John Morris: *The Age of Arthur*, London, 1984, p20.

24 Denis Rixson: *The West Highland Galley*, Edinburgh, 1998, p171.
   Alasdair Moffat: *Before Scotland*, London, 2005, p70 sqq.

25 *Treasures of the National Museum of Ireland*, p129, [1-14].

26 John Marsden: *The Illustrated Columcille*, London, 1991, p182.

27 Adamnan, p82.

28 Francis J Byrne: *Irish Kings and High Kings*, Dublin, 2001. According to Francis Byrne the word Cruithni is the Q-Celtic version of Pretani (Welsh = Prydyn) used for the Picts of north Britain and found in early Welsh texts meaning the people to the north of the Antonine Wall, ie the Picts, although Prydain and Pritani are often found as meaning the whole island and its inhabitants, whence 'ancient Britons', a vague term applied to the inhabitants of England, Wales and southern Scotland before the arrival of the Saxons.

29 Adamnan, pp79-80.

30 O'Donnell, p185.

CHAPTER III

1 *St Patrick's World*, ed., Liam de Paor, Dublin, 1996, p133.

2 Adamnan: *Vita Columbae*, ed., William Reeves, Lampeter, 1988, p17.

3 Manus O'Donnell: *The Life of Colum Cille (Beatha Cholaim Chille)*, ed. Brian Lacey, Dublin, 1998, p97.

4 ibid., pp140-1.

5 Adamnan, p83.

6 Edward Dwelly: *The Illustrated Gaelic-English Dictionary*, Glasgow, 1988, p254.

7 Donald B MacCulloch: *Romantic Lochaber, Arisaig and Morar*, Edinburgh, 1971, pp321-3.

8 Adamnan, p83.

9 ibid., p84.

10 ibid., p96.

11 Charles MacDonald: *Moidart or among the Clanranalds*, Edinburgh, 1989, pp115-6.

12 William J Watson: *The History of the Celtic Placenames of Scotland*, Dublin, 1986, p286.

13 Adamnan, p78.

14 William Mackay: *Urquhart and Glenmoriston*, Inverness, 1893, pp334-5.

15 Alexander MacDonald: *Song and Story from Loch Ness-Side*, Inverness, 1914, pp61-2.

16 Adamnan, p120.

17 Norman Newton: *The Life and Times of Inverness*, Edinburgh, 1996, p6.

18 ibid., p8.

19 John Morris: *The Age of Arthur*, London, 1984, p20.

20 Wynford Vaughan Thomas: *Wales – A History*, London, 1985, p54.

21 Miles Dillon and Nora Chadwick: *The Celtic Realms*, London, 2000, pp79-80.

22 O'Donnell, p159.

23 Adamnan, p95.

24 ibid., p95.

25 ibid., p88.

26 O'Donnell, p158.

27 Adamnan, p91.

28 O'Donnell, p168.
29 Liam de Paor, p186.
30 Adamnan, p110.
31 ibid., p93.
32 ibid., p93.
33 John Marsden: *The Illustrated Colmcille*, London, 1991, p178.
In the 12th century the Norman knight, John de Courcy, ruled Co Antrim, Co Down and part of Co Derry. The native clergy were upset by the arrival of monks from England and to conciliate them he deposited, or pretended to deposit, the bones of the three patron saints of Ireland, St Patrick, St Brigid and St Columba, in a vault in Downpatrick Cathedral.

CHAPTER IV
1   Dalriada, the kingdom founded by Scotti from Ireland in an area roughly where Argyll is today.
2   *Annals of Innisfallen*, ed., Sean Mac Airt, 1951.
3   Peter Berresford Ellis: *Macbeth High King of Scotland*, Belfast, 1990, pp38-9.
4   Archibald AM Duncan: *Scotland, the Making of the Kingdom*, 1975.
5   Norman Newton: *The Life and Times of Inverness*, Edinburgh, 1996, p9.
    James Miller: *Inverness*, Edinburgh, 2004, p7.
6   Douglas Hyde: *The Literary History of Ireland*, Dublin, 1967, p164.
7   *Duanaire na Sracaire. Anthology of Medieval Gaelic Poetry*, ed., Wilson McLeod and Meg Bateman, Edinburgh, 2007, no21, lines 61-8.
8   ibid., no24, lines 117-44.
9   *Orkneyinga Saga*, ed., Joseph Anderson, Edinburgh, 1977, xxv.
10 *Annals of Tigernach 1045*.
11 Marquis Curzon of Kedleston: *A Viceroy's India*, London, 1985, 116-7.
12 Nick Aitchison: *Macbeth, Man and Myth*, Stroud, 1999. pp101-5.
    Peter Berresford Ellis, p63.
13 Nick Aitchison, pp105-8.
14 ibid., pp108-14.
    Peter Berresford Ellis, p94.
15 ibid., p96.
    Nick Aitchison, pp116-22.
16 ibid., pp122-3.
    Peter Berresford Ellis, pp117-8.
17 Nick Aitchison, p128.
18 Dean Monro: *The Western Isles of Scotland*, 1549.
    E Mairi MacArthur: *Columba's Island*, Edinburgh, 1995, pp25-8.

CHAPTER V
1   James Fraser: *Chronicles of the Frasers*, The Wardlaw Manuscript, Edinburgh (Scottish History Society), 1903, p108.
2   *Acts of the Lords of the Isles, 1336-1493*. Edinburgh (Scottish History Society), 1986, xxxi.
3   ibid., pp292 and 296.

4   Norman H MacDonald: *The Clan Ranald of Lochaber*, Edinburgh (published by the author), undated. p33.

5   *Acts*, xli.

6   John Sadler: *Clan Donald's Greatest Defeat*, Stroud, 2005, 146-7.
    LF Grant: *The Lordship of the Isles*, Edinburgh, 1982, pp189-90.

7   David H Caldwell: *Having the right kit; gallowglass fighting in Ireland*, in: *History Ireland*, 2008, vol 16., no1., pp20-1.
    Acts, xli.

8   *Duanaire na Sracaire. Anthology of Medieval Gaelic Poetry*, ed., Wilson McLeod and Meg Bateman, Edinburgh, 2007, no78, lines 448-53.

9   Anne Lorne Gillies: *Songs of Gaelic Scotland*, Edinburgh, 2005, p126.

10 Anne Lorne Gillies explains this fully in ibid., p126.

11 *Duanaire na Sracaire*, 446-8.

12 Gillies, pp127 and 128.

13 Norman H MacDonald: *The Clan Ranald of Lochaber*, published by the author, undated, pp3-4.

14 Donald J MacDonald of Castleton: *Clan Donald*, Loanhead, Midlothian, 1978, p97.

15 *Acts*, xxxi.

CHAPTER VI

1   James Fraser: *Chronicles of the Frasers, The Wardlaw Manuscript*, ed. William Mackay, Edinburgh (Scottish History Society), 1903.

2   Fraser, p138.

3   Donald Gregory: *The History of the Western Highlands and Isles of Scotland*, Edinburgh, 1975, p158.

4   Fraser, p134.

5   Gregory, p158.

6   Fraser, p133.

7   Donald J Macdonald of Castleton: *Clan Donald*, Loanhead, 1978, p293.
    Gregory, p160.

8   Fraser, p135. Foynes is probably Phoineas, which lies a mile or two east of Beaufort (Dounie) Castle, Lovat's stronghold.

9   The Laird of Grant had to get to Strathspey, so to turn off at the Water of Gloy would be his quickest way home, but this route would be right out of Grant of Glenmoriston's way as he could cut over the hills from Cill Chumein into his glen.

10 Fraser, p135.

11 ibid., p135.

12 ibid., p136.

13 ibid., p137.

14 ibid., pp136-7.
    David H Caldwell: *Having the right kit; gallowglass fighting in Ireland*, in: *History Ireland*, 2008, vol 16, no 1, pp21-2.

15 Fraser, p137.

16 ibid., p136.

17 ibid., p136.
18 ibid., p137.
19 ibid., p138.
20 George Buchanan: *Historia*, 1582, Book 18, p548.
21 Fraser, pp140-1.
22 Nick Bridgland: *Urquhart Castle and the Great Glen*, London (Historic Scotland), 2005, p96.
23 John Stewart of Ardvorlich: *The Camerons*, Clan Cameron Association, 1975, p29.

CHAPTER VII

1   James Fraser: *Chronicles of the Frasers, The Wardlaw Manuscript*, ed. William Mackay, Edinburgh (Scottish History Society), 1903, p352.
2   *Collected Poems of James Graham, First Marquis of Montrose*, ed., Robin Graham Bell, Hitchin, 1990, pages unnumbered.
3   *Orain Iain Luim*, ed., Annie M Mackenzie, Edinburgh (Scottish Gaelic Texts Society), 1973, 142, lines 1764-6.
4   David Stevenson: *Alasdair MacColla and the Highland Problem in the Seventeenth Century*, Edinburgh, 1980.
5   *Reliquiae Celticae, Texts Papers and Studies in Gaelic Literature and Philology*, ed., Alexander Macbain and John Kennedy, Inverness, 1894, vol II, p183.
6   Rev George Wishart: *The Memoirs of James Marquis of Montrose 1639-1650*, London, 1893, p81.
7   *Reliquiae Celticae*, vol II, p183
8   John Buchan: *Montrose*, London, Edinburgh, 1928, opposite page 218.
9   Catriona Fforde: *A Summer in Lochaber. The Jacobite Rising of 1689*, Colonsay, 2002, p2.
10 *Wishart*, p82.
    William Forbes Leith: *Memoirs of Scottish Catholics during the Seventeenth and Eighteenth Centuries*, 1909, vol I, p323.
11 ibid., p323.
12 *Orain Iain Luim*, 20, lines 190-4.
13 Mark Napier: *Memoirs of the Marquis of Montrose*, Edinburgh, 1856, vol II, p285.
14 Personal communication from Ronnie Campbell of Bohuntin in whose family the story has been handed down.
15 Orain Iain Luim, 22, line 213.
16. John Wilcock: *The Great Marquess, Life and Times of Archibald, 8th Earl and 1st (and only) Marquess of Argyll (1607-1661)*, Edinburgh and London, 1903, p175.
17 Kevin Byrne: *Colkitto!*, Colonsay, 1997, p145.
    Angus Matheson: *Traditions of Alasdair Mac Colla* in: *Transactions of the Gaelic Society of Glasgow*, vol 5 1958, p38.
18 Mark Napier, vol II, p485.
19 ibid., p485.
20 ibid., p485.
21 *Orain Iain Luim*, 20-5.
22 Mark Napier, vol II, p485.
23 Fraser, pp353-4.

CHAPTER VIII

1 John Drummond of Balhaldy: *Memoirs of Sir Ewen Cameron of Locheill, Chief of the Clan Cameron*, Edinburgh, 1842, pp77-81.

2 ibid., p100.

3 ibid., pp104-5.

4 ibid., pp106-7.

5 ibid., pp110-2.

6 ibid., pp112-20.

7 ibid., pp120-1.

8 ibid., pp124-5.

9 ibid., pp141-6.

10 Bruce Lenman: *The Jacobite Clans of the Great Glen 1650-1784*, London, 1984, p33.

11 Balhaldy, pp149-50.

12 James Fraser: *Chronicles of the Frasers, The Wardlaw Manuscript*, ed. William Mackay, Edinburgh (Scottish History Society), 1903, p454.

13 Balhaldy, pp188-92.

14 William Buchanan of Auchmar: *An Enquiry into the Genealogy and Present State of Ancient Surnames*, etc., p129.

15 Balhaldy, editor's introduction, p24.

16 Norman H MacDonald: *The Clan Ranald of Lochaber*, published by the author, undated, pp18-9.

17 ibid., p19.

18 *Orain Iain Luim*, ed., Annie M Mackenzie, Edinburgh (Scottish Gaelic Texts Society), 1964, lines 1021-9.

19 Norman H MacDonald, p6.

20 *Orain Iain Luim*, lines 974-1173.

21 ibid., lines 1436-41.

22 ibid., lines 1442-45.

23 ibid., lines 1618-37.

24 Stuart Macdonald: *Back to Lochaber*, Edinburgh, 1994, p132.

25 Norman H MacDonald, pp24-5.

26 *Privy Council Records*, vol II, p110.

CHAPTER IX

1 James Philip of Almericlose: *The Grameid an heroic poem descriptive of the Campaign of Viscount Dundee in 1689*, Edinburgh (Scottish History Society), 1888, IV, line 34.

2 ibid., II, line 713.

3 ibid., III, lines 242-53.

4 Samuel Johnson: *A Journey to the Western Isles*, ed., Finlay J MacDonald, London 1983, p149.

5 John Drummond of Balhaldy: *Memoirs of Sir Ewen Cameron of Locheill*; Edinburgh, 1842.

6 *The Grameid*, IV, lines 179-199.

7 Gallowglass, from gall oglach = foreign soldier. They were Highlanders recruited by Irish chiefs and they usually did not return to Scotland. They were succeeded by Highlanders known as Redshanks, because of their bare legs; they were recruited in the same way but gen-

erally returned to Scotland after their particular service was completed.

8   For a full account of all those who took part in the Rising see Catriona Fforde: *A Summer in Lochaber. The Jacobite Rising of 1689*, Colonsay, 2002.

9   *The Grameid*, IV, line 10.

10 ibid., lines 82-4.

11 *Bàrdachd Shìlis na Ceapaich*, ed., Colm Ó Baoill, Edinburgh, (Scottish Gaelic Texts Society), 1973, pp70-2.

12 Balhaldy, pp260-1.

13 Quoted in William A Gillies: *In Famed Breadalbane*, Strathtay, 1987, p163.

14 *The Grameid*, III, lines 620-38.

15 Balhaldy, p258.

16 *Orain Iain Luim*, p185, lines 2362-4.

17 ibid., p187, lines 2374-5.

CHAPTER X

1   John Drummond of Balhaldy: *Memoirs of Sir Ewen Cameron of Locheill, Chief of the Clan Cameron*, Edinburgh, 1842, p283.

2   ibid., pp322-3.

3   Samuel Johnson: *A Journey to the Western Isles*, ed., Finlay J MacDonald, London 1983, p53.

4   William Taylor: *The Military Roads in Scotland*, Colonsay, 1996, p18.

5   William Mackay: *Urquhart and Glenmoriston. Olden Times in a Highland Parish*, Inverness, 1893, p171.

6   James Fraser: *Chronicles of the Frasers, The Wardlaw Manuscript*, ed. William Mackay, Edinburgh (Scottish History Society), 1905, pp415-6.

7   *Burt's Letters from the North of Scotland*, Edinburgh, 1998, p75.

8   ibid., p299.

9   ibid., p299.

10 ibid., p168.

11 ibid., pp168-178.

12 ibid., p295.

13 ibid., p294.

14 Neil Munro: *The New Road*, Edinburgh, 1994, pp73-5.

15 Brian Doogan: *The Guardian of Blackmount. A History of Kingshouse Inn, Glencoe*, Glencoe, 1998, p11 sqq.

16 Dorothy Wordsworth: *A Tour in Scotland in 1803*, Edinburgh, 1981, pp176-8.

17 William Taylor, p35.

18 Paula Martin: *Lochaber. An Historical Guide*, Edinburgh, 2005, p166.

19 William Taylor, pp32-3.

20 Samuel Johnson, pp47-54.
    James Boswell: *The Journal of a Tour to the Hebrides with Samuel Johnson*, London and Glasgow, 1955, pp93-9.

21 Thought to be an anglicised version of Coire Ghearraig (Dwelly's *Gaelic Dictionary* gives it in this form, see p1010) which could mean 'corrie of the young hare'. People from the Badenoch end of the pass, however, have been known to call it An Coire Dearg (the red corrie), although

the 'y' of 'yairack' is much closer in sound to the Gaelic 'Gh' than to the Gaelic 'De'.

22 ARB Haldane: *New Ways Through the Glens*, Newton Abbot, 1973, p6.

23 William Taylor, pp24-5.

24 Burt, p75.

25 William Hague: *William Pitt the Younger*, London, 2004, p25.

26 William Taylor, p68.

27 Thomas Pennant: *A Tour in Scotland and Voyage to the Hebrides, 1772*, Edinburgh, 1998, p336.

28 Boswell, pp93-9.
    Johnson, pp47-54.

29 Burt, pp298-9.

30 ibid., p296.

31 ibid., p297.

32 Quoted in: Dom Odo Blundell: *Kilcumein and Fort-Augustus, Fort Augustus*, undated, p9.

33 Munro, p46.

34 ibid., p33.

35 ibid., p29.

36 Burt, p155.

37 ibid., p157.

38 Munro, p269.

CHAPTER XI

1   John Watts: *Hugh Macdonald: Highlander, Jacobite and Bishop*, Edinburgh, 2002, pp109-10.

2   *Highland Songs of the Fortyfive*, ed., and translated by John Lorne Campbell, Edinburgh, 1933, poem IV, lines 1-8.

3   Donald MacCulloch: *Route of Prince Charlie's Army from Fassifern to Moy* in: *Jacobite Anthology*, Aberdeen, 1995, pp12-3.

4   Walter Biggar Blaikie: *Itinerary of Prince Charles Edward Stuart*, Edinburgh, 1975, p8, note 6.

5   Eric Linklater: *The Prince in the Heather*, 1966, p22.

6   Fitzroy Maclean: *Bonnie Prince Charlie*, London, 1988, p223.

7   The question of whether the copy of these orders was forged is fully discussed in: WA Speck: *The Butcher*, Caernarvon, 1995, pp148-56.

8   *The Lyon in Mourning*, ed., the Rev Robert Forbes and Henry Paton, Edinburgh, 1975, vol III, pp54-5.

9   ibid., vol III, pp155-7.

10 ibid., vol I, p215.

11 William Mackay: *Urquhart and Glenmoriston. Olden Times in a Highland Parish*, Inverness, 1893, pp280-5.

12 *The Muster Roll of Prince Charles Edward Stuart's Army*, ed., Alistair Livingstone of Bachuil, Christian WH Aikman and Betty Stuart Hart, Aberdeen, 1984, pp149-60.

13 Thomas Wynne: *The Forgetten Cameron of the '45*, published privately, Roy Bridge, 2011, pp79-91.

14 Eric Linklater, p133.

15 John Watts, p169 and pp263-4.

16 William Mackay, pp277-8.

17 Eric Linklater, p129.

18 ibid., p34.

19 Catriona Fforde: *A Summer in Lochaber. The Jacobite Rising of 1689*, Colonsay, 2002, p47.

20 *The Lyon*, vol III, p45.

21 Much more detailed accounts of the sieges of the three forts and, particularly, of the Battle of Culloden are to be found in: Christopher Duffy: *The '45*, London, 2003, pp447-8, 451-7 and 501-24.

CHAPTER XII

1 LTC Rolt: *Thomas Telford*, Stroud, 2007, p232.

2 ibid., p74.

3 Alexander Mackenzie: *The Prophecies of the Brahan Seer*, London, 1983, p35.

4 ibid., pp113-7.

5 James Anderson: *An Account of the Present State of the Hebrides and Western Coasts of Scotland*, Dublin, 1786.

6 ibid., p387.

7 ibid., pp385-6.

8 ibid., pp378-94.

9 LTC Rolt, pp80-1.

10 ibid., p73.

11 AD Cameron: *The Caledonian Canal*, Edinburgh, 2005, p29.

12 Brian D Osborne: *The Last of the Chiefs*, Glendaruel, Argyll, 2001, 174.

13 Tom Weir: The Scottish Lochs, London, 1970, vol I, p168.

14 Joseph Mitchell: *Reminiscences of My Life in the Highlands*, London, 1884, vol I.

15 AD Cameron, pp93-4.

16 ibid., p47.

17 Puddling. Applying a mixture of light clay, sand or gravel and water. It was worked in with the feet, wearing special boots.

18 *Inverness Courier*, 31st October, 1822.

19 *Queen Victoria's Highland Journals*, ed., David Duff, Exeter, 1994, pp180-2.

20 ibid., pp58-9.

EPILOGUE

1 See Chapter 7.

2 See Chapter 9.

3 See Chapter 8.

4 *Orain Iain Luim*, ed., Annie M Mackenzie, Edinburgh (Scottish Gaelic Texts Society), 1973, p222.

5 See Chapter 5.

6 *Duanaire na Sracaire*, ed., Wilson McLeod and Meg Batemen, Edinburgh, 2007, no 68, lines 25-8.

7 ibid., no 68, lines pp85-8.

8 *Bàrdachd Shìlis na Ceapaich*, ed., Colm Ó Baoill, Edinburgh, (Scottish Gaelic Texts Society),

1972, poem XIV, lines pp847-54.

9   ibid., poem XXI, lines 1261-5 and 1321-4.

10 *An Lasair*, ed., Ronald Black, Edinburgh, 2001, no 34, lines 9-12 and 21-2.

11 ibid., lines 25-8.

12 See Chapter 5.

BIBLIOGRAPHY

Acts of the Lords of the Isles, 1336-1493, Edinburgh (Scottish History Society), 1986.

Adamnan: Vita Columbae, ed., William Reeves, Lampeter, 1988.

Aitchison, Nick: *Macbeth, Man and Myth*, Stroud, 1999.

Alcock, Leslie: *Arthur's Britain*, London, 2001

Anderson, James: *An Account of the Present State of the Hebrides and Western Coasts of Scotland*, Dublin, 1786.

Argyll, Duke of: *Iona*, 1884.

Balhaldy, John Drummond of: *Memoirs of Sir Ewen Cameron of Locheill, Chief of the Clan Cameron*, Edinburgh, 1842.

Bàrdachd Shìlis na Ceapaich, ed., Colm Ó Baoill, Edinburgh (Scottish Gaelic Texts Society), 1972.

Barrington, Michael: *Grahame of Claverhouse, Viscount Dundee*, London, 1911 .

Blaikie, Walter Biggar: *Itinerary of Prince Char les Edward Stuart*, Edinburgh, 1975.

Blundell, Dom Odo: *Kilcumein and Fort-Augustus*, Fort Augustus, undated.

Boswell, James: *The Journal of a Tour to the Hebrides with Samuel Johnson*, London and Glasgow, 1955.

Bridgland, Nick: *Urquhart Castle and the Great Glen*, Historic Scotland, 2005.

Buchan, John: *Montrose*, London, Edinburgh, 1928

Burt's Letters from the North of Scotland, Edinburgh, 1998.

Byrne, Francis: *Irish Kings and High Kings*, Dublin, 2001.

Byrne, Kevin: *Colkitto!*, Colonsay, 1997.

Cahill, Thomas: *How the Irish Saved Civilization*, London, 1995.

Caldwell, David H: *Having the right kit; galloglas fighting in Ireland*, in: *History Ireland*, vol 16, no.1, 2008.

Cameron, AD: *The Caledonian Canal*, Edinburgh, 2005.

Carmina Gadelica, ed., Alexander Carmichael, Edinburgh, 1928.

Chadwick, Nora: *The Celts*, London, 1979.

Companion to Gaelic Scotland, ed., Derick S Thomson, Oxford, 1983.

Dillon, Miles and Nora Chadwick: *The Celtic Realms*, London, 2000.

Doogan, Brian: *The Guardian of Blackmount: A History of Kingshouse Inn, Glencoe*, Glencoe, 1998.

Duke, John A: *The Columban Church*, Edinburgh, 1950.

Duanaire na Sracaire, Anthology of Medieval Gaelic Poetry, ed. Wilson McLeod and Meg Bateman, Edinburgh, 2007.

Dwelly, Edward: *The Illustrated Gaelic-English Dictionary*, Glasgow, 1988.

Ellis, Peter Berresford: *Celtic Inheritance*, London, 1992.

Macbeth High King of Scotland, Belfast, 1990.

Fforde, Catriona: *A Summer in Lochaber: The Jacobite Rising of 1689*, Colonsay, 2002.

Finlay, Ian: *Columba*, Glasgow, 1979.

Forbes Leith, *William: Memoirs of Scottish Catholics during the Seventeenth and Eighteenth Centuries*, London, 1909.

Fraser, James: *Chronicles of the Frasers, The Wardlaw Manuscript*, ed., William Mackay, Edinburgh (Scottish History Society), 1903.

Fraser, Simon: *The Airs and Melodies Peculiar to the Highlands of Scotland*, Edinburgh, 1816.

Grant, IF: *The Lordship of the Isles*, Edinburgh, 1982.

Gregory, Donald: *The History of the Western Highlands and Isles of Scotland*, Edinburgh, 1975.

Haldane, ARS: *New Ways Through the Glens*, Newton Abbot, 1973.

Hastings, Max: *Montrose The King's Champion*, London, 1977.

Highland Songs of the Fortyfive, ed., John Lorne Campbell, Edinburgh, 1933.

Hyde, Douglas: *The Story of Early Gaelic Literature*, London, 1920.

A Jacobite Anthology, Aberdeen (The 1745 Association), 1995.

Johnson, Samuuel: *A Journey to the Western Isles*, retraced by Finlay J Macdonald, London, 1983.

Lane, Alan and Ewan Campbell: *Dunadd*, Oxford, 2000.

An Lasair: An Anthology of Eighteenth Century Scottish Gaelic Verse, ed., Ronald Black, Edinburgh, 2001.

Lenman, Bruce: *The Jacobite Clans of the Great Glen 1650-1784*, London, 1984.

Linklater, Eric: *The Prince in the Heather*, London 1966.

The Lyon in Mourning, ed., the Rev Robert Forbes and Henry Paton, Edinburgh, 1975.

MacArthur, E Mairi: *Columba's Island, Iona from Past to Present*, Edinburgh, 1995.

MacCulloch, Donald B: *Romantic Lochaber Arisaig and Morar*, Edinburgh, 1971.

MacDonald, Alexander: *Song and Story from Loch Ness-Side*, Inverness, 1914.

MacDonald, Charles: *Moidart or Among the Clanranalds*, Edinburgh, 1989.

MacDonald, Norman: *The Clan Ranald of Lochaber*, Edinburgh, undated.

MacDonald, Stuart: *Back to Lochaber*, Edinburgh, 1994.

Mackay, William: *Urquhart and Glenmoriston, Olden Times in a Highland Parish*, Inverness, 1893.

Mackenzie, Alexander: *The Prophesies of the Brahan Seer*, London, 1983.

MacLean, Fitzroy: *Bonnie Prince Charlie*, London, 1988.

MacLennan, Duncan M: *The Cathach of Colum Cille* in: *Transactions of the Gaelic Society of Inverness*, vol XXXV, Inverness, 1929.

Marsden, John: *The Illustrated Columcille*, London, 1991.

Sea-Road of the Saints, Edinburgh, 1995.

Martin, Paula: *Lochaber A Historical Guide*, Edinburgh, 2005.

The Memoirs of James Marquis of Montrose, 1639-1650, ed., Rev George Wishart, London, 1895.

Menzies, Lucy: *Saint Columba of Iona*, London and Toronto, 1920.

Mitchell, Joseph: *Reminiscences of My Life in the Highlands*, London, 1884, vol I.

Moffat, Alasdair: *Before Scotland*, London 2005.

Morris, John: *The Age of Arthur*, London 1984.

Munro, Neil: *The New Road*, Edinburgh, 1994.

Muster Roll of Prince Charles Edward Stuart's Army, ed., Alistair Livingstone of Bachuil, Christian WH Aikman and Betty Stuart Hart, Aberdeen, 1984.

Napier, Mark: *Memo:irs of the Marquis of Montrose*, two vols, Edinburgh, 1856.
   Memoirs of Dundee 1643-1689. Life and Times of John Graham of Claverhouse, Viscount Dundee, three vols, Edinburgh, 1859.

Newton, Norman: *The Life and Times of Inverness*, Edinburgh, 1996.

O'Donnell, Manus: *The Life of Colum Cille (Beatha Cholaim Chille)*, ed., Brian Lacey, Dublin, 1998.

Orain Iain Luim, ed., Annie M Mackenzie, Edinburgh (Scottish Gaelic Texts Society), 1973.

Osborne, Brian D: *The Last of the Chiefs*, Glendaruel, 2001.

The Oxford Companion to Irish History, ed., SJ Connolly, Oxford, 1998.

Orkneyinga Saga, ed., Joseph Anderson, Edinburgh, 1977.

Paterson, Raymond Campbell: *The Lords of the Isles*, Edinburgh, 2001.

Pennant, Thomas: *A Tour in Scotland and Voyage to the Hebrides 1772*, Edinburgh, 1998.

Philip, James, of Almerieclose: *The Grameid, an heroic poem descriptive of the Campaign of Viscount Dundee in 1689*, Edinburgh (Scottish History Society), 1888.

Purser, John: *Scotland's Music*, Edinburgh, 2007.

Queen Victoria's Highland Journal, ed., David Duff, Exeter, 1994.

Rees, Elizabeth: *Celtic Saints. Passionate Wanderers*, New York, 2000.

Reliquiae Celticae, ed., Alexander MacBain and Rev John Kennedy, Inverness, 1892.

Rixson, Denis: *The West Highland Galley*, Edinburgh, 1998.

Rolt, LTC: *Thomas Telford*, Stroud, 2007.

Sadler, John: *Clan Donald's Greatest Defeat*, Stroud, 2005.

Sellar, Walter Carruthers and Robert Julian Yeatman: *1066 And All That, A Memorable History of England*, London, 1934.

Songs of Gaelic Scotland, ed., Anne Lorne Gillies, Edinburgh, 2005.

Spes Scotorum, Hope of Scots, Saint Columba, Iona and Scotland, ed., Dauvit Broun and Thomas Owen Clancy, Edinburgh, 1999.

St Patrick's World, ed., Liam de Paor, Dublin, 1996.

Stevenson, David: *Alasdair MacColla and the Highland Problem in the Seventeenth Century*, Edinburgh, 1980.

Stewart, John, of Ardvorlich: *The Camerons*, Clan Cameron Association, 1975.

Sutherland, Elizabeth: *In Search of the Picts, A Celtic Dark Age Nation*, London, 1994.

Tabraham, Chris: *Urquhart Castle Loch Ness*, Historic Scotland, 2002.

Taylor, William: *The Military Roads in Scotland*, Colonsay, 1996.

Treasures of the National Museum of Ireland. Irish Antiquities, ed: Patrick F Wallace and Raghnall F Ó Flionn. Dublin, 2002.

Vaughan Thomas, Wynford: *Wales A History*, London, 1985.

Watson, WJ: *The History of the Celtic Placenames of Scotland*, Dublin, 1896.

Watts, John: *Hugh MacDonald, Highlander, Jacobite and Bishop*, Edinburgh, 2002.

Wedgwood, CV: *Montrose*, Stroud, 1995.

Weir, Tom: *The Scottish Lochs*, London, 1973.

Wilcock, John : *The Great Marquess, Life and Times of Archibald, 8th Earl and 1st (and only) Marquess of Argyll (1607-1661)*, Edinburgh and London, 1903.

Williams, Ronald: *Montrose, Cavalier in Mourning*, Glasgow, undated.

Wordsworth, Dorothy: *A Tour in Scotland in 1803*, Edinburgh, 1981.

Wynne, Thomas: *The Forgotten Cameron of the '45*, published privately, Roy Bridge, 2011.

INDEX

INDEX